P9-ECV-965

On Reading the
Bible

Thoughts and Reflections
of Over 500 Men and Women,
from St. Augustine to Oprah Winfrey

Edited by
Bill Bradfield

DOVER PUBLICATIONS, INC.
Mineola, New York

Copyright

Copyright © 2005 by Bill Bradfield
All rights reserved.

Bibliographical Note

On Reading the Bible: Thoughts and Reflections of Over 500 Men and Women, from St. Augustine to Oprah Winfrey is a new work, first published by Dover Publications, Inc., in 2005.

Library of Congress Cataloging-in-Publication Data

On reading the Bible : thoughts and reflections of over 500 men and women, from St. Augustine to Oprah Winfrey / edited by Bill Bradfield.
  p. cm.
  ISBN 0-486-43708-6 (pbk.)
  1. Bible—Reading. I. Bradfield, Bill, 1927–

BS617.O5 2005
220.1—dc22   2004058233

Manufactured in the United States of America
Dover Publications, Inc., 31 East 2nd Street, Mineola, N.Y. 11501

A Dedication to Sowers of the Word

THIS anthology of quotations about the Bible and Bible-reading is dedicated to the thousands of Gideons who effectively have become Sowers of the Word, exemplified in the New Testament by Christ's parable of the sower.

Three traveling salesmen—John H. Nicholson, Sam E. Hill, and Will J. Knights—organized the Gideons as a Christian evangelical fellowship in 1899, meeting at a YMCA building in Janesville, Wisconsin.

Choosing to name their organization for a biblical character, the trio of founders picked one from the Old Testament described in the Book of Judges as a man willing to do exactly what God wanted him to do, at any time and any place, regardless of his own judgment as to plans or results. They agreed that they wanted to follow Gideon's example in showing qualities of humility, faith, and obedience to God's will.

The association grew rapidly—large enough by 1908 to hold a convention in Louisville, Kentucky. During the convention, members adopted a plan to provide Bibles to hotel bedrooms. In 1916, Gideons began placement of Bibles also at the bedside of hospital patients, a program broadened in later years to prisons, military chapels, nursing homes, offices of doctors and dentists, and foreign refugee camps.

Besides providing Bibles in places where God's Word would be available to those who might not otherwise encounter it, Gideons also engaged in hand distribution of Scriptures from time to time, most notably as a large-scale effort to supply pocket editions to servicemen during and since World War II.

Early in its history the organization spread to Toronto, Canada, and subsequently to several other countries. International membership surged during the mid-century period. By 1980 the Gideon ministry was organized in 122 countries and Scriptures were being distributed in fifty languages.

Since 1964, Nashville has been the association's headquarters city.

Major changes in printing technology, coupled with membership growth, enabled the Gideons to expand remarkably their distribution of Bibles during the twentieth century's later years to a point where the average exceeded a million copies per week. In mid 2001, leaders calculated that the total since 1908 had just passed the one billion mark.

Membership including the women's auxiliary numbered 133,944 in the United States and 250,079 worldwide in September 2004.

Acknowledgments

Quotations that represented early, significant contributions to *On Reading the Bible* came from two multitalented writers: JAMES REAPSOME of Wheaton, Illinois, and DR. JAMES E. ROSSCUP of Whittier, California.

During his notable career as a Christian journalist, Jim Reapsome was managing editor of *Christianity Today* magazine, later serving as editor of the Billy Graham Center's *Evangelical Missions Quarterly* and its *World Pulse* newsletter. Jim Rosscup, an Arizonan who received his Ph.D. at the University of Aberdeen, Scotland, headed the department of Bible Exposition at Talbot Theological Seminary from 1965 until 1987. Since then, he has been a professor on the faculty of The Master's Seminary at Sun Valley, California.

Our friendship traces back memorably to newspaper days when the two Jims were young award-winning columnists and sports editors with whom I shared the pressure of many press deadlines.

My thanks go to them and to others who have given thoughtful suggestions and encouragement for this quotation anthology—Tom and Ruth Loney, Jim Gregory, Charlotte Maceo, Dr. Charles Baker, Ron Maness, Bob Thomas, Wallace Finfrock, Ann Shelton, Clay Bradfield, Stacy Obenhaus, Bill Reed, and Dr. Don Umphrey.

I am grateful also to Christopher Pope, whose Christian Authors database became a valued source of information via the internet.

Most of all, I want to thank my wife, Clare, who continues to amaze me with her keen skills in copyediting, proofreading, and solving *New York Times* crossword puzzles.

Contents

Quotations

JOHN QUINCY ADAMS

So great is my veneration for the Bible that the earlier my children begin to read it, the more confident will be my hope that they will prove useful citizens to their country and respectable members of society.

I speak as a man of the world to men of the world, and I say to you, search the Scriptures! The Bible is the book of all others, to be read at all ages, and in all conditions of human life—not to be read once or twice through and then laid aside, but to be read in small portions of one or two chapters every day, and never to be intermitted unless by some overruling necessity.

MARILYN McCORD ADAMS

However much it divides, the Bible also has a marvelous way of bringing people together.

NA'IM AKBAR

Black women "didn't know nothing" about Dr. Spock, but they did know the Bible. Raise up a child in the way he should go and when he is old he will not depart from it.

WILLIAM FOXWELL ALBRIGHT

Thanks to the Qumran discoveries, the New Testament proves to be in fact what it was formerly believed to be: the teaching of Christ and his immediate followers between circa 25 and circa 80 A.D. In the light of these finds, the New Testament becomes more Jewish than we thought—as truly Jewish as the Old Testament is Israelite. Yet both parts of our Bible are deeply indebted to the world in which they arose . . . The non-Jewish streams which flowed through Judaism into nascent Christianity were transfigured by the Cross and given a spiritual depth which was to transform the world.

From the Stone Age to Christianity

There can be no doubt that archaeology has confirmed the substantial historicity of the Old Testament. The excessive skepticism shown toward the Bible by important historical schools of the eighteenth and nineteenth centuries . . . has been progressively discredited. Discovery after discovery has established the accuracy of innumerable details, and has brought increased recognition to the value of the Bible as a source of history.   *The Archaeology of Palestine* (rev. ed.)

WICK ALLISON

Even if there were little external evidence of Jesus's life, the actions of His disciples and the written record produced by His followers hardly seem possible without a real person to inspire and motivate them. The fact that many of His early followers, including the Apostles themselves, were put to death on account of their fidelity to the mission they believed He had sent them on seems inconsistent with the notion that He was a fabrication.
That's in the Bible?

ROBERT ALTER

Genesis begins with the making of heaven and earth and all life, and ends with the image of a mummy—Joseph's—in a coffin. But implicit in the end is a promise of more life to come, of irrepressible procreation, and that renewal of creation will be manifested, even under the weight of oppression, at the beginning of Exodus . . . Although it looks forward to sequel, it stands as a book, inviting our attention as an audience that follows the tale from beginning to end.
Genesis: Translation and Commentary

MAX ANDERS

Without the Bible, we might believe that there was a God, but we would not know who He was, whether he wanted or expected anything from us, or how to get to know Him. The Bible fills in those gaps, and through the Scripture we can be led into an understanding of who God is and how to develop a relationship with Him.   *The New Christian's Handbook*

The word "inspired," when it is used in reference to the Bible, is a technical term meaning "God-breathed" . . . When God revealed His word to humans for the Bible, He supernaturally oversaw the writing down of the Scriptures so that without the loss of the writers' own personalities, they composed and recorded without error God's revelation in the original manuscripts and letters.   *The New Christian's Handbook*

PAUL M. ANDERSON

I recall one evening reading a statement made by a 19th century professor of natural sciences, Henry Drummond: "Willpower does not change men. Time does not change men. Christ does." I was somewhat startled—and excited—to realize that I understood its meaning. Subsequently, I bought a New Testament and read most of it in about three weeks. It amazed me. Here was a blueprint for living and a description and explanation of the sense of separation from God that I had been experiencing . . . I came to understand that one of the ways God communicates with us is through the writings of godly people as collected in the Bible, and that understanding its message is also a gift.

Professors Who Believe

SAINT THOMAS AQUINAS

It is one of the glories of the Bible that it can enshrine many meanings in a single passage . . . Each man marvels to find in the divine Scriptures truths which he has himself thought out.

De Potentia

MICHAEL C. ARMOUR

It is only natural to ask why the impact of the Bible has been so monumental. What accounts for its attractiveness over the centuries? And why is it still the best- selling book in the world? The answer lies in the great ideas conveyed by the Bible, the great truths it unfolds. No other book has ever surpassed its exalted view of God and His love for mankind. In a word, the Bible stretches our sense of who God is and what we have the potential to become because of His love.

A Newcomer's Guide to the Bible

WILLIAM ARNDT

In reading and studying the books of the New Testament, we are doing what in other fields of learning would be considered beyond the scope or ability of the average person. Consulting primary sources is ordinarily the task of scholars and experts. When they have finished their work and written down their findings for us, we are satisfied. But in examining the books of the New Testament, we have access to the original documents in translation and do the research work ourselves.

MATTHEW W. ARNOLD
He will find one English book and one only, where, as in the *Iliad* itself, perfect plainness of speech is allied with perfect nobleness, and that book is the Bible.

KAY ARTHUR
The Bible was written so that anyone who wants to know who God is and how they are to live in a way that pleases Him can read it and find out. God wants to bring us into intimacy with Himself . . . He also wants us to understand the blessings of a life of obedience to His Word and the consequences of disobeying Him. And He wants us to know the truth about life and what is going to happen in the future.   *How to Study Your Bible*

GAIUS GLENN ATKINS
The Bible furnished good Christians an armor for their warfare, a guide for their conduct, a solace for their sorrows, food for their soul.

SAINT AUGUSTINE OF HIPPO
Scripture, which proves the truth of its historical statements by the accomplishment of its prophecies, gives no false information.
                                    The City of God, Book XVI

If you believe what you like in the Gospels and reject what you don't like, it is not the Gospels you believe, but yourself.

PAUL AZINGER
. . . During this time I faithfully attended a Bible Study Fellowship group in our hometown. I had been reading the Bible regularly since my first chemo. After recommitting my life to the Lord, I found that the Bible was no longer a dusty book, but a living Word. I knew I couldn't live without it ever again. My initial

meeting of the Bible study impressed me in many ways: the number of men there, the demographic diversity—wealthy and poor, black and white, young and old. But all the guys had a common goal—to discover in the Bible how Jesus Christ could be more real in their lives. My Bible study group became a mainstay in my physical and spiritual improvement.

Zinger: A Champion's Story of Determination, Courage, and Charging Back

JOHANN SEBASTIAN BACH

This is the great fountain of music, and every musician should play to the glory of its Author.

FRANCIS BACON

Prosperity is the blessing of the Old Testament; adversity is the blessing of the New.   *Essays*

JIM BALL

The Scripture passages attest (that) this land is not my land, this land is not your land, this land is God's land. This land was not made for you and me, it was made by and for Christ.

Creation Care

SAL BANDO

God's gift, the Bible, is my manual on how to live a fruitful and meaningful life. I have found the Bible's truth and authority to be restorative. In both my personal life and my professional baseball life, the Bible has been a foundation and a guide to work through life's highs and lows. The Bible provides peace and strength for all my tomorrows.

WILLIAM BARCLAY

The Gospels are not primarily historical documents; they are not intended to be regarded as biographies of Jesus. They are in fact the preaching material of the early church . . . They are attempts to show the mind and heart and the character of Jesus; and they make this attempt, not simply as a matter of interest, and not simply as a contribution to history, but so that those who read may see the mind of God in Jesus. The Gospels are not

simply descriptions of Jesus—they are invitations to believe in
him as the Son of God.   *Introducing the Bible*

GEORGE BARNA

Almost all believers own a Bible (99 percent); in fact, more
than three-quarters of them own three or more Bibles. Most of
them read from the Bible, other than during church services, in a
typical week. Three out of four believers indicate that during a
typical week they have at least one "quiet time" or private
devotional time. Most Christians take the Bible seriously.

Growing True Disciples

ALBERT BARNES

The Bible, as a revelation from God, was not designed to give
us all the information we might desire, nor to solve all the
questions about which the human soul is perplexed, but to impart
enough to be a safe guide to the haven of eternal rest.

WILLIAM BARNES

It does not require great learning to be a Christian and to be
convinced of the truth of the Bible. It requires only an honest
heart and a willingness to obey God.

WILLIE BARROW

When I get down really low, I just go back to the Bible. He
promised us that He would be our mother, our father, our sister,
our brother, and I just keep going over that . . . Lord, I don't have
nobody but you—you've got to come and lift my spirit.

Will the Circle Be Unbroken?

KARL BARTH

Any Christian who wishes to live responsibly must read two
things: the Bible and the daily newspaper—and never one
without the other.

The Holy Scriptures will interpret themselves in spite of our
human limitations. We need only to follow this drive, this spirit,
this river, to grow out beyond ourselves toward the highest
answer. This daring is faith; and we read the Bible rightly, not
when we do so with false modesty, restraint, and attempted
sobriety, for these are passive qualities, but when we read it in

faith. And the invitation to dare and to reach toward the highest, even though we do not deserve it, is the expression of grace in the Bible.

It is not the right human thoughts about God which form the content of the Bible, but the right divine thoughts about men. The Bible tells us not how we should talk with God but what He says to us, not how we find the way to Him, but how He has sought and found the way to us; not the right relation in which we must place ourselves to Him, but the covenant which He has made with all who are Abraham's spiritual children and which He has sealed once and for all in Jesus Christ. It is this which is within the Bible. The Word of God is within the Bible.

The Strange New World Within the Bible

BRUCE BARTON

The Bible rose to the place it now occupies because it deserved to rise to that place, and not because God sent anybody with a box of tricks to prove its divine authority.

The Man and the Book Nobody Knows

JACQUES BARZUN

The Bible was a whole literature, a library. It was an anthology of poetry and short stories. It taught history, biography, biology, geography, philosophy, political science, psychology, hygiene, and sociology (statistical at that), in addition to cosmogony, ethics, and theology. What gives the Bible so strong a hold on minds that once grow familiar with its contents is its dramatic reporting of human affairs. For all its piety, it presents a worldly panorama, and with particulars so varied that it is hard to think of a domestic or social situation without a biblical example to match and turn to moral ends.

From Dawn to Decadence

MARY BATCHELOR

Stained-glass windows . . . were once the ordinary person's Bible. Before the invention of printing or the spread of literacy, men and women learned the Bible and the basics of their faith from the scenes depicted in church and cathedral windows . . . The original techniques of making stained glass have survived the centuries, although these days most sheets of coloured glass are produced commercially. But one artist explained why she still prefers the much more expensive hand-made glass. "We pay for the imperfections," she acknowledged. The light is reflected through these small flaws and in this way every window makes its own unique and beautiful impact on the beholder. The men and women whose stories the Bible tells have flaws and imperfections too, and the Bible never tries to hide them. Often, as God impinges on their lives, these very imperfections become the means of reflecting the light of God's love and power . . .

Windows on the Bible

HENRY WARD BEECHER

The Bible is God's chart for you to steer by, to keep you from the bottom of the sea, to show you where the harbor is, and how to reach it without running on rocks and bars . . . Sink the Bible to the bottom of the ocean and man's obligations to God would be unchanged. He would have the same path to tread, only his lamp and guide would be gone. He would have the same voyage to make, only his compass and chart would be overboard.

D. R. BENSEN
The Tower of Babel

Their tower's impressive statistics
Pleased architects, boosters, and mystics,
But their excess of pride
Caused the Lord to decide
It was time they studied linguistics.

Biblical Limericks

ROBERT BENSON

I know a little girl who claims that she talks with God and that God talks back. She is not the only little one who has ever made such a claim, but she is the only one who has made such a claim around me, so I listen to her. I am afraid not to. If the Bible is to be believed on any sort of basis at all, then God has certainly done stranger things than talk to five-year-old girls. People whose view of the Scriptures is literal will tell you that they believe that God created the world in a few days, including kangaroos, trees that lose their leaves every year and some others that do not, broccoli and other assorted vegetables that masquerade as edible foods, and a couple of hundred different species of monkeys—the last, presumably, for pure entertainment value.

Between the Dreaming and the Coming True

WENDELL BERRY

The Bible leaves no doubt at all about (it) . . . We are holy creatures living among other holy creatures in a world that is holy. Some people know this and some do not. Nobody, of course, knows it all the time. But what keeps it from being far better known than it is? Why is it apparently unknown to millions of professed students of the Bible? How can modern Christianity have so solemnly folded its hands while so much of the work of God was and is being destroyed?

MARY MCLEOD BETHUNE

"Whosoever," it said. No Jew nor Gentile, no Catholic nor Protestant, no black nor white, just "whosoever." It meant that I, a humble Negro girl, had just as much chance as anybody in the sight and love of God. Those words stored up a battery of faith and confidence and determination in my heart, which has not failed me to this day.

GILBERT BILEZIKIAN

In majestic tones, the opening words of the Bible announce that before time began and all things were created, there existed nothing and no one but God. Before anything else, God was. Human life cannot exist outside of time and space. We need time to breathe, to think, to work, and to play. We need places where we can move, rest, and rise. Not so with God. He created time, space, and everything that exists within them. He was before creation.

Christianity 101

JOSH BILLINGS

Almost any fool can prove the Bible ain't so. It takes a wise man to believe it.

WILLIAM BLADES

The custom of fastening books to their shelves by chains was common in an early period throughout all Europe . . . Large collections of chained books were for the use of particular bodies of students. But when religious zeal made many people feel the want of spiritual food, it led to the chaining of single volumes in churches, where any parishioner able to read could satisfy his soul. The Bible was, of course, one of the most common, and among others were Foxe's *Book of Martyrs,* the various works of Bishop Jewel, and other divines.

ALLAN BLOOM

My grandparents were ignorant people by our standards, and my grandfather held only lowly jobs. But their home was spiritually rich, because all the things done in it, not only what was specifically ritual, found their origin in the Bible's commandments, and their explanation in the Bible's stories and the commentaries on them, and had their imaginative counterparts in the deeds of the myriad of exemplary heroes. My grandparents found reasons for the existence of their family and the fulfillment of their duties in serious writings, and they interpreted their special sufferings with respect to a great and ennobling past.   *The Closing of the American Mind*

HAROLD BLOOM

No one in the West can now hope to read the Bible without having been conditioned by it, or by the various misreadings it has engendered.   *The Book of J*

BENSON BOBRICK

Up to the Middle Ages, the Bible was known only in Latin, and the Church had cast itself in the role of the sole proper authority to interpret what the text said. It had interposed itself between the text and the reader . . . A movement developed in England under John Wycliffe—he was the representative of it in the late 14th century—to see that the Scriptures were rendered into the vernacular and made available to the people. He was succeeded by a number of other translators despite tremendous resistance from the Church, and subsequent translations were also christened by martyrs' blood, but ultimately, by the middle of the 16th century, the Scriptures were widely available in English. Once the people had direct access to the Scriptures, it fostered habits of reading and reflection . . . At the same time, once the people were free to interpret the word of God according to the light of their own understanding, they began to question the authority of all their inherited institutions, which led to reform within in the Church.

Daniel Webster once remarked that the tavern was the headquarters of the American Revolution—meaning, in part, that ideas of self-determination could only emerge in a setting where free discussion naturally took place. That discussion was free because the English Reformation had established the ground and right to it, by virtue of the place the English Bible had in people's lives. Already, in 1546, Henry VIII had complained to Parliament that the Bible was being "disputed, rhymed, sung and jangled in every ale house and tavern," and there is a kind of poetic rightness to the notion that it was the tavern where the Reformation was also born. *Wide As the Waters*

LORAINE BOETTNER

As we proclaim the word of life from the pulpit, or in the classroom; as we attempt to give comfort at some bed of sickness, or in a bereaved home; or as we see our fellow men struggling against temptation or weighed down with care, and would give them encouragement and hope for this world and the next, how thankful we are then for a fully trustworthy Bible!

The Inspiration of Scripture

JAMES MONTGOMERY BOICE

The Scriptures of the Old and New Testaments were given by inspiration of God, and are the only sufficient, certain, and authoritative rule of all saving, knowledge, faith, and obedience.

Abstract of Principles

MARTHA BOLTON

Scripture doesn't say that the cheerful heart has joy only in the good times. It says it has a *continual* feast—in the good times, the bad times, when we get that grocery cart with all four wheels going in opposite directions, when that instant teller machine pretends it's never heard of us and swallows our card, when we get a flat tire in front of our children's school. We can have a feast of joy 24 hours a day, no matter what comes our way.

Lamp unto My Feet

NAPOLEON BONAPARTE

If the Bible is not true religion, one is very excusable in being deceived, for everything in it is grand and worthy of God. The more I consider the Gospel, the more I am assured there is nothing there which is not beyond the march of events and above the human mind.

DIETRICH BONHOEFFER

It is implicit in the New Testament statement concerning the incarnation of God in Christ that all men are taken up, enclosed and borne within the body of Christ, and that this is just what the congregation of the faithful are to make known to the world by their words and by their lives. What is intended here is . . . the summoning of the world into the fellowship of this body of Christ, to which in truth it already belongs.   *Ethics*

A concert audience does not come to watch a conductor, but to hear the music. A church congregation should not come to watch or hear the preacher, but to listen to the Word of God.

It is not with the next world that we are concerned, but with this world as created and preserved and set subject to laws and atoned for and made new. What is above the world is, in the Gospel, intended to exist *for* this world . . . in the Bible sense of the creation and of the incarnation, crucifixion, and resurrection of Jesus Christ.   *Letters and Papers from Prison*

DAVE BOONE

Most books fill a place in your library. This one fills a place in your life.

DANIEL J. BOORSTIN

God is the celebrity-author of the world's best-seller.

MARCUS J. BORG

As the foundation of the Christian tradition, the Bible is the source of our images and stories for speaking of God's passion. Thus its interpretation shapes our vision of what it means to take the God of the Bible seriously. The Bible is also a sacrament of the same sacred mystery, a means whereby God speaks to us still today. Through and within the Bible's many voices, we are called to discern *the voice* that addresses us in our time. And listen. What we hear matters greatly.

Reading the Bible Again for the First Time

MARTHA BOSHART

There are many "higher powers" but there is only one Jesus and only one way. There is only one instruction manual . . . If you don't read another book in your life, read that one. If you don't even finish reading the book you have in your hands right now, read that one.   *Heaven—Who's Got the Tickets*

WILLIAM D. BOSWELL

It was said by some that by the 20th century, the Bible would be obsolete. Ingersoll said that in 100 years from his time there wouldn't be a copy of the Bible left. Poor Ingersoll has long since gone the way of all the earth, and the very printing press he used to print his poisonous literature has been converted into a press to print Bibles . . . During the past fifty years, the Bible has had its greatest increase in circulation and influence.

Boswell's Sermons

ALLEN BOWMAN

The thousands of promises in the Bible are set forth as proceeding from God Himself. Some of them are unconditional, pointing to an inevitable fulfillment regardless of what people do. Most of them are conditional, assuring the reader that if he meets stated conditions, God will do certain things . . . For the conditional promises, we have the vast materials of church history as well as thousands of diaries, autobiographies, and biographies of spiritually minded people who have actually ventured out on the assurance the Bible gives.

JAMES PETIGRU BOYCE

Q. How came the Bible to be written?
A. God inspired holy men to write it.
Q. Did they write it exactly as God wished?
A. Yes, as much as if he had written every word himself.
Q. Ought it, therefore, to be believed and obeyed?
A. Yes, as much as though God had spoken directly to us.

Brief Catechism of Bible Doctrine

DAVID JOSIAH BREWER

The American nation, from its first settlement at Jamestown to the present hour, is based upon and permeated by the principles of the Bible. The more this Bible enters into our national life the grander and purer and better that life will become.

JOHN ALBERT BROADUS

It is entirely possible that we may have no creed or system of theology, no professors or even preachers, nor even newspaper writers, nor writers of tracts, that can always interpret the Bible with infallible success. But our persuasion is that the real meaning of the Bible is true.

Paramount and Permanent Authority of the Bible

DAVID BROOKS

In the political sphere, there is conflict and rigid partisanship. In the religious sphere, there is mobility, ecumenical understanding, and blurry boundaries. If George Bush and Howard Dean met each other on a political platform, they would fight and feud. If they met in a Bible study group and talked about their eternal souls, they'd probably embrace.

New York Times, 12/30/2003

PHILLIPS BROOKS

The Bible is like a telescope. If a man looks *through* his telescope, then he sees worlds beyond—but if he looks *at* his telescope, then he does not see anything but that. The Bible is a thing to be looked through, to see that which is beyond.

LEWIS BROWNE

When read intelligently, the Bible reveals itself as the immortal epic of a people's confused, faltering, but indomitable struggle for a nobler life in a happier world.   *The Graphic Bible*

F. F. BRUCE

The people and events described in the Bible were very much down-to-earth. They did not belong to some never-never land above the clouds. Some of the men and women we meet in the Bible lived all their lives in the same place. Many others travelled widely. While Jesus taught for three years only, mainly within Palestine, Paul's extensive journeys took him through the Roman empire around the Mediterranean Sea. If we can envisage them in their various geographical settings, it helps us to understand many of the things that are recorded about them.

Jesus and Paul: Places They Knew

A Bible version of a different kind is the *Picture Bible for All Ages,* issued in six paperback volumes by Scripture Union (1974). This strip cartoon version takes us back to the earliest days of English Christianity, when the Bible story was brought home to the people by wall-paintings and relief-drawings in churches and by carved panels, representing scenes from the Gospels, like those on the Ruthwell Cross and similar monuments. Have we thus, in the course of the centuries, come full circle from pre-literacy to post-literacy?   *History of the Bible in English*

There is, I imagine, no body of literature in the world that has been exposed to the stringent analytical study that the four Gospels have sustained for the past 200 years. This is not something to be regretted; it is something to be accepted with satisfaction. Scholars today who treat the Gospels as credible historic documents do so in the full light of this analytical study, not by closing their minds to it.

JOHN F. BRUG

The Book of Psalms is a miniature Bible, a miniature history of God's people. It expresses all the feelings and experiences they will ever have.   *People's Bible Commentary: Psalms II*

ROBERT WILLIAMS BUCHANAN

Alone at nights, I read my Bible more and Euclid less.

PEARL BUCK

As I write, it occurs to me that the Bible has another meaning. It is an Asian book, for Christianity came out of the East. It seems a contradiction that today the West, facing conflict with the East, should nevertheless find its own source of spiritual life in a volume of Asia, centering around the Jews, who, though they have wandered far, nevertheless remain in many ways true to their ancient history which is Asian. It may be that in this very fact we shall find the means of a common understanding, a basic agreement on the constitution for a peaceful world.

The Story Bible

JAMIE BUCKINGHAM

Read the Bible devotionally, and let God meet you at your place of greatest need—perhaps through a simple verse and a small reminder at your elbow. Ask questions. The Bible is not so sacred that it cannot stand honest examination. Ask *when* a thing took place. Ask *why* it was included in the Bible. Ask *where* it happened. Ask *who* was writing, *whom* it was written about. Ask *what* it meant at that time and *what* it should mean to you. Don't be frustrated if your study raises more questions than you can answer. You are dipping into a great well of spiritual knowledge that has no limits but will quench all thirst.

JOSEPH BUCKINGHAM

I have no recollection of any time when I could not read . . . In December 1784, the month in which I was five years old, I went to a master's school, and, on being asked whether I could read, I said I could read in the Bible. The master placed me on his chair and presented a Bible opened at the fifth chapter of Acts. I read the story of Ananias and Sapphira falling down dead for telling a lie. He patted me on the head and commended my reading.

WILLIAM F. BUCKLEY, JR.

We cannot . . . confidently assume that we have heard correctly the word of God as given to us in the Bible. That word is best likened to the Lost Chord about which Arthur Sullivan wrote, the chord perhaps accidentally, perhaps providentially, struck one day by the discursive fingers of the organist. He struggles to finger again the same notes that produced that sound, musically, spiritually, orgasmic. He does not, in Arthur Sullivan's account, ever succeed. It is a Christian postulate that those who struggle to decipher that chord will one day hear it. Anyone looking for God, Pascal said, will find Him.

Nearer to God: An Autobiography of Faith

FREDERICK BUECHNER

How many ways are there to read the Bible? You can read it
devotionally, and I suppose I do that somewhat, St. Paul
especially. But I don't want to give the impression I'm a great
Bible reader. I don't sit down every day and read for an hour
through the Bible. But I really do read it with a great deal of
pleasure . . . which is the last thing I would have suspected. It's
fun to read. So I read it sometimes as a devotional, but really
more, not for fun, but because it's fascinating.

The Door Interviews

JOHN BUNYAN

God's book of grace is just like his book of nature: it is his
thoughts written out. This great book, the Bible, this most
precious volume is the heart of God made legible. It is the gold of
God's love beaten out into gold leaf, so that therewith our
thoughts might be plated, and we also might have golden, good
and holy thoughts concerning him.

Read and read again, and do not despair of help to understand
the will and mind of God though you may think they are fast
locked up from you. Neither trouble your heads though you have
not commentaries and exposition. Pray and read, read and pray;
for a little from God is better than a great deal from men.

I never had in all my life so great an inlet in the Word of God
as now (in prison). The Scriptures that I saw nothing in before are
made in this place to shine upon me. Jesus Christ also was never
more real and apparent than now. Here I have seen him and felt
him indeed . . . I have seen (such things) here that I am
persuaded I shall never while in this world be able to express . . .
Being very tender of me, (God) hath not suffered me to be
molested, but would with one scripture and another strengthen
me against all; insomuch that I have often said, were it lawful I
could pray for greater trouble for the greater comfort's sake.

Grace Abounding to the Chief of Sinners

ABE BURROWS and JOE SWERLING

Maybe the Bible don't read as lively as the scratch sheet, but it is at least twice as accurate.

Guys and Dolls

JOHN BURTON

Holy Bible, book divine,
Precious treasure, thou art mine;
Mine to teach me whence I came,
Mine to teach me what I am.
Mine to chide me when I rove;
Mine to show a Savior's love.
Mine thou art to guide and guard;
Mine to punish or reward.

"Holy Bible, Book Divine" (hymn)

SAMUEL BUTLER

The Bible is like the poor: we have it always with us, but we know very little about it.   *Notebooks*

GEORGE A. BUTTRICK

There is obviously interpretation in the Gospels. They are indeed a faith-proclamation, necessarily written in the language and thought-forms of their time, and they involve mythic elements. But their core is history, not myth . . . The Bible at base is history.   *Christ and History*

MILDRED CABLE and FRANCESCA FRENCH

Every Gobi trade route carries all these people and many more, and the missionary's problem is now to convey a message which fits every one of them. Only one book can do this, because it is the Word of God which is for every man of every nation, but it must be taken to him in his own language or it is of no use to him. This means that one must learn the language so well that he can translate the Bible into it.

THOMAS CAHILL

The Bible is the record *par excellence* of the Jewish religious experience, an experience that remains fresh and even shocking when it is read against the myths of other ancient literatures. The word *bible* comes from the Greek plural form *biblia*, meaning "books." And though the Bible is rightly considered *the* book of the Western world—its foundation document—it is actually a collection of books, a various library written almost entirely in Hebrew over the course of a thousand years . . . To most readers today, the Bible is a confusing hodge-podge; and those who take up the daunting task of reading it from cover to cover seldom maintain their resolve beyond a book or two. Though the Bible is full of literature's two great themes, love and death (as well as its exciting caricatures, sex and violence), it is also full of tedious ritual prescriptions and interminable battles. More than anything, because the Bible is the product of so many hands over so many ages, it is full of confusion for the modern reader who attempts to decode what it might be about.   *The Gifts of the Jews*

We can read the Bible (as postmodernists do) as a jumble of unrelated texts, given a false and superficial unity by redactors of the exile period and later. But this is to ignore not only the powerful emotional and spiritual effect that much of the Bible has on readers, even on readers who would rather not be moved, but also its cumulative impact on whole societies.

(We cannot) imagine the great liberation movements of modern history without reference to the Bible. Without the Bible we would never have known the abolitionist movement, the prison-reform movement, the antiwar movement, the labor movement, the civil rights movement, the movements of indigenous and dispossessed peoples for their human rights, the antiapartheid movement in South Africa, the Solidarity movement in Poland, the free-speech and pro-democracy movements in such Far Eastern countries as South Korea, the Philippines, and even China. These movements in modern times have all employed the language of the Bible; and it is even impossible to understand their great heroes and heroines—people like Harriet Tubman, Sojourner Truth, Mother Jones, Mahatma Ghandi, Martin Luther King, Cesar Chavez, Helder Camara, Oscar Romero, Rigoberta Menchu, Corazon Aquino, Nelson Mandela, Desmond Tutu, Charity Kaluki Ngilu, Harry Wu—without recourse to the Bible.   *The Gifts of the Jews*

JOHN CALVIN

It is only in the Scriptures that the Lord hath been pleased to preserve his truth in perpetual remembrance. It obtains the same complete credit and authority with believers, where they are satisfied of its divine origin, as if they heard the very words pronounced by God Himself.   *Institutes*

Scripture, carrying its own evidence along with it . . . owes the full conviction with which we ought to receive it to the testimony of the Spirit. Enlightened by him, we . . . feel perfectly assured— as much so as if we beheld the divine image visibly impressed on it—that it came to us, by the instrumentality of men, from the very mouth of God . . . we feel a divine energy living and breathing in it . . .

PETER CALVOCORESSI

The Bible's main characters have lived on, in the imagination of later generations and in their works of art. For 2000 years, artists have retold the Bible's stories in stone and glass, in prose and verse, in paint and music. Generation by generation, these works have shaped the biblical figures who were first presented to us by the Bible itself.

ALEXANDER CAMPBELL

The works of God and the words of God, or the things done and spoken by God, are those facts which are laid down and exhibited in the Bible as the foundation of all faith, hope, love, piety, and humility.

STAN CAMPBELL

We can study Scripture by using all the resources at our disposal, and we can meditate on what it says until our gray matter hurts, but only God Himself in the form of the Holy Spirit can clarify certain passages so that they make sense to those who have placed faith in Him. Much of the Old Testament was (intentionally) a mystery until Jesus appeared and revealed how He would make sense of it all. Similarly, other portions of Scripture remain vague and foggy until we connect with God through His Holy Spirit and are enabled to see more clearly what He is revealing to us.

"The World's Easiest Guide" to Understanding the Bible

JAMES CANTELEON

Paul had a problem with women's rights? Amos wrote from the perspective of a rustic, and Isaiah from that of a courtier? Solomon was bitter with life? John thought he was Jesus' favorite? So what? What impresses me is the uniformity and universality of the timeless message coming through these human filters. I read the Bible and I hear from God. His Word speaks to me and my generation. What's more, it challenges me to change myself and my world. In preparation for its promise of a new heaven and a new earth on the horizon. It leads, I'll follow, because I trust the Author.   *Theology for Non-Theologians*

MICHAEL CARD

Long ago I realized that one purpose of the Bible was to turn an eye into an ear. "Pay careful attention to what you have heard," the writer of Hebrews warns his readers. The author intends for his readers to become *hearers* of the Word in the truest sense. Music provides a means toward this transformation. I suppose that's what attracted me to songwriting in the first place. It offers another vehicle for experiencing what the Bible has to say. Another way to *hear*.

> There is a hunger, a longing for bread
> And so comes the call for the poor to be fed.
> More hungry by far are a billion and more
> Who wait for the Bread of the Word of the Lord.
> So many books, so little time
> So many hungry, so many blind.
> Starving for words, they must wait in the night
> To open a Bible and move towards the Light.
> *So Many Books, So Little Time*

NORMAN CARLISLE

There is no joy in getting by on your job—doing as little as you can. There is a lot of pleasure in doing more than you have to. "And whosoever shall compel you to go a mile, go with him twain," says the Bible, wisely.

THOMAS CARLYLE

It must have been a most blessed discovery, that of an old Latin Bible which he found in the Erfurt Library about this time.

He had never seen the Book before. It taught him another lesson than that of fasts and vigils... Luther learned now that a man was saved not by singing masses, but by the infinite grace of God: a more credible hypothesis. He gradually got himself founded, as on the rock. No wonder he should venerate the Bible, which had brought this blessed help to him. He prized it as the Word of the Highest must be prized by such a man. He determined to hold by that, as through life and to death he firmly did.

What built St. John's Cathedral? Look at the heart of the matter. It was that divine Hebrew book—the word partly of the man Moses, an outlaw tending his Midianitish herds four thousand years ago in the wilderness of Sinai! It is the strangest of things, yet nothing is truer!   *Heroes and Hero-Worship*

The period of the Reformation was a judgment day for Europe, when all the nations were presented with an open Bible, and all the emancipation of heart and intellect which an open Bible involves.

S. E. CARPENTER
The Bible contains the revelation of the living God, the God who acts, who has a purpose for the world and carries it forward in what men call history.

JIMMY CARTER
It is interesting now to go back into the Old Testament, to correlate the prophecies with what we know from the Gospels about Jesus as a human being, and then to try to apply this awareness to our own lives.

All of us can try to live an average life—nothing special, but good enough to get along and to make us feel self-satisfied. But an important reason to study the Scriptures is to help each of us define and strive for a transcendent life—a life that reaches above and beyond what is normally expected of us. From Scripture, we can learn how Jesus Christ lived and what he set forth as proper priorities for human existence. We are aware of this opportunity in moments of exaltation or inspiration, when we are embarrassed by our own inadequacies, or perhaps when we are in total despair.

The Bible offers concrete guidance for overcoming our
weaknesses and striving toward the transcendent life for which we
were created.   *Sources of Strength*

GEORGE WASHINGTON CARVER

The secret of my success? It is found in the Bible: "In all thy
ways acknowledge Him, and He shall direct thy paths."

ANGIER CAUDLE

In Genesis 1, we can locate a range of images of God. For one
thing, we get a sense of the immensity of God—an immensity
increased all the more by what modern science reveals about
creation: more than one hundred billion stars in our own galaxy,
for example, and maybe a hundred billion galaxies! Surely a God
who can create all that can contain even our experiences of exile
and despair. We also get a sense of the nearness of this God, who
not only speaks us into being on the sixth day, but also speaks
directly to us, inviting and even trusting our participation in
creation.   *Faith @ Work* magazine, Spring 2004

TERESA CAVALCANTI

The cry of the women prophets of the Bible is in line with the
cries of Israel in Egypt, and it will lead to the cry of Jesus, who,
throughout his life and until the time of his death, took up the cry
of the suffering and oppressed of the world.

RICHARD CECIL

The history of all the great characters of the Bible is summed
up in this one sentence: They acquainted themselves with God,
and acquiesced in His will in all things.

SAMUEL CHADWICK

Give no heed to people that discredit it, for they speak without
knowledge. It is the Word of God in the inspired speech of
humanity. Read it for yourself. Read it thoroughly. Study it
according to its own directions. Live by its principles.

No man is uneducated who knows the Bible, and no man is
wise who is ignorant of its teaching.

OSWALD CHAMBERS

The Bible treats us as human life does—roughly.

The Bible does not thrill, the Bible nourishes. Give time to the reading of the Bible, and the recreating effect is as real as that of fresh air physically.

If you have no vision from God, no enthusiasm in your life, and no one watching and encouraging you, it requires the grace of Almighty God to take the next step in your devotion to Him, in the reading and studying of His Word, in your family life, or in your duty to Him. It takes much more of the grace of God, and a much greater awareness of drawing upon Him . . . We lose interest and give up when we have no vision, no encouragement, no improvement, but only experience our everyday life with its trivial tasks. The thing that testifies for God and for the people of God in the long run is steady perseverance, even when the work cannot be seen by others.   *My Utmost for His Highest*

God's Book is packed full of overwhelming riches. They are unsearchable—the more we have, the more there is to have.

WHITTAKER CHAMBERS

The Bible is, I suppose, the single greatest anti-intellectual book ever put together, but it is full of those magical simple phrasings—bread on the water, etc. It is full of them, of course, because it is, at its best, about simple life; because Job's question ("Why me?"), the central theme, remains unanswered, and because Jonah does not lie, but says, "I do well to be angry."

WILLIAM ELLERY CHANNING

We ought indeed to expect occasional obscurity in such a book as the Bible . . . but God's wisdom is a pledge that whatever is necessary for us, and necessary for salvation, is revealed too plainly to be mistaken.

In the New Testament I learn that God regards the human soul with unutterable interest and love; that in an important sense it bears the impress of His own infinity, its powers being germs, which may expand without limit or end; that He loves it, even when fallen, and desires its restoration; that He has sent His Son

to redeem and cleanse it from all iniquity; that He forever seeks
to communicate to it a divine virtue which shall spring up, by
perennial bloom and fruitfulness, into everlasting life.

The Perfect Life

JOHN JAY CHAPMAN

The New Testament is the Thesaurus of sacred wisdom,
compared to which there is no book or monument that deserves
to be named.

RAY CHARLES

There's nothing written in the Bible, Old or New Testament,
that says if you believe in Me you ain't going to have troubles.

Brother Ray

E. La B. CHERBONNIER

According to the Bible, life confronts every man and nation
with a decisive either/or. Choose the true God and live, or choose
a false god, and perish. There remains one final device by which
men have sought to escape this choice. It is cynicism, the attempt
to avoid entanglement with the fickle gods of idealism by
espousing none at all . . . An examination of cynicism reveals
exactly what the biblical analysis would lead one to expect. Every
cynic turns out to be a covert idealist, in the sense that he does
gravitate toward some standard outside himself as the criterion of
his decision.   *Hardness of Heart*

GILBERT K. CHESTERTON

The Bible tells us to love our neighbors, and also to love our
enemies, probably because they are generally the same people.

RUFUS CHOATE

No lawyer can afford to be ignorant of the Bible.

JOHN CHRYSOSTOM

When God saw that many men were lazy and gave themselves
only with difficulty to spiritual reading, He wished to make it easy
for them. He added melody to the words, that all being rejoiced
by the charm of the music should sing hymns to Him with
gladness.

ELDRIDGE CLEAVER

When Kathleen left the United States she brought with her a very small bag, and instead of grabbing the Communist Manifesto or *Das Kapital*, she packed that Bible. That is the Bible I grabbed from the shelf that night and in which I turned to the 23rd Psalm. I discovered that my memory really had not served me that well. I got lost somewhere between the Valley of the Shadow of Death and the overflowing cup. But it was the Bible in which I searched and found that psalm. I read through it. At the time, I didn't even know where to find the Lord's Prayer. Pretty soon the type started swimming before my eyes, and I lay down on the bed and went to sleep. That night, I slept the most peaceful sleep I have ever known in my life.   *Soul on Fire*

VAN CLIBURN

My parents had me memorize verses of Scripture when I was three years old. I have lived with them all my life. King Solomon, the writer of Proverbs, expresses it all so eloquently . . .
Lamp unto My Feet

DAVID CLINES

The great prophets whose messages we have in the Old Testament appeared on the scene only at times of crisis in the nation's history. They were God's men for the moment and their messages were generally concerned with particular times and places. They remain valid and helpful because the same kinds of situations have recurred again and again in history.
The Lion Encyclopedia of the Bible

KIMBERLEE H. COLBY

In the big picture, most Christian parents understand that objective teaching is better than ignoring or suppressing the Bible.   *The New York Times,* 11/12/99

SAMUEL TAYLOR COLERIDGE

Intense study of the Bible will keep any writer from being vulgar in point of style.   *Table Talk*

I have found in the Bible words for my innermost thoughts, songs for my joy, utterance for my hidden griefs, and pleadings for my shame and feebleness.

For more than a thousand years, the Bible, collectively taken, has gone hand-in-hand with civilization, science, law—in short, with the moral and intellectual cultivation of the species, always supporting and often leading the way.

CHARLES COLSON

Who speaks for God? He does quite nicely for Himself. Through His holy and infallible Word and the quiet obedience of His servants.

The Bible is not like any other book, but you have to read it like any other book. Parables are parables. Poetry is poetry. Metaphors are metaphors. Where you have to be very careful is reading a didactic teaching as didactic teaching, reading historical accounts as clearly historical accounts, and reading parables as parables. When it says that the heavens declare the glory of God, well, we know that the heavens don't speak. We use the same expressions in modern American language. We say the mountains clap their hands. We say that the sun rises. But the sun doesn't rise. Obviously. We know that. But that's a figure of speech. And the Bible is replete with figures of speech that people could understand. And they have to be read as figures of speech.

Searching for God in America

CHRISTOPHER COLUMBUS

It was the Lord who put into my mind (I could feel his hand upon me) that it would be possible to sail from here to the Indies. All who heard of my project rejected it with laughter, ridiculing me. There is no question that the inspiration was from the Holy Spirit, because He comforted me with rays of marvelous inspiration from the Holy Scriptures.

JOSEPH COOK

Do you know a book that you are willing to put under your head for a pillow when you are dying? Very well, that is the book you want to study when you are living. There is only one such book in the world.

CALVIN COOLIDGE

It is hard to see how a great man can be an atheist. Skeptics do not contribute. Cynics do not create. Faith is the great motive power, and no man realizes his full possibilities unless he has the deep conviction that life is eternally important and that his work, well done, is a part of an unending plan.

M. F. COTTRELL

We have referred to the Bible as the Way of Life Exposed . . . By this we mean nothing less than the application of the teachings of God for happy, successful daily living. To live in harmony with the teaching of God is not only being good, it is being smart. Conversely, failing to do so is not only sinful, it is stupid.
Refocusing God: The Bible and the Church

WILLIAM COWPER

A glory gilds the sacred page,
Majestic like the sun;
It gives a light to every age—
It gives, but borrows none.
The hand that gave it still supplies
The gracious light and heat;
His truths upon the nations rise—
They rise, but never set.
The Light and Glory

HARVEY COX

The Bible does not provide a model for family life. Nor does it supply many images of truly emancipated women, though there are a few. Rather, the importance of biblical faith for the freeing of women from the cultural and religious images by which they have been held for so long in bondage lies elsewhere. It lies in the inclusive vision of biblical religion which sees God's ultimate purpose as the liberation and maturation of all human beings, and of all creation, to their full potential in a cosmic feast of love and joy.   *The Seduction of the Spirit*

THOMAS CRANMER

Therefore, every man that cometh to the reading of this holy book ought to bring with him first and foremost this fear of Almighty God, and then next a firm and stable purpose to reform his own self according thereto.

In the Scriptures be the fat pastures of the soul. Therein is no venomous meat, no unwholesome thing—they be the very dainty and pure feeding. He that is ignorant shall find there what he should learn.

W. A. CRISWELL

The Bible works. Its truth transforms the hearts and lives of men and women. It converts to better life the small and great. The beggar on the street and the king on his throne, the poor woman weeping in an attic room and the philosopher in his endowed chair, the profoundest thinker and the uncultured savage, are all changed by the power of this Book. The drunkard, the thief, the libertine leave their sins to walk in the light of God's precepts. The proudest atheist becomes an humble believer in Christ by the truths of the Bible.

The creative power of the Bible is one of the miracles of history. John Bunyan was locked up for twelve years in a Bedford jail with his Bible for his constant companion. In that jail he composed an immortal dream written in the beauty of style and in the simple manner of the King James Version of the Bible. So matchless was the intellectual and spiritual culture of this unlearned tinker of Bedford that the scholarly John Owen testified before the king, "Your majesty, if I could write as does that tinker in Bedford jail, I would gladly lay down my learning." *Pilgrim's Progress* is truly one of the greatest classics in human literature. Where did John Bunyan get his culture? He obtained it in glorious fellowship with Moses and the Law, with David and the Psalms, with Isaiah and the prophets, and with Jesus and the apostles. Living with them, he came to speak, like them, the language of the Bible.

Why I Preach That the Bible is Literally True

DAVID DANIELL

To try to understand the literature, philosophy, art, politics, and society of the centuries from the sixteenth to the early twentieth without knowledge of the Bible is to be crippled.

Apart from manuscript translations into English from the Latin, made at the time of Chaucer, and linked with the Lollards, the Bible had been only in that Latin translation made a thousand years before, and few could understand it (in the 15th century). Tyndale, before he left England for his life's work, said to a learned man, "If God spare my life, ere many years I will cause a boy that driveth the plough shall know more of the Scripture than thou dost." He succeeded.   *William Tyndale: A Biography*

Both Old and New Testaments were locked away from the people, the Bible considered too sacred to be touched by any but the most learned. It remained inaccessible in Latin for a thousand years, and the "common version" of it, the Vulgate, came to be regarded as the true original. To translate it for the people became heresy, punishable by a solitary lingering death as a heretic, or, as it had happened to the Cathers in southern France, or to the Hussites in Bohemia and Lollards in England, official and bloody attempts to exterminate the species.

The Bible in English

In the history of the world, the fact that reading the Word of God either alone or in company can change lives is overwhelmingly attested. For this to happen, the Word has to be understandable. The history of the Bible is a story of translation.

DANTE ALIGHIERI

Thou art my Master and my Author. Thou alone art he from whom I took the good style that hath done me honor.

Divine Comedy

T. H. DARLOW

Men do not reject the Bible because it contradicts itself but because it contradicts them.

ROBERTSON DAVIES

It took me some time to discover the Bible as a repository not only of salty, hardbitten wisdom, but as a never-failing book of wonders and inspiration that are timeless . . .

It's a very great thing in any culture to have some classical literature to which you can refer with confidence that most of the people you're talking to share it and know what's in it. That used to be the case with the Bible because it is a classical literature . . . which everybody used to know. But they *don't* know it anymore and that means a big frame of reference has been lost.

Every day of my life, from the time I began to go to school as a little boy, until I emerged from school at the age of 18 or 19, I heard the Bible read to me and that meant that every day of my life I had an example of some of the finest prose in English read to me first thing in the morning. I didn't think of it as that, but that was what I heard, and it's amazing how it imposes itself upon you as a standard of exposition and concise expression. Because the Bible's written almost in shorthand, all of it.

Conversations with Robertson Davies

An enormous amount of the Bible is written in the present tense as though it were happening right now, which is a different way of thinking about the past. And this is like Welsh . . . In Welsh, if you talk about something that has happened, you indicate that it has happened in the past and then you tend to describe it in the present tense, which gives it great vividness.

Acta Victoriana (1973)

In my opinion, the society from which the Bible is disappearing is a society which is moving toward barbarism. Because one of the elements of a civilized society is that it has a congruous body of common knowledge, generally of classical literature. And that is what the Bible was, quite apart from what it had to say on religious subjects, which was another thing . . . There was a common frame of reference for conversation, oratory, and opinion, right from the top of society to the bottom, and when somebody in parliament made a biblical reference, he

was literally talking to a nation which understood him, not making
a classical allusion which went over the heads of most of the
people who might hear him. We have lost that great classical
background.

CECIL B. DE MILLE

After more than sixty years of almost daily reading of the Bible,
I never fail to find it always new and marvelously in tune with the
changing needs of every day.

L. HAROLD DEWOLF

All the biblical testimonies concerning the word of God refer
to God's revelation or disclosure of himself and his instruction to
men . . . God is known to Jews and Christians as personal. This
does not mean that he is reduced to the form or limits of human
beings. The God who created us and all things and who reigns
over all is obviously not a big man, in the sky or elsewhere.
Besides being invisible in our eyes he has powers beyond our
imagination and understanding. Yet with all his unmeasured
mystery he is one who thinks, acts with purpose, and loves.
Interpreter's One-Volume Commentary

The belief that the earth was flat, with the realm of the dead
beneath it, was part of the popular science in the ancient world.
So likewise was the description of many diseases as due to
possession by demons. Such ideas are found in the Bible, not
because it is a record of revelation, but because it was written
when such ideas were taken for granted. If we would find the
element of revealed truth in the Scriptures, we must give special
attention to teachings which differentiate the scriptural writings
from others current in the same periods of time.
Interpreter's One-Volume Commentary

CHARLES DICKENS

The New Testament is the best book the world has ever known
or will know.

ERNEST VON DOBSCHUTZ

There is a small book: one can put it one's pocket, and yet all
the libraries of America, numerous as they are, would hardly be
large enough to hold all of the books which have been inspired by

this one little volume. The reader will know what I am speaking of. It is the Bible, as we call it—the Book, the book of mankind, as it has properly been called.

The Influence of the Bible on Civilization

JAMES DOBSON

Clearly, Scripture tells us that we lack the capacity to grasp God's infinite mind or the way He intervenes in our lives. How arrogant of us to think otherwise! Trying to analyze His omnipotence is like an amoeba attempting to comprehend the behavior of man. Romans 11:33 indicates that God's judgments are "unsearchable" and his ways "past finding out." Similar language is found in I Corinthians 2:16: "For who has known the mind of the Lord that he may instruct Him?" Clearly, unless the Lord chooses to explain Himself to us, which often He does not, His motivation and purposes are beyond the reach of mortal man. What this means in practical terms is that many of our questions—especially those that begin with the word *why*—will have to remain unanswered for the time being.

When God Doesn't Make Sense

DAVID S. DOCKERY

While the final book in the Bible had immediate relevance to the first-century church, it also speaks powerfully to us about the return of Christ, his judgment of the world, and God's ultimate eschatological victory over the power of evil.

MERYL DONEY

The first thing is to get a Bible. You may have been given one by some well-meaning relative—and all you have to do is blow off the dust! But make sure it is a version you can understand.There are so many new ones on the market that it would be a pity to be put off by old-fashioned words . . . The Bible is God's own story. If people want to know who God is and what he has done, the Bible will tell them.

How the Bible Came to Us

FREDERICK DOUGLASS

There is a class of people who seem to believe that if a man should fall overboard into the sea with a Bible in his pocket, it would hardly be possible to drown.

North Star

JOHN W. DRANE

The Bible may be an ancient book, but it is part of an unfinished story. Its characters no doubt had a very different lifestyle from 20th Century people. But their story is the first installment in our own story. Their experience with God was the same as ours, and modern Christians are united with them across the centuries in the same story of salvation.

The Lion Encyclopedia of the Bible

JOHN DRYDEN

Then for the style, majestic and divine,
It speaks no less than God in every line.

Religio Luici

MARY BAKER EDDY

The central fact of the Bible is the superiority of spiritual power over physical power.

Science and Health with Key to the Scriptures

The Bible is the learned man's masterpiece, the ignorant man's dictionary, the wise man's directory.					*Miscellaneous Writings*

ANDREW EDINGTON
Hezekiah Thanks the Lord

Things looked mighty dark to me,
Facing death so early.
No more would my friends I see;
No wonder I am surly.
Delirious I chattered as a bird,
Mourning also like a dove;
Praying, praying, not yet heard,
Knowing my boil came from above.
But heal me, Lord, heal me quick.
Thank you, Lord, I needed that!
I know you're wise to make me sick,
But now I'm well and getting fat.

The Word Made Flesh: A Down to Earth
Version of the Old Testament

BRIAN EDWARDS

The inspiration of Scripture is a harmony of the active mind of the writer and the sovereign direction of the Holy Spirit to produce God's inerrant and infallible Word to mankind.

JONATHAN EDWARDS

The devil has ever shown a mortal spite and hatred towards that holy book the Bible. He has done all in his power to extinguish that light . . . He is engaged against the Bible, and hates every word in it.

JAMES M. EFIRD

For the person who believes that the Bible is God's revelation to the world, the question is not *whether* these teachings are relevant but rather *how* can the application of these teachings be made in and to contemporary society and individual lives today. The assumption for such people is that these documents are more than mere literature or history from another time and place.

How to Interpret the Bible

CHARLES DAVID ELDRIDGE

The Old Testament prophets and the New Testament writers denounce the exclusive privileges of the rich and the usurpation of rights of the poor, and strenuously enforce their demands for righteous dealings among men. The Bible, like an unfailing arsenal, has supplied the ammunition for the agelong struggle for liberty.

DUKE ELLINGTON

On becoming more acquainted with the word of the Bible, I began to understand so much more of what I had been taught, and of what I had learned about life and about the people in mine.

RALPH WALDO EMERSON

People imagine that the place which the Bible holds in the world, it owes to miracles. It owes it simply to the fact that it came out of a profounder depth of thought than any other book.

The vice of our theology is seen in the claim that the Bible is a closed book and that the age of inspiration is past.

The Bible is like an old Cremona. It has been played upon by the devotion of thousands of years until every word and particle is public and tunable.

DESIDERIUS ERASMUS

I believe firmly what I read in the holy Scriptures, and the Creed, called the Apostles', and I don't trouble my head any further. I leave the rest to be disputed and defined by the clergy, if they please; and if any Thing is in common use with the Christians that is not repugnant to the holy Scriptures, I observe it for this Reason, that I may not offend other people.

Colloquia

LOUIS H. EVANS

The Bible has in it the "life principle." Simply plant it in your heart and see what happens. That will prove the divine authorship of the book. Let a man read it, it will lead him to God. Let a man study it, he will know the heart of God. Let a man ask his questions and he will find his answers. Let him test the Christ of these pages and he will find the power that Christ has to give. *Life Principle*

TONY EVANS

One day some men were reading the story of Moses when they noticed one little statement that said Moses' mother made a basket for Moses with tar and pitch. Those men said, "Tar and pitch?" They knew that wherever there is tar, there is oil. That began a process of going to the Middle East with machinery to discover that the greatest oil deposits are located in the Middle East—because the two men read the Bible and saw a reference to tar and pitch. The Bible is absolutely true. It's not a science book, but whenever it speaks scientifically, it speaks perfectly. It's not just a history book, but whenever it speaks historically, it speaks perfectly. That's why you must know the Word of God, because it is absolute truth. *Our God Is Awesome*

To meditate on God's Word means to have it rolling around in your mind as a way of life. It doesn't mean sitting down all day

practicing yoga, but having the Word so filter your thought
processes that God can ride the wings of His Word into your
heart. There, he can give direction to your life, leading you in the
path of everlasting life and in the way you ought to go.

Our God Is Awesome

Wisdom is seeing and interpreting life from God's perspective
and then making life's decisions based on that understanding. We
know that wisdom is important because the word itself occurs
hundreds of times in the Bible—and more than one hundred
times in the book of Proverbs alone. God is deeply concerned
that we learn to live wisely according to his definition of wisdom.

MICHAEL FARADAY
Why will people go astray when they have this blessed Book to
guide them?

W. A. FARBSTEIN
The dog is mentioned in the Bible eighteen times, the cat not
even once.

FREDERIC WILLIAM FARRAR
Men have misused Scripture just as they have misused light or
food.

We must never lose sight of the fact that the Bible is not a
single nor even homogeneous book. The Bible is, strictly
speaking, not a book but a library.

WILLIAM FAULKNER
You don't need to choose. The heart already knows. He didn't
have His Book written to be read by what must elect and choose,
but by the heart, not by the wise of the earth because maybe they
don't need it or maybe the wise no longer have any heart, but by
the doomed and lowly of the earth who have nothing else to read
with but the heart. Because the men who wrote this Book for
Him were writing about truth and there is only one truth and it
covers all things that touch the heart.   *Go Down, Moses*

WILLIAM H. P. FAUNCE

Not one of you would think of looking in a book of medicine which was published 50 years ago; not one of you would think of using a compendium of science 50 years old; not one of you would think of taking as authoritative the statements in a book of psychology that was even 20 years old. Mr. Wells's *Outline of History* had to be revised even before it was published. Here is a book which remains the standard guide of the world after all these centuries.

JOHN FAWCETT

How precious is the Book divine
  By inspiration giv'n!
Bright as a lamp its precepts shine
  To guide my way to heav'n.

The lamp through all the tedious night
  Of life shall guide my way,
Till I behold the clearer light
  Of an eternal day.

BRUCE FEILER

The Bible is not an abstraction in the Middle East, nor even just a book; it's a living, breathing entity, undiminished by the passage of time. If anything, the Bible has been elevated to that rare stature of being indefinitely immediate. That's the principal reason few people ultimately care when the Bible was written; the text is forever applicable. It's always now. The ability of the Bible to continually reinvent itself is matched only by its ability to make itself relevant to anyone who encounters it.

Walking the Bible: A Journey by Land Through the Five Books of Moses

JOHN FERGUSON

The New Testament is the story of Jesus of Nazareth, the central figure in one of the world's great religions, and acknowledged as a prophet or divinely inspired person in other faiths; it goes on to tell the beginnings of the community he inspired. The story is sometimes beautiful, sometimes terrible and shocking, often dramatic, always fascinating.

Great Events of Bible Times

ROGER FERLO

There is no one single person whose intention has made the
Bible the coherent document that it is. No single person, but
an entire culture. And I, being a religious reader, would say that,
as it was a culture that was God-shaped, so the language is
God-shaped.   Quoted by Ann Monroe in *The Word*

A lot of Bible readers are very well-intentioned but ill-trained.
Reading the Bible with a fifth-grade sensibility is not always
innocuous . . . To ignore the words and the play of words, and
playfulness of the words, and the myriad of words—to ignore the
generative energy of those words—is to ignore the Bible.

W. C. FIELDS

I have spent a lot of time reading the Bible, looking for loopholes.

JOHN FISKE

Great consequences have flowed from the fact that the first
truly popular literature in England—the first which stirred the
hearts of all classes of people . . . was the literature comprised
within the Bible.   *The Beginnings of New England*

WILLIAM FITCH

What a story lies behind this miracle of the divine library.
Nearly 2,000 years were needed to complete it. At least 30
authors took part in writing it, most of them living long
generations apart from one another. Three continents—Asia,
Africa, Europe—shared in the creation. Every literary form is
employed—biography, law, history, letters, poetry, philosophy,
oratory, and much else. Yet the book is one, an amazing unity, and
a literary phenomenon without parallel.
                    The Impregnable Rock of Holy Scripture

JOHN FLAVEL

The Scriptures teach us the best way of living, the noblest way
of suffering, and the most comfortable way of dying.

TED FLETCHER

While I was reading my Bible one day, the Lord spoke to me
from a verse that in later years led me to launch a new mission

agency called Pioneers aimed at the unreached people of the world. That verse was Psalm 2:8. The words came with terrific authority and I knew it was God speaking. Today, after more than 15 years, God has answered prayer and blessed Pioneers with more than 550 missionaries and 150 national workers in thirty-nine countries. *Lamp unto My Feet*

MARCIA FORD

True understanding, the kind the Bible encourages us to seek out and learn from, comes only from God himself. He is the one who created and understands all things; to seek wisdom from another source is to act foolishly and risk serious misunderstanding. "Lean not on your own understanding," Proverbs 3:5 tells us, and with good reason. Ours is incomplete. God alone can provide complete understanding.
101 Most Powerful Promises in the Bible

GEORGE FOX

These things I did not see by the help of man, nor by the letter, though they are written in the letter, but I saw them in the light of the Lord Jesus Christ, and by his immediate Spirit and power, as did the Holy men of God, by whom the Holy Scriptures were written. Yet I had no slight esteem of the Holy Scriptures; they were very precious to me, for I was in that spirit by which they were given forth; and what the Lord opened in me, I afterwards found was agreeable to them.

ERICH FRANK

When the Bible speaks of God as Judge, Savior, Creator, Sovereign, it seeks to characterize the nature of the ultimately determinative power that faith sees operating in personal life and history . . . Biblical faith makes the affirmation that (our world) is a purposive, meaningful creation and that a creative power works through people and the events of history in a definable direction.
A Varied Harvest

HARRY THOMAS FRANK

The Bible is a universal book, restricted neither by time nor place. Over the centuries on all continents its words have carried a message of hope, solace and salvation for the believer, and on the authority of the Holy Word societies have been shaped and great events set afoot. Moreover, for the individual person of faith, now as in the past, the Bible is both an indispensable guide and a fundamental point of reference. *Atlas of the Bible Lands*

BENJAMIN FRANKLIN

A Bible and a newspaper in every house, a good school in every district—all studied and appreciated as they merit—are the principal support of virtue, morality, and civil liberty.

IAN FRAZIER

The Bible's dreary statement that a life span is "three-score years and ten" and its tired talk about times to be born and times to die now smell strongly of plain old defeatism. Determined individuals like Noah and Dick Clark have shown that people can live indefinitely beyond what is thought of as normal chronology. The members of the rock group Arrowsmith, by suspending their pulse rate and similar techniques, have managed to survive and remain a touring band since the days of the French and Indian War.   *The New Yorker,* 10/27/2003

WILLIAM FREEL

The Word of God is not just for domestic consumption; it is also for export.

SIGMUND FREUD

It was the Holy Book, and the study of it, that kept the scattered people together.

ZSA ZSA GABOR

Conrad Hilton was very generous to me in the divorce settlement. He gave me five thousand Gideon Bibles.

FRANK E. GAEBELEIN

The Bible speaks to us about who we are and about our aesthetic responsibility under God. Moreover, we must never overlook the fact, so often forgotten by Christians, that God's inspired Word is itself a supremely great piece of art.
          The Christian, The Arts, and Truth

JOHN KENNETH GALBRAITH

Had the Bible been in clear straightforward language, had the ambiguities and contradictions been edited out, and had the language been constantly modernized to accord with contemporary taste it would almost certainly have been, or become, a work of lesser influence.

Economics, Peace, and Laughter

ROY A. GALLANT

If we interpret the Bible literally, we find in Genesis 2:19 in the Old Testament that man was given language at the time he was created. In the 1600s, the Swedish language scholar Andreas Kemke complicated things by suggesting that in the Garden of Eden God spoke Swedish, while Adam spoke Danish, and the serpent spoke French.

Man Must Speak: The Story of Language

GEORGE GALLUP, JR., and TIMOTHY JONES

New ways are needed to bring the Bible into our lives in a regular, deep, and meaningful way—and to remind people that reading the Bible is more than a a polite exercise. The most cited benefit from (survey) respondents' Bible reading is the "closeness" they feel to God after reading—76 percent. That can be encouraged. We also need to remind them that they find in the Bible a bracing—and necessary—dose of reality.

The Next American Spirituality

JOHN WILLIAM GARDNER

One of my less pleasant chores when I was young was to read the Bible from one end to the other. Reading the Bible straight through is at least 70 percent discipline, like learning Latin. But the good parts are, of course, simply amazing. God is an extremely uneven writer, but when He's good, nobody can touch him.

LEROY GARRETT

I view the Bible as Holy Scripture—the term Jesus used— rather than as the word of God, for only our Lord is ultimately "the Word of God" (Revelation 19:13). God speaks through

Scripture, though some Scripture is not His word. But where God does speak through Scripture, it can be called the *written* word of God. Sometimes, as in most of the Psalms and much of Job, it is man's word—man speaking to God, not God speaking to man. But it is still Scripture, and it informs us.

The Bible is a record of God's disclosure of himself through mighty deeds toward the redemption of humankind—what he says and what he does (facts). The Bible is also a record of the human response to that revelation. While I believe in the reliability and integrity of Scripture—and in its inspiration—in that it adequately conveys what God intends, I do not believe in its inerrancy, a claim that it does not make for itself. I also believe that modern biblical research is useful, if not necessary, to understanding the nature of Scripture.

SUSAN R. GARRETT and AMY PLANTINGA PAUW
"Recite them to your children," Moses tells the people of Israel after he speaks the Ten Commandments. "Talk about them when you are at home and when you are away, when you lie down and when you rise." Many of us who care for children earnestly desire to do what Moses instructed. We want to give our children more than physical nurture—more, even, than love and security. We want to give them confident assurance that the Creator of the universe knows them by name, loves them, and desires their love in return. We want to give them knowledge of the Bible and instill in them a lifelong hunger to know both the questions it raises and the answers it provides.
Making Time for God: Daily Devotions for Children and Families to Share

PHILIP J. GERSMEHL
The God who speaks to me through the Bible has placed at the center of his message a Redeemer who spent much of his public ministry doing precisely that: ministering to the public, feeding the hungry, counseling the disturbed, consoling those who mourn. His spoken message was not complex—"Love one another." The relevance of the Christian message is not just in the simple but profound command to love one another. It is also in the equally

simple but profound central phrase of the Lord's Prayer: "Forgive
us . . . As we also have forgiven."

Professors Who Believe

JOE GIBBS

The Bible was written by more than 35 authors over 1,500
years, and still it's perfect. When I think of how one simple
football play gets distorted when it goes from a coach to a player
and then to the quarterback, I'm amazed that anything in the
Bible fits together. Yet it all does.

GIDEONS INTERNATIONAL

The Bible contains the mind of God, the state of man, the
way of salvation, the doom of sinners, and the happiness of
believers. Its doctrines are holy, its precepts are binding, its
histories are true, and its decisions are immutable. Read it to
be wise, believe it to be safe, and practice it to be holy. It
contains light to direct you, food to support you, and comfort to
cheer you. It is the traveler's map, the pilgrim's staff, the pilot's
compass, the soldier's sword, and the Christian's charter. Here
Paradise is restored, Heaven opened, and the gates of hell
disclosed. Christ is its grand subject, our good the design, and
the glory of God its end. It should fill the memory, rule the
heart, and guide the feet. Read it slowly, frequently, and
prayerfully. It is a mine of wealth, a paradise of glory and a
river of pleasure. It is given you in life, will be opened at the
judgment, and be remembered forever. It involves the highest
responsibility, will reward the greatest labor, and will condemn
all who trifle with its sacred contents.

Introduction to the New Testament with Psalms and
Proverbs, published by The Gideons International

OWEN GINGERICH

The first chapter of Genesis is not a scientific textbook but a
magnificent, universal statement of God's creative powers. It rises
to a climax in Genesis 1:27, which tells us there is a divine spark
in each of us, including those godly attributes of consciousness,
creativity, and conscience.   *Lamp unto My Feet*

TERRY W. GLASPY

I can remember as a young Christian being counseled against reading Bible commentaries and works of theology because, I was told, all I really needed was the Bible itself. If I were to read only the Bible, then all that I needed to know could be drawn from its pages. This idea troubled me for some time until I realized the hidden arrogance of believing that I did not need the insights and revelations of those who had preceded me. To suggest that I would be harmed by the insights of brilliant and godly men and women of the past and present is a folly that is truly dangerous.

Great Books of the Christian Tradition

If you make it a goal in life to constantly keep your mind open to new ideas and to better understand the beliefs and values you already hold, then books become a necessary companion on the journey of life. How important are books? Well, God himself chose the medium of a book as a primary way to communicate to us the truth of his love and grace. And the exploits of the great heroes of the faith and the life of Christ himself are also forever revealed and offered to us in this same book.

Book Lover's Guide to Great Reading

BRIAN GODAWA

The ultimate source book of most sex-and-violence media watchdogs is the Bible. And it ought to be, because without its definition of universal morality that transcends individual choice, we as a society have no absolute reference point of truth. We are left with nothing but a sea of relativity that logically results in the violence of personal wills in conflict, the ethical fruit of survival of the fittest. Without God and His Law that defines absolute right and wrong, there can be no ultimate value difference between the acts of Jeffrey Dahmer and the acts of Mother Teresa . . . It is the Bible alone that provides a rational meaningful standard to make moral judgments that transcend the arbitrariness of personal opinion.   *The Christian Imagination*

"GODSPEAKS" ADVERTISING CAMPAIGN°

Have you read My #1 best-seller?
(There will be a test.)—God

It's quite a best-seller, these works, words, and loves that come from Heaven. Worth a serious "read." Oh, and a reminder: there will—eventually—be a test. It wouldn't be wise to wait until the last minute to cram. Take the time you have and enjoy.

JOHANN WOLFGANG VON GOETHE

The Bible grows more beautiful as we grow in our understanding of it.

The greater the intellectual progress of the ages, the more fully it will be possible to employ the Bible not only as the Foundation, but also as the instrument of education.

DAVID GOLDSTEIN

The Old Testament is the backbone of Western civilisation. It is the foundation of the Judaeo-Christian heritage, and as such it has provided the moral and spiritual basis for the lives of countless millions of people in Europe, the Americas, and wherever the Bible has been cherished. The great figures of Biblical history, such as Abraham, Moses, David, and the prophets have impressed themselves on human consciousness, and the events described in its pages, from the Flood and the building of the Tower of Babel, which are shrouded in mystery, to the conflicts between empires, which affected Judah and Israel so crucially, are an integral part of our own literary and religious traditions.   *Great Events of Bible Times*

°Hired in 1998 by a person requesting anonymity, a Fort Lauderdale advertising agency developed a billboard campaign to get people thinking about God. The roadside announcements in south Florida, were the work of the agency's Andy Smith and Charlie Robb. With support from the Outdoor Advertising Association of America as a public service, the messages-from-God project grew to ten thousand billboards in more than 200 cities, described as a cultural and spiritual phenomenon around the world.

PETER J. GOMES

What engages the reader of the Bible is the fact that it is filled
with people very much like the reader, people who are confused
and confusing, who are less than exemplary but who nevertheless
participate in a developing encounter with God. If the Bible were
just about the successful and the pious it would be little more
than a collection of Horatio Alger tales or Barbara Cartland
romances . . . What makes the Bible interesting and compelling is
the company of human beings who through its pages play their
parts in the drama of the human and the divine. In the sense that
the Bible stories tell our story, the human story in relation to the
divine, they are true. They are not true because they are in the
Bible; they are in the Bible because they are true to the
experience of men and of women.   *The Good Book*

Admiring literature won't get you into heaven . . . If you come
to the Bible thinking it's an interesting book and you want to
know more about it, you get what you can and away you go. But if
your assumption is that this book is not like any other, that in this
book God is talking to you in ways that are essential for you to
understand, then you ask how you are going to enter into it.
Quoted by Ann Monroe in *The Word*

JUSTO L. GONZALEZ

What makes the Bible the word of God is not that it is
infallible, nor that it can serve as a source of authority for
theological and religious debate. The Bible is the Word of God
because in it Jesus, the Word incarnate, comes to us. Any who
read the Bible and somehow do not find Jesus in it, have not
encountered the Word of God.
The Story of Christianity

B. C. GOODPASTURE

The nature and contents of the Bible are such that the rank
and file of its readers in all generations have recognized God as
its author. Man would not have written such a book, if he could;
and could not, if he would.

EDGAR J. GOODSPEED

There are two ways to use the Bible. One is the old childhood way of using a text from here or there, regardless of the time and circumstances of its origin. The other is the grown person's way, of reading it a book at a time, as it was written to be read, and with some understanding of the time and circumstances in which each book was written. It is obvious that only in this latter way can the major value of the Bible be realized. The Bible is far from being a child's book. No book in the world is more definitely addressed to the mature mind.   *The Story of the Bible*

BILLY GRAHAM

Christianity finds all its doctrines stated in the Bible, and Christianity denies no part nor attempts to add anything to the Word of God.

Read the Bible. Work hard and honestly. And don't complain.
"A Message to the Chinese"
International Herald Tribune, 4/18/1988

A knowledge of the Bible is essential to a rich and meaningful life.

Why do I believe in the Devil? For three reasons: (1) Because the Bible plainly says he exists. (2) Because I see his work everywhere. (3) Because great scholars have recognized his existence.

Like Joseph storing up grain during the years of plenty to be used during the years of famine that lay ahead, may we store up the truth of God's Word in our hearts as much as possible, so that we are prepared for whatever suffering we are called upon to endure.   *Till Armageddon*

The fact of Jesus Christ is the eternal message of the Bible. It is the story of life, peace, eternity, and heaven. The Bible has no hidden purpose. It has no need for special interpretation. It has a single, clear, bold message for every living being—the message of Christ and His offer of peace with God.

Millions of people today are searching for a reliable voice of authority. The Word of God is the only real authority we have. His Word sheds light on human nature, world problems, and human suffering. But beyond that, it clearly reveals the way to God.   *What the Bible Is All About* (foreword)

When we approach the Bible as history and biography, we approach the Bible in the wrong way. We must read the Bible, not primarily as historians seeking information, but as men and women seeking God.

The human tendency is to let the Bible be closed. We hide behind many excuses, saying it is hard to understand, or that we are too busy, or we advance any of a thousand other reasons; but the fact still remains that the Bible has met the deepest needs of multitudes, and to this day it continues to demonstrate its ancient power to mend broken lives and give peace of soul to those who stand upon its promises and heed its claims.

His Unchanging Word in a Changing World

FRANKLIN GRAHAM

If you're a woman who wants to get in sync with God, it's important for you to understand the mighty things God has done through women in the past. Scripture is full of stories that extol the special virtues of women who know how to touch the heart of God, who walk with Him, and who are eager to be used by Him and live a life that is beyond the culture of stereotypes.

Living Beyond the Limits

RUTH BELL GRAHAM

If our children have the background of a godly, happy home and the unshakable faith that the Bible is indeed the Word of God, they will have a foundation that the forces of hell cannot shake.

ULYSSES S. GRANT

To the influence of the Bible we are indebted for the progress made in our civilization, and to it we must look as our guide to the future.

HORACE GREELEY

It is impossible to mentally or socially enslave a Bible-reading people. The principles of the Bible are the groundwork of human freedom.

BRIAN GREENAWAY

I got a lot of strength from my Bible reading. Especially when I read about the disciples of Jesus. It was good to find that these men were no plaster saints. But God still used them. Even in prison, ordinary men like Peter served God.

S. L. GREENSLADE

In the 1954 Bible supplement to *The Times* (London), Basil Willey went so far as to say that since the Bible societies began their work, "the dissemination of Bibles has proceeded in inverse ratio to the amount of Bible reading done at home." The school now becomes of major importance. Quite apart from the religious issues, it will be an absurd failure in educational perspec- tive if generations grow up in ignorance of one of the foundations of western civilization.

The Cambridge History of the Bible

To the modern mind the Bible cannot be an easy book. The old Christian Fathers used to say that in it all the necessary things are clear, and faith knows in what sense that is true. It is one of the blessings of the Bible that we do not have to be intellectuals to hear what it says to us. Though Coleridge's "I do not find the Bible, the Bible finds me" is not an adequate theory of biblical inspiration, it is an excellent statement of fact.

ANGELINA GRIMKE

I have not placed reading before praying because I regard it more important, but because, in order to pray aright, we must understand what we are praying for.

VERNON C. GROUNDS

Consider how extraordinary it is that this collection of ancient Jewish history, poetry, and prophecy has lived on for thousands of years. That in itself is a very strange and significant fact.

Hundreds of centuries have slowly ticked away since the Bible was written; a score or so of powerful civilizations have flourished, decayed, and vanished, leaving scarcely a trace of their existence; war and fire and human negligence have wiped out the records of antiquity to so large an extent that the books of such nations of antiquity as the Phoenicians and the Hittites and the Cretans are lost to us. And yet for some reason these ancient writings of the Hebrews have survived . . . So perhaps, after all, there is something to what the Bible says, when it declares in reference to itself, "The grass withereth and the flower thereof falleth away. But the word of the Lord endureth forever." (I Peter 1:24-25)

The Reason for Our Hope

OS GUINNESS

"You shall not bear false witness," the ninth commandment thundered from Sinai. From beginning to end, the Bible declares that God detests lying and that deception is a major root of evil in our world. Defined as "an attempt to deceive without the other's consent," a lie is a fundamental breach of the human contract to speak the truth. Thus to treat lying, falsehood, evasiveness, mendacity, and carelessness with words as only minor problems—whimsies with words—hands a dangerous alibi to the powerful . . .   *Time for Truth*

HENRY H. HALLEY

Authors may pray for God's help and guidance—God does help and guide—and there are many good books in the world which unmistakably God has helped the authors to write. But even so, even the most saintly of authors would hardly presume to claim for his books that God wrote them. But that is claimed for the Bible. God Himself superintended and directed and dictated the writing of the Bible books, with the human authors so completely under His control that the writing was the writing of God.

Halley's Bible Handbook

EDITH HAMILTON

The Bible is the only literature in the world up to our century which looks at women as human beings, no better and no worse than men.   *Spokesmen for God*

MARGUERITTE HARMON-BRO

Somehow the Bible is not just one more book in a book-filled world. It's the only book we have ever read which we know for sure our grandparents read, too. And their grandparents, and theirs . . . It's a family book.   *Book of Our Fathers*

DOROTHY C. HASKIN

The Bible is a wonderful book. Full blessing from it is received not by listening to others quote it, but by reading it for oneself. It is a book of ethical moderation, and by listening to the entire truth revealed in it, a person can learn to live a balanced, abundant life.   *God in My Home*

H. L. HASTINGS

Infidels with all their assaults make about as much impression on this book as a man with a tack hammer would make on the Pyramids of Egypt . . . If this book had not been the book of God, men would have destroyed it long ago. Emperors and kings, princes and rulers, even spiritual authorities have all tried their hand at it. They die, and the Bible still lives.

RICHARD B. HAYS and JUDITH C. HAYS

The Scriptures are filled with stories of God's breaking into the individual lives of older persons to confer a particular gift or vocation. Equally important, perhaps, are the things not said about older characters in the New Testament. Nowhere in the biblical canon are they pitied, patronized, or treated with condescension. Nowhere is growing old itself described as a problem. Nowhere are elders described as pitiable, irrelevant, or behind the curve, as inactive or unproductive . . . On the contrary, they are seen as the bearers of wisdom by virtue of their age. *Growing Old in Christ*

ROGER HAZELTON

The faithful reader of the Bible is not provided automatically with a kind of measuring device for taking, as it were, the temperature of events. But he is placed within a temporal context of engagements with God, of entering into those events which are ordered by God for our good and for his glory.
                              God's Way with Man

HEINRICH HEINE

Strange, after having passed the whole of my life in gliding about the dancing floors of philosophy, and abandoning myself to all the orgies of the intellect, and dallying with systems without ever being satisfied, I have suddenly arrived at the same point of view as Uncle Tom, taking my stand on the Bible and kneeling beside my black brother in prayer in the same act of devotion.

The Bible is a plain old book, modest as nature itself . . . a book of unpretending workday appearance, like the sun that warms us or the bread that nourishes us.   *Scintillations*

The Bible, what a book! Large and wise as the world based on the abysses of creation, and towering aloft into the blue secrets of heaven. Sunrise and sunset, promise and fulfillment, birth and death—the whole drama of humanity—are contained in this one book. It is the Book of Books.
Quoted in Wick Allison's *That's in the Bible?*

ERNEST HELLO

The Holy Bible is an abyss. It is impossible to explain how profound it is, impossible to explain how simple it is.

MAX HELTON

Three things are noted in Joshua 1:8—to know the Word of God, to meditate on it, and to do it. I believe these will produce a successful life for anyone, and this is why Bible study is so important. In our country, it's interesting that so many people have a copy of the Bible. They would probably fight for it and maybe even die for it. And yet, so many people don't know what's in it.   *Lamp unto My Feet*

TONY HENDRA and SEAN KELLY

Old Testament book of Genesis, *unauthorized* version:

Chapter 1, Verse 26: And God saw everything He had made, and He saw that it was very good; and God said, "It *just* goes to show Me what the private sector can accomplish. With a lot of fool regulations, this could have taken *billions of years.*"

Chapter 1, Verse 27: And on the evening of the fifth day, *which had been* the roughest day yet, God said, "Thank Me it's Friday." And God made the weekend.

"The Book of Creation," *Playboy,* September 1982

HOWARD HENDRICKS

Dusty Bibles always lead to dirty lives. In fact, you are either in the Word and the Word is conforming you to the image of Jesus Christ, or you are in the world and the world is squeezing you into its mold.

CARL F. H. HENRY

Skepticism toward the reliability of Scripture seems to survive in many academic circles despite the repeated collapse of critical theories. One still finds a disposition to trust secular writers whose credentials in providing historical testimony are often far less adequate than those of the biblical writers. Not long ago many scholars who rejected the historicity of the patriarchal accounts denied that writing existed in Moses' day and ascribed the Gospels and Epistles to second-century writers. But higher criticism has sustained some spectacular and even stunning reverses, mainly through the findings of archaeology.

The Bible remains the world's most indispensable reading, and a personal walk with God remains man's unsurpassable privilege.

MATTHEW HENRY

We have now before us the holy Bible, or *book,* for so *bible* signifies. We call it *the book,* by way of eminency, for it is unquestionably the best book that ever was written, the book of *books,* shining like the sun in the firmament of learning, other valuable and useful books, like the moon and stars, borrowing their light from it.   *Matthew Henry's Commentaries*

It was a common saying among the Puritans—"Brown bread and the Gospels is good fare."   *Commentaries: Isaiah*

PATRICK HENRY

The Bible is worth all other books which have ever been printed.

GEORGE HERBERT

Of all the creatures, both in the sea and land,
Only to man thou hast made known thy ways
And put the pen alone into his hand,
And made him secretary of thy praise.

"Providence"

OREL HERSHISER

Late one night I pulled the Gideon Bible from the nightstand
and began reading from the Gospel of John. Without any
prompting, I slipped to my knees next to the bed. Openly
confessing my sin, I invited Jesus Christ into my life and received
Him as my Savior by faith. As I crawled back in bed at the
Buckaroo Motel and continued to read from the Bible, I knew
that this would be the beginning of a new journey.

"Trust," Focus on the Family, July 2002

CHARLTON HESTON

Perhaps the most ironic moment in the entire Bible comes at
the end of the story of the crucifixion. "It is finished," Jesus cries
out. He is referring to his mission on earth. But in a larger sense,
this moment is more a beginning than an end. Jesus has died. But
by doing so, he has overcome death and granted mankind the
promise of eternal life.   *Charlton Heston Presents the Bible*

For millions of people, of course, the Bible's literary merits are
secondary. They read the Bible in the way that its authors
intended it to be read: as the Word of God. But the beauty of the
Bible is that it can be profitably read by everyone—archbishops
and atheists alike.

HUGH HEWITT

The book of Scripture named Ecclesiastes is a hard book, and
many incorrectly believe that it leads a reader to despair. It
actually should lead a reader to bold witness, because its narrative
demolishes the idea of competing priorities. If the voice of
Ecclesiastes is heard, believers recognize that nothing else
matters, nothing else endures, except the relationship between
the believer and God. What possible source of scorn could matter
in comparison? What loss of status, power, influence, or money

could count? . . . All of our pastimes, pursuits, careers, hobbies, hopes and fears boil down to a chasing after wind. Once that central fact is grasped—really understood—the believer cannot be embarrassed. *The Embarrassed Believer*

CRAIG C. HILL

Many contemporary Christians have a hard time getting beyond questions about the literal meaning of a passage. "Is the Bible true?" is for us mainly a question of factual accuracy. By contrast, it was possible for ancient authors—Paul, say—to hold to the truth of a scriptural passage while at the same time rewriting it to suit their own purposes. The New Testament authors may at times appear heavy-handed in their use of the Hebrew Bible, but they were no more so than some of their non-Christian Jewish contemporaries.

In God's Time: The Bible and the Future

BOBBY HILLIN, JR.

Proverbs is the most useful book in the Bible for anyone to read and receive day-to-day living instructions. Proverbs 3:5 is my reminder that God's wisdom is much greater than mine; therefore, I will lean on Him always. *Lamp unto My Feet*

EDWIN HODDER

Thy Word is like a garden, Lord,
With flowers bright and fair;
And every one who seeks may pluck
A lovely cluster there.
Thy Word is like a deep, deep mine;
And jewels rich and rare
Are hidden in its mighty depths
For every searcher there.
"Thy Word Is Like a Garden" (hymn)

CHARLES HODGE

The best evidence of the Bible's being the Word of God is found between its covers.

OLIVER WENDELL HOLMES, SR.

What you bring away from the Bible depends to some extent on what you carry to it.

LAUREN B. HOMER

James 1:25 has become the keynote verse for my activities in bringing the rule of law to Russia and other former Soviet republics. The Bible is replete with verses that state that God's law and adherence to it will provide every form of material and spiritual blessing, while departure from it will bring only defeat and disorder.   *Lamp unto My Feet*

SIDNEY HOOK

No book has been read more widely, more carefully, more sympathetically, more critically. Yet no book has been subject to greater variety of interpretations, many of them mutually incompatible.   *Education for Modern Man*

J. EDGAR HOOVER

Juvenile delinquency can be prevented. It is not a scourge which rules with inevitable necessity. One of the best weapons with which to attack this malady is religious training. The young boy and girl trained in the teachings of the Bible have a moral reliance which serves as a compass for everyday living. They know the difference between right and wrong, good and evil. They are able to conquer the temptations of life.

MICHAEL HORTON

For the Pharisees, the Scriptures were a source of trivia for life's dilemmas. To be sure, Scripture provides God-centered and divinely-revealed wisdom for life—but if this were its primary objective, Christianity would be a religion of self-improvement by following examples and exhortations, not a religion of the Cross.

LOUISA "SUE" HULETT

The book of Genesis reveals the origin and history of humankind, the evolution of God's chosen people, the emergence of key prophets and servants of God like Abraham, and the declaration of God's character, plans, teachings and promises such as transcendence, omnipotence, and nature and consequences of sin, judgment, reconciliation, messiah, and salvation. Abraham believed in and experienced God . . . I don't claim to know God as Abraham did, but I know that God exists because I have experienced his presence in my life.   *Professors Who Believe*

TODD HUNTER

The Bible is the Holy Spirit's book. God always works in
agreement with his Word. His Spirit inspires it, he shines God's light
on it, he speaks through it, and he gives us the power to obey it.

EARL HUTTO

There are many verses in the Bible that guide me, but one
took on special meaning when I went to Congress in 1978. At that
time, my brother-in-law, Albert Myers, gave me a plaque with
Philippians 4:13 inscribed on it. It was placed on the door of my
inner office and served as a constant reminder that I needed the
Lord's involvement in the decisions I had to make.

Lamp unto My Feet

JOHN A. HUTTON

The New Testament holds up a strong light by which a man
can read even the fine print of his soul.

The Bible is a great and responsible book, not a sad book. The
last thing about it that one can say justly is that it is a sad book.
The Bible is a brave, strong book. It seldom speaks easily about
life, but it never speaks desperately about it . . .The Bible never
locks us up in a cell, leaving us to mere anger or despair or
remorse. In the Bible, there is always a way out. It may not be an
easy way; it may not be the way that we would have chosen, but a
way out there always is.

THOMAS HUXLEY

Throughout the history of the Western world, the Scriptures
have been the great instigators of revolt against the worst forms of
clerical and political despotism.   *Controverted Questions*

The Bible has been the Magna Carta of the poor and oppressed.
The human race is not in a position to dispense with it.

BILL HYBELS

I would be remiss if I didn't point you to the surest, most
productive, and most effective way to receive God's guidance—
the Bible. Almost all that we need to know is right there. Often

the only things missing are the details. God has already told us in general terms how He wants us to live, love, talk, take care of our bodies, handle our money, pray, function as a family member or employee, and any number of other issues. I'm sometimes struck by how many of the decisions we face are really no-brainers. The course of action is clearly laid out for us in the Bible.

The God You're Looking For

The clearest, most direct route to the guidance of God is through His revealed Word, the Bible. We ignore it at our own peril. But sometimes we need more specific guidance on how to *apply* Scripture, and for that, God gives us His Holy Spirit.

RODNEY D. ICE
God has entrusted me with the Word as a reference standard with which to assess every step of my daily walk . . . The unchanging, always illuminating gospel, entrusted to believers, provides that reference for me.   *Lamp unto My Feet*

T. D. JAKES
The book of Ephesians is the New Testament equivalent of the Old Testament book of Joshua, and neither one of these books is for wimps! The book of Joshua is a picture of a people who have ceased wandering, come to know their God, embraced the promises of God, and who are now ready to seize what God has promised them. The book of Ephesians translates the natural warfare of Joshua into the spiritual warfare of the believer . . . This is the book where the apostle Paul commands, "Be strong in the Lord and in the power of his might," just as God commanded Joshua, "Be strong and of good courage."

Overcoming the Enemy

KEVIN JENKINS
As a Christian, I have found that my most important job is to maintain and nurture my relationship with God. The best way to accomplish this is to regularly read the Bible and pray. Once I understood my most important job, it changed my life. I realized that a branch not connected to the vine will never bear fruit. It is useless. Therefore, for over a year, I have prayed every day. Two things that have helped me are that I choose a different Bible

verse to meditate on each day, and at the beginning of the day I
ask God to guide me in every meeting, phone call, or other
interaction on my calendar for that day.

PHILIP JENKINS

In understanding what can look like the oddities of Third
World churches, it is helpful to recall one basic and astonishing
fact, which is that they take the Bible very seriously indeed. To
quote Richard Shaull, "In Pentecostalism, poor and broken
people discover that what they read in the Gospels is happening
now in their midst." For Christians of the Southern Hemisphere,
and not only for Pentecostals, the apostolic world as described in
the New Testament is not just a historical account of the ancient
Levant, but an ever-present reality open to any modern believer,
and that includes the whole culture of signs and wonders.
The Next Christendom

Millions of Christians around the world do in fact live in
constant danger of persecution or forced conversion, from either
governments or local vigilantes. For modern Christians in
Nigeria, Egypt, the Sudan, or Indonesia, it is quite conceivable
that they might someday find themselves before a tribunal that
would demand that they renounce their faith upon pain of death.
In all these varied situations, ordinary believers are forced to
understand why they are facing these sufferings, and repeatedly
they do so in the language of the Bible and of the earliest
Christianity . . . In Guatemala or Rwanda, as in the Sudan,
martyrdom is not merely a subject for historical research, it is a
real prospect.   *The Next Christendom*

IRVING L. JENSEN

The Bible has survived the hammer blows of the skeptics. The
inscription on the monument to the Huguenots of Paris expresses
this so vividly: "Hammer away, ye hostile hands. Your hammers
break, God's anvil stands."

The Bible is living communication from the Holy Spirit.
Because of this, Bible study can be instructive, comforting,
challenging, and inspiring.

SAINT JEROME

Everything in the Sacred Book shines and glistens, even in its outer shell. But the marrow of it is sweeter. If you want the kernel, you must break through.   *Epistula LXIX*

A. WETHERELL JOHNSON

I remember when I first started to seriously read the Bible. I was reading John 2. I asked myself the third question, "What does this mean to me?" At once I remembered the text in the passage, "Whatsoever he saith unto you, do it." I knelt and asked God what He wanted me to do that day. God answered me in my thoughts, "I want you to talk to one of your work companions about Me." I did so, and God's blessing resulted.
Created for Commitment

HERRICK JOHNSON

The Bible is the most thought-suggesting book in the world. No other deals with such grand themes.

If God is a reality and the soul is a reality and you are an immortal being, what are you doing with your Bible shut?

PAUL JOHNSON

Science, having once appeared to destroy the historicity of the Bible, now seems more likely, on the whole, to corroborate it . . . Some years ago, I remember listening, or half-listening, to a talk on radio about the Big Bang which set the entire universe in motion. I suddenly sprang into consciousness and exclaimed, "But this is the first chapter of Genesis, told in scientific terminology!" The Big Bang theory of the origins of the universe is now accepted by virtually all astrophysicists.
The Quest for God: A Personal Pilgrimage

VICTORIA JOHNSON

The Bible is the record of a sovereign God at work in a world of mere mortals. Through history, poetry, biography, and prophecy God's Word instructs and inspires. It helps us see God and ourselves in the proper light, and lets us in on the plan of the Almighty for humanity . . . Satan does not want you to study

God's Word and he will try to discourage and distract you. Even
your own human nature will resist the discipline study takes, so
you'll need to seek God's help in persevering from the start.

Many Christians approach the Bible without confidence,
feeling that they cannot understand its great teachings on their
own . . . To gain more insight, look up cross-references on various
words in your Bible's study notes or in references in the margins.
After you have done your best, consult a good Bible commentary
to add to your understanding.

Practical Principles of Bible Study

LARRY S. JULIAN

The Bible is the greatest leadership book for today's business
leader.

TOYOHIKO KAGAWA

When you start a Bible movement, it means revolution—a
quiet revolution against darkness and crime.   *Behold the Man*

IMMANUEL KANT

The Bible is the greatest benefit which the human race has
ever experienced . . . Every attempt to belittle it is a crime against
humanity . . . A single line in the Bible has consoled me more
than all the books I ever read besides.

KENNETH S. KANTZER

How can God sovereignly control the writing of the Bible
down to the very words that compose it if the Bible is truly a
human book, stemming from the mind and heart of the human
author? This is not a problem from the viewpoint of the God of
the Bible. The God of some people is not big enough to run a
peanut stand. But the Bible presents us with a true theism—a
god who is sovereign over all and who therefore can work all
things together for good to them who love him. He can do so,
moreover, without destroying human freedom or human
responsibility for sin. If God can use the freedom of a wicked
king like Nebuchadnezzar to secure his own ends, surely he can
use his own prophets or apostles to convey exactly the message he
wishes without destroying the freedom and true human
authorship of biblical writing.   *Tough Questions Christians Ask*

In writing the Bible, its authors used figures of speech, allegory, symbolic language, and the various genre of literature employed by other human authors. Moreover, because they wrote in the language of the common man of two or more millennia ago, they frequently chose not to provide specific technical data where that was not important to their purpose. Never do they speak in the vocabulary of modern science. They felt no more obligation to be precise and exact in many of their statements than we do in our ordinary conversation. Divine inspiration guaranteed only the truth of what they wrote. God preserved them from error both of ignorance and of deception. But he did not prevent them from speaking as humans.

Encyclopedia of Bible Difficulties (foreword)

The real Jesus, the only Jesus for whom we have any evidence whatsoever, believed that the Bible was true and that it was the very Word of God. He commanded his disciples to believe it and obey it. He rebuked those who disregarded it or sought to interpret away its obvious instructions. And he held its teachings binding over himself.

WILLIAM KATERBERG

The wisdom found in Scripture addresses all areas of life. It is authoritative and divinely inspired. And God's Spirit is with us when we read, interpret, and apply it. Yet, to understand what biblical wisdom means today, in a world that the Apostle Paul, the Psalmist, or Moses could hardly imagine, we also need to draw on human traditions more widely, with appreciation and criticism. Besides God's special revelation and saving grace, there is a creational grace that all people continue to receive.

SIR ARTHUR KEITH

The Bible remained for me a book of books—still divine, but divine in the sense that all great books are divine which teach men to live righteously.

HELEN KELLER

Gradually I came to see that I could use the Bible, which had so baffled me, as an instrument for digging out precious truths, just as I could use my hindered, halting body for the high behests of my spirit.

PHILLIP KELLER

To a great extent, the Bible is a collection of books written by men of humble origin who penned under the guidance of God's Spirit. Much of its terminology and teaching is couched in rural language, dealing with outdoor subjects and natural phenomena . . . Many who either read or study the Scriptures in the 20th century come from an urban, man-made environment. City people, especially, are often unfamiliar with such subjects as livestock, crops, land, fruit, or wildlife. They miss much of the truth taught in God's Word because they are not familiar with such things as sheep, wheat, soil, or grapes.

A Shepherd Looks at Psalm 23

WERNER KELLER

The opinion has been, and still is, widely held that the Bible is nothing but the story of man's salvation, a guarantee of the validity of their faith for Christians everywhere. At the same time it is a book about things that actually happened . . . The events themselves are historical facts and have been recorded with an accuracy that is nothing less than startling. Thanks to the findings of the archaeologists, many of the Biblical narratives can be understood better now than ever before. There are, of course, theological insights which can only be dealt with in terms of the Word of God.

The Bible as History: A Confirmation of the Book of Books

THOMAS À KEMPIS

Truth is to be sought for in the Holy Scriptures, not eloquence. Holy Scripture ought to be read with the same spirit wherewith it was written (Romans 15:4). We would rather search after profit in the Scriptures than subtlety of speech. We ought to read devout and simple books as willingly as the high and profound. Let not the authority of the writer offend you, whether he be of great or small learning, but let the love of pure truth draw you to read.

The Imitation of Christ

CARROLL KENDRICK

Persons who take up the book, open it at random, read a chapter, perhaps hastily, and with little thought; and only after about a week or more do about the same thing, making a dozen or more hasty and careless readings in a year, will never understand or rightly value the Bible. Even the recent and thrilling history of the United States could never be understood that way—nor with Fourth of July speeches added.

Rules of Bible Study

D. JAMES KENNEDY

Never has a skeptic been able to overturn or overthrow the evidences for the inspiration of the Scriptures.

GERALD KENNEDY

Revelation is not confined to the New Testament nor is it an exclusive doctrine of the Fourth Gospel. But John has set forth in classic language the philosophy of Revelation and gives a Christian climax and fulfillment. When he says that the Word became flesh, he is placing Jesus in a cosmic setting and he is making clear that this is God's revelation of Himself. It is important to note that revelation comes from God and reaches us through a divine initiative.

God's Good News

PAUL B. KERN

Man must be forever trying his spirit against the spirit of the world. Calamity smites him; confusion overtakes him; fortune smiles, then suddenly frowns upon him. Out of all this welter of conflicting emotions he cries for a sure word of direction, a solace to his wounded spirit, a light amid his surrounding darkness. These he must have or perish. With grateful heart he finds them unerringly in the Bible. It speaks his language; it "finds" him where he is, and points him to the place to which he wishes to go . . . As long as men desire reality and seek for God, they will turn wistfully the pages of this immortal epic of the soul.

Why Men Treasure the Bible

SOREN KIERKEGAARD

The Bible is a letter from God with our personal address on it.

When you read God's Word, you must constantly be saying to yourself, "It is talking to me and about me."

For Self-Examination

CLYDE S. KILBY

The greatest artist of all, the greatest imaginer of all, is the one who appears at the opening of Genesis. Esthetics has to do with form, design, harmony, beauty. Perhaps the key word is "form." Now the earth, says Genesis, was without form. God shaped the creation into form—light and darkness, the heavens, the teeming waters, the multitudinous fauna and flora . . . And we are told that he looked upon each thing he had shaped and saw that it was good. The whole he saw to be *"very* good." Even after the fall of man the Bible treats nature as beautiful, with God as its maker and wielder.   *Christian Herald,* 1969

LINDA KING

After the English Bible appeared in the 1500s, thanks to such heroes of the Reformation as Thomas Cranmer, God's word could speak directly to prelate and peasant alike. It has been said that no single incident in our history has done more to implement the Reformation doctrine of the priesthood of all Believers than the introduction of the English Bible. We take this gift for granted, but it was a revolutionary event.
The Transforming of a Tradition

JOHN KNOX

If you look for a life to come, of necessity it is that you exercise yourselves in the book of the Lord your God. Let no day slip or want some comfort received from the mouth of God. Open your ears, and he will speak even pleasant things to your heart. Close not your eyes, but diligently let them behold what portion of substance is left to you within your Father's testament . . . Above all things, study to practice in life that which the Lord commands.
Selected Writings of John Knox

RONALD KNOX

The differences between the Old and the New Testament is the difference between a man who said, "There is nothing new under the sun" and a God who says, "Behold, I make all things new."   *Stimuli*

DONALD E. KNUTH

For thousands of years, the book of Genesis was the most rational account available about the world's origins. Therefore people began to regard it as a scientific document as well as a work of theology; they forgot that a book of such antiquity had to be consistent with the outline of its own time. Some people even today expect this book to have the precision that we require of a modern historian or scientist. The surprising thing is that Genesis is as accurate as it is. Archaeology keeps shedding new light on long-forgotten facts recorded in this book, indicating that centuries of orally-transmitted history did not actually blur the details very much.   *3:16 Bible Texts Illuminated*

TOM KOK

I often think of Heaven; I think of a choir that is singing the praises of God continually. I think of a lovely garden, like the Garden of Eden must have been. The Bible talks about a new Heaven and a new Earth. I tell my kids all the time, I'm looking forward to walking in the grass and playing baseball. My golf game probably won't be any better, but I won't care. A new Heaven and a new Earth, that's the promise of Scripture.
                    Will the Circle Be Unbroken?

J. NELSON KRAYBILL

The Book of Revelation is the Jurassic Park of biblical interpretation. Two thousand years after it was written, it can still startle the daylights out of a casual reader—or even a lifelong reader of the book.

Let anyone who is alert note that sincere Christians interpret the Book of Revelation in different ways . . . The Word of God cannot be tethered to any one school of interpretation. I believe that much of Revelation describes the first century, but the Holy Spirit enables us to see a new layer of fulfillment and application for our future.   *Christianity Today*, 10/25/99

PETER KREEFT

Will there be nature in Heaven? Scripture tells us there will be "a new heaven (that is, sky) and a new Earth." If we have a new body, we need a new Earth—bodies are not for drifting in empty space. And if a world, why a dead world like the moon, rather than a world brimming with life, like this Earth. I think we will have a much more intimate relationship with nature than we do now, not less.

NICHOLAS D. KRISTOF

Bibles, like history, are written by the winners. There were innumerable early gospels and teachings (some 85 percent of Christian literature from the first two centuries has been lost). Some won approval and entered the New Testament and the rest were condemned as heresies or died out on their own. The Gnostic gospels and other early writings suggest that initially the role of women was hotly debated, but ultimately the idea prevailed that men should dominate.

The New York Times, 2/28/04

HAROLD KUSHNER

I have been studying biblical Hebrew for fifty years, I earned my doctorate in biblical Hebrew, and I still can't say for certain what *timshol* and many other key biblical words mean. No one can. We can only make the best guess we can, colored inevitably by our theological biases. Many biblical verses are like inkblot tests, revealing more about us than about the text in question . . .

How Good Do We Have to Be?

For me, the biblical Scriptures are human beings writing down what they have come to understand as the will of God: how you live, how you treat each other, how you treat yourself, how you learn to control your impulses instead of being controlled by them. For me the Scriptures are sacred because they represent what some of the wisest souls in human history have understood as the will of God.   *Searching for God in America*

TIM F. LaHAYE

It is improper to say that America was founded on Christian principles, for that would unnecessarily exclude the Jewish community. America was founded on biblical principles, all of which are found in the Old Testament and therefore should not exclude any but the most anti-God, antimoral humanist thinkers of our day . . . Such thinkers comprise scarcely 4 percent of our nation's population.   *The Battle for the Mind*

TOM LANDRY

I realize that a lot of people think the idea of a "personal relationship" with God sounds disturbingly exclusive, somehow presumptive, and more than a little pious. I thought the same thing before I read what the Bible said and decided to become a Christian. According to the Bible, this idea of having a personal relationship with God isn't at all presumptive. It was God's idea. And it's not at all exclusive. It's available to anyone who accepts God's offer. It's that belief, that faith, more than anything else that enabled me to last 29 years on the sidelines of the Dallas Cowboys. It's that faith that has allowed me to keep my perspective and not feel devastated or bitter about being fired. And it's that faith that gives me hope for whatever the future holds for me . . .   *Landry: An Autobiography*

J. CARL LANEY

The Bible endures forever. It does not offer mere opinions which may lose their value with the passing of time. Unlike science textbooks, it doesn't need revision when new discoveries are made or theories corrected.

MARY A. LATHBURY

Break Thou the bread of life, dear Lord, to me
As Thou didst break the loaves beside the sea.
Beyond the sacred page I seek Thee, Lord;
My spirit pants for Thee, O living Word.
                    Break Thou the Bread of Life

FRANK LAUBACH

I still remember the delight with which as a boy I first read the gospels and met Jesus face to face . . . Reading the Bible is different from reading other books. It leaps across two thousand years. It brings Bible times up to this very minute . . . The highest value of the Bible comes when it makes us vividly aware that Jesus lives.

ROBERT E. LEE

The Bible is a book in comparison with which all others in my eyes are of minor importance, and which in all my perplexities and distresses never failed to give me light and strength.

SUSAN LEE

There is good reason that the Bible has not only endured for thousands of years but has been read by millions and millions of people and is read over and over again—its dense polyvalency allows it to be meaningful in many ways to many people in many times. It used to be thought that a person wasn't truly literate, or even civilized, unless he or she knew the Bible.

The Wall Street Journal

UMPHREY LEE

One of the richest fruits of the literary study of the Bible is the realization that the books which compose the New Testament were written in definite, concrete situations to meet definite, concrete human needs. They were not written "at" people but "to" them. This is true of that strange book we call the Book of Revelation, written to hearten early Christian communities which were under the shadow of a threatened persecution. The book exhorts the communities to stand fast in the faith, and assures them that their faith will not be in vain.

Christianity has a meaning for our own crowded days in that it does set things in a new perspective. Where we have lost sight of the woods because of the trees, where life has become just one thing after another, and all seems vanity, Christianity offers a new outlook, shows a door that opens out on virgin meadows. The method of Christianity is to take a man when he is discouraged and disgusted, and to point out to him an entirely new scene, so that he exclaims, "I never saw it this way before." The Bible is full of illustrations of this.   *Jesus the Pioneer and Other Sermons*

MADELEINE L'ENGLE

I'm particularly grateful that I was allowed to read my Bible as I read my other books, to read it as a story, that story which is a revelation of truth. People are sometimes kept from reading the Bible itself by what they are taught about it, and I'm grateful that I was able to read the Book with the same wonder and joy with which I read *The Ice Princess* or *The Tempest*.

C. S. LEWIS

I have been suspected of being what is called a Fundamentalist. That is because I never regard any narrative as unhistorical simply on the ground that it includes the miraculous.

The New Testament has lots to say about self-denial, but not about self-denial as an end to itself. We are told to deny ourselves and to take up our crosses in order that we may follow Christ; and nearly every description of what we ultimately find if we do so contains an appeal to desire. If there lurks in most modern minds the notion that to desire our own good and earnestly to hope for the enjoyment of it is a bad thing, I submit that this notion has crept in from Kant and the Stoics and is no part of the Christian faith. Indeed, if we consider the unblushing promises of reward and the staggering nature of the rewards promised in the gospels, it would seem that Our Lord finds our desires not too strong, but too weak.   *The Weight of Glory*

In Scripture, the visitation of an angel is always alarming. It has to begin by saying, "Fear not." (In the arts) the Victorian angel looks as if it were going to say, "There, there." Humanity falls into two equal and opposite errors concerning the devil. Either they take him altogether too seriously or they do not take him seriously enough.

LEXINGTON (Kentucky) *LEADER*

The Bible continues to be the best-selling book. It is regarded as the most economical of all fire escapes.

NEIL R. LIGHTFOOT

Tracing the Bible down through the centuries presents the human side of how we got the Bible. From a different standpoint, the story of how we got the Bible begins and ends with God. God is Light, the Source of Light, both physical and spiritual. Ultimately, then, the story of how we got the Bible leads us to the throne of God. In Mark 13:31 Jesus said, "Heaven and earth will pass away, but my words will not pass away." Here Jesus makes two claims. First, he claims that his words are divine: the world will pass away but his words will not. Therefore, his words are not from the world. Second, because his words are divine, Jesus claims his words will stand forever.   *How We Got the Bible*

HALDOR LILLENAS

The Bible stands like a rock undaunted
'Mid the raging storms of time;
Its pages burn with truth eternal,
And they glow with a light sublime.

> The Bible stands every test we give it,
> For its Author is divine;
> By grace alone I expect to live it,
> And to prove and make it mine.

"The Bible Stands," hymn

ABRAHAM LINCOLN

The Bible is the best gift God has given to man. All the good the Savior gave to the world was communicated through this book. But for it we could not know right from wrong. All things most desirable for man's welfare, here and hereafter, are to be found portrayed in it.

Read this book for what on reason you can accept, and take the rest on faith. You will live and die a better man.

DAVID LIVINGSTONE

All I am I owe to Jesus Christ, revealed to me in His divine book.

MARTYN LLOYD-JONES

The trouble today, as it has been for many years, is that Christian people have not been reading their Scriptures, nor troubling to understand them . . . But our forefathers, who worked much harder and for much longer hours, and for much smaller wages, found the time. Those men used to read their Scriptures and study them. They generally bought a Bible which had a commentary at the bottom of each page, and they studied it and spent time with it. They also read other books which helped them to understand the Scriptures. They were "exercising their senses," and that is what made them strong.

"That Christ may dwell in your heart by faith . . . " (Ephesians 3:17). But how difficult it is to keep this feeling and desire in the mind! The only way to do it is to read your Bible, and especially passages such as this and similar ones, and then to think about it frequently and deliberately cause your mind to turn to it.

The Unsearchable Riches of Christ

JOHN LOCKE

The Bible is one of the greatest blessings bestowed by God on the children of men. It has God for its author, salvation for its end, and truth without any mixture for its matter. It is all pure, all sincere, nothing too much. Nothing wanting.

J. G. LOCKHART

Sir Walter Scott expressed to me, as he lay dying, that I should read to him, and when I asked him what book, he said, "Need you ask? There is but one." I chose the 14th chapter of St. John's Gospel. Then Sir Walter Scott said, "Well, this is great comfort."

Life of Sir Walter Scott

HERBERT LOCKYER

Approaching the Scriptures, we must believe them to be the infallible source of truth. Our attitude must be that God cannot make a mistake; therefore, in His Word we have the authoritative revelation of His mind and will. We must have equal faith in the Old and New Testaments. If both sections are not the Word of God, neither part is the Word of God. One inspiring mind and one developing purpose runs through the whole.

An unregenerate or unspiritual man may extract features from the Bible common to other books, like historic interest, dramatic force, poetic pathos, etc. The distinguishing feature of the Bible, however, is its revelation of God, which can be fully understood and enjoyed only by those who are in harmony with the mind of God.   *All About Bible Study*

TREMPER LONGMAN III

To say that the Bible comes to us as stories and poems does not mean that the biblical events are mythological or historically untrue. No, these stories accurately tell us what actually happened. But they do so in a gripping, vivid style that keeps us on the edge of our seats. And they do it in a manner that celebrates God and His ways in the world. As such, the Bible speaks to the whole person. Its stories seize our imaginations. Its poems pluck at our heartstrings. The events and images do more than simply inform us; they suck us into the "story" of our God, bringing us into His life. And none of this will let go of us until we are changed people.

Reading the Bible with Heart and Mind

ANNE GRAHAM LOTZ

Success from God's point of view is not measured by the accumulation of wealth, a problem-free life, or good health. Rather, it is measured by the individual's observance of and obedience to the Word of God. I want to be successful in God's eyes.

MAX LUCADO

The purpose of the Bible is to proclaim God's plan and passion to save his children. That is the reason this book has endured through the centuries. It dares to tackle the toughest questions about life: Where do I go after I die? Is there a God? What do I do with my fears? The Bible offers answers to these crucial questions. It is the treasure map that leads us to God's highest treasure, eternal life. *Life Lessons*

The Bible's durability is not found on earth; it is found in heaven. For millions who have tested its claims and claimed its promises there is but one answer—the Bible is God's book and God's voice. *God's Inspirational Promise Book*

The Bible is a fence full of knotholes through which we can peek but not see the whole picture. It's a scrapbook full of snapshots capturing people in encounters with God, but not always recording the result.

HENRY LUCE

Time did not invent personality journalism. The Bible did.

ROGER LUNDIN

The Bible, especially the Old Testament, contains many accounts of God's questioning of humanity. In fact, the very first time God speaks to Adam and Eve after the fall, he addresses them with questions: Where are you? Have you eaten from the

tree of which I commanded you not to eat? What is this that you
have done? By means of questions, God calls us to account and
makes us responsible for the thoughts of our minds, the deeds of
our hands, and the inclinations of our hearts.

The Bible is the Word of God while the greatest classics are
only supreme embodiments of human insight. Nevertheless, there
is something like a divine weight to the questions that the classics
ask of our lives. The writer of the letter to the Hebrews in the
New Testament says that "the word of God is living and active,
sharper than any two-edged sword, piercing until it divides soul
from spirit, joints from marrow; it is able to judge the thoughts
and intentions of the heart." In an age such as ours, when
cynicism and suspicion can make it difficult for us to take
seriously anything that fails to meet our own standards or to
gratify our desires, the great classics of literature have a unique
power to speak to us of our potential and our peril.

Invitation to the Classics

MARTIN LUTHER

If a theologian does not want to err, he must have all Scripture
before his eyes, must compare apparently contradictory passages
and, like the two cherubim facing each other from opposite sides,
must find agreement of the difference in the middle of the mercy
seat.

The Bible is alive. It speaks to me. It has feet, it runs after me.
It has hands, it lays hold of me.

I would advise no one to send his child where the Holy
Scriptures are not supreme. Every institution that does not
unceasingly pursue the study of God's Word becomes corrupt . . .
I greatly fear that the universities, unless they teach the Holy
Scriptures diligently and impress them on the young students, are
wide gates to hell.

To the Christian Nobility of the German Nation, 1520

Everything the apostles have taught and written they have
derived from the Old Testament, for everything that would take
place in the future in Christ and would be preached has been

proclaimed in it . . . For this reason, they based all their preaching on the Old Testament, and there is no word in the New Testament for which one does not see behind it the Old Testament in which it was previously proclaimed.

There is no need for bloodshed. The world will be conquered by the Word of God, and by the Word the Church will be rebuilt and reformed.

Christ is the Master. The Scriptures are only the servant. The true way to test all the Books is to see whether they work the will of Christ or not.

I have observed that all the heresies and errors have arisen not from Scripture's own plain statements, but when that plainness of statement is ignored and men follow the scholastic arguments of their own brains.

With this book (Psalms), I have occupied, delighted, and trained myself from my youth, and thanks be to God, not without great benefit. Yea, I would not exchange the blessing of the Holy Spirit which I have obtained by enjoying and considering the psalms for all the thrones and kingdoms of this world.

Studies in the Psalter

J. MARY LUTI

A fascinating story. Full of divine wonder and awe, it is also a tale of human mystery and drama, suffering and joy, heroism and devotion, irony and humor. It is, above all, a life story that presents us at every turn with a deep sense of God's enduring care for His people and His people's flawed but persistent desire to be faithful. It is a majestic story that deserves a good telling by able tellers. And in this volume we have just that!

The Reforming Power of the Scriptures (foreword)

GEN. DOUGLAS MACARTHUR

Believe me, sir, never a night goes by, be I ever so tired, but I read the Word of God before I go to bed.

JOHN MACARTHUR

Why is God's Word so important? Because it contains God's will for your life . . . Bible study is not complete until we ask ourselves, "What does this mean for my life, and how can I practically apply it?" We must take the knowledge we have gained from our reading and draw out the practical principles that apply to our personal lives.

MacArthur's Quick Reference Guide to the Bible

The power of God is not found in some mystical, extra-biblical source of knowledge, the use of signs and wonders and ecstatic utterances, the insights of secular psychology and philosophy, or clever insights into people's felt needs. But rather the power of God resides only in the inspired, infallible, and inerrant Word of God. When believers read, study, obey, and apply Scripture, they will realize it has sufficient power to deal with any situation in life . . . Scripture is the answer to all of life's challenges.

Think Biblically: Recovering a Christian Worldview

CLARENCE EDWARD MACARTNEY

The Bible is the supreme Book on human personality . . . From Adam in Genesis to Satan in the Apocalypse, its portraits are unforgettable . . . Augustine wrote how men wander over the earth and wonder at the rivers and the mountains and the sea and the stars, while all the time man himself is the great wonder . . . How fearful and how wonderful are man's terrible and glorious capacities and possibilities . . . It is said that every man's life contains sufficient material for a great novel.

Preaching Without Notes

THOMAS BABINGTON MACAULAY

If everything else in our language should perish, the Bible would alone suffice to show the whole extent of its beauty and power.   *Edinburgh Review,* January 1826

GEORGE MACDONALD

Every man must read the Word for himself. One may read it in one shape, another in another. All will be right if it be indeed the

Word they read, and they read it by the lamp of obedience. He who is willing to do the will of the Father shall know the truth of the teaching of Jesus. The spirit is "given to them that obey him."

Unspoken Sermons

JAMES MACDONALD

How badly we need a source of stability when circumstances shake our world. We never have to worry that God's Word may be out-of-date or in need of revision. It is just as relevant as the day it was written. Circumstances may change, cultures and world leaders may come and go, but God's Word is always current because it deals with two things that never change—the God who made us and the deepest needs of the human heart.

God Wrote a Book

Let me tell you, picking up the Bible and starting in Revelation is like asking a first grader to begin with algebra or calculus. Until you've done 2 + 2 = 4, you can't do calculus. And until you've read the Gospel of John and some other basic passages, you cannot do the Book of Revelation. With a good strategy of where to begin, you *will* understand the Bible.   *God Wrote a Book*

If you were to read through the whole Bible and circle every time it says, "And God said," and "Thus says the Lord," and "The word of the Lord came to," you would discover that more than 4,000 times the writers of Scripture say without embarrassment or apology that what they are saying and writing is the very Word of God. For this reason, the early church knew that if the specific writing under consideration was in fact God's Word, then all would agree that it communicated a sense of divine authority.

God Wrote a Book

One of the greatest proofs for the reliability of the Bible to me is the fact that the Old Testament is filled with prophecies that have come true.

WILLIAM C. MACDONALD

The books of the Bible were written over a long period of time. It took God longer to write the Bible than it took him to build the British empire.   *Modern Evangelism*

IAN MACPHERSON

There are countless thousands to whom, as David Reed remarks, "Genesis is only a biological term." There are multitudes whose limited knowledge of the Word of God is as narrow as that of the ignoramus of whom Andrew Blackwood reports that he thought Sodom and Gomorrah were husband and wife.

ADMIRAL ALFRED T. MAHAN

After much experience of bad and good, of religion and irreligion, I assure you—with the full force of the conviction of a lifetime—that to one who has mastered the Word of God even imperfectly, it brings a light, a motive, a strength, and a support which nothing else does.

G. T. MANLEY

The Bible contains the most wonderful histories, but is yet no history book. It is a treasury of truth concerning right and wrong, but it is not a textbook of ethics. It goes deeper than any other into the problems of life, but in no sense is it a handbook of philosophy.   *The New Bible Handbook*

GERALD MANN

I do not worship the Bible, so I am not afraid that a scientist will discover something the Bible can't account for. I worship the God whose actions and revelations were recorded by my spiritual ancestors. And I find that my own experiences with God are remarkably corroborated by theirs.   *Common Sense Religion*

PETER MARSHALL

The Bible is the chief moral cause of all that is good, and the best book for regulating the concerns of men . . . The man, therefore, who weakens or destroys the divine authority of that book may be accessory to all of the public disorders which society is doomed to suffer.

EVERETT D. MARTIN

Private interpretation meant that any group of men, however ignorant, need only be able to read the Bible to be in possession

of the ultimate, undeniable truth about almost any important
question of human life.   *Liberty,* 1930

MARTIN E. MARTY

When one rereads the Bible as a Jew, Protestant, Orthodox or
Roman Catholic, he may read it as a mirror of his preconceptions.
When encouraged to read it in the contexts of other traditions, he
is apt to find something hitherto overlooked.

The New York Post, 5/17/64

T. B. MASTON

The Bible is the most important possession of the Christian
churches, far more important than all of their buildings,
institutions, and endowments. Protestants who give to it a "unique
and unrivaled place of authority" need in a special way to be
acquainted with it and to see the relevance of its basic concepts
and principles to the life of the individual and the world in which
he lives.   *Biblical Ethics*

There is no portion of the Old Testament that speaks more
pointedly to the needs of our day than the prophets. The
relevance of their messages stems from the fact that the problems
they dealt with were human problems and those problems are
basically the same from generation to generation.

Biblical Ethics

LOUIS B. MAYER

The number one book of the ages was written by a committee,
and it was called The Bible.

RICHARD MAYHUE

The truth about God illuminating Scripture should greatly
encourage us. While it does not eliminate the need for gifted men
to teach us, or the hard labor of serious Bible study, it does
promise that we do not need to be enslaved to church dogma or
be led astray by false teachers. Our primary dependence for
learning Scripture needs to be upon the Author of Scripture—
God Himself. Thus we can be like the Bereans who compared
every teaching of man with God's Word to determine if man's
words were true or not.   *Spiritual Maturity*

The writer of Psalm 119 knew that he was dependent upon God for light, sight, insight, and wisdom. This became so important to him that he promised God that he would not forget God's Word. He put a premium upon possessing Scripture for immediate recall; he unquestionably memorized Scripture for this to become reality. God's ministry of illumination by which He gives us light on the meaning of Scripture is in view here. Paul and John affirm this also in the New Testament.

Spiritual Maturity

DAVID C. McCASLAND

The Bible is not a spiritual mail-order catalog, but in its pages we vividly see ourselves both as we are today and as we hope to be . . . Far more than a book of wishful thinking; it is a book of well-founded confidence in God's purpose and plan for us as believers. Whatever we are like today, we know that in Christ we have a living hope, and it will not end in disappointment.

ROBERT MURRAY McCHEYNE

One gem from that ocean is worth all the pebbles from earthly streams.

JAMES McCOSH

The book to read is not the one which thinks for you, but the one which makes you think. No book in the world equals the Bible for that.

The Laws of Discursive Thought

JOSH McDOWELL

The Bible should be on the top shelf all by itself. The Bible is unique.

DONALD McGAVRAN

Being a Christian means believing the Bible, and willing to live the Bible, and willing to do what God commands us to do in the Bible.

J. VERNON McGEE

All great spiritual movements among the people of God have come about through a revival of Bible study.

ALISTER E. McGRATH

That the gospel is deeply satisfying, with the power to change human lives . . . is no delusion, no human invention to ease the pain of life. It is grounded in the bedrock of truth. The New Testament offers us hints as to how we can proclaim the gospel in a variety of contexts. But above all, it reassures us that the truth and relevance are intrinsic to the gospel, part of its very fabric.

In a series of lectures at Cambridge University during the First World War, Sir Arthur Quiller-Couch declared that the King James Bible was "the very greatest" literary achievement in the English language. The only possible challenger for this title came from the complete works of Shakespeare. His audience had no quarrel with this judgment. It was the accepted wisdom of the age. The King James Bible was a landmark in the history of the English language, and an inspiration to poets, dramatists, artists, and politicians. The influence of this work has been incalculable.

In the Beginning

DOUG McINTOSH

Meditation is the adoring believer's interaction with the God of the Bible by means of the Bible. When I meditate, I realize, from reading and study, the truth of God as it is contained in the Scriptures. I reflect upon that truth, considering its implications for me personally and for the world. I respond to God in thanksgiving, worship, and obedience because of that truth.

God Up Close

FRANK S. MEAD

The Bible is a portrait gallery. Down its pages from Adam walking the mists of the cooling earth to the last dreaming seer of Revelation, moves a deathless procession of the most interesting men and women in the history of the world . . . good men and bad, noble women and low, cowards and heroes, saints and devils, martyrs, apostates and apostles. They run the gamut of character from Jesus to Jezebel. Some were great and some were puny.

Saints and Sinners in the Bible

HENRIETTA C. MEARS

Hold the Bible in your hand and turn to the middle of the book. It is the Psalms. Not merely is this true physically. There is a deeper truth. It is central also in human experience. This book is used by Hebrew and Christian alike, even in our day. The Psalms were for use in the temple, for which many were prepared. They were written for the heart to worship God out under the open heavens, or in the pit of despair, or in a cave of hiding. When you find yourself in deep need, you can always find a psalm which expresses your innermost feeling. Or if you have an abounding joy, the words are there for you, too.

What the Bible Is All About

C. D. MEIGS

What is home without a Bible?
'Tis a home where daily bread
For the body is provided,
But the soul is never fed.

Home Without a Bible

THOMAS MERTON

By the reading of Scripture, I am so renewed that all nature seems renewed around me and with me. The sky seems to be a pure, a cooler blue, the trees a deeper green. Light is sharper on the outlines of the forest and the hills, and the whole world is charged with the glory of God—and I feel fire and music in the earth under my feet.   *The Sign of Jonas*

BRUCE M. METZGER

Of all the "helps" which assist the reader to understand the New Testament, the Old Testament is by far the most important. In that collection of 39 books one finds the religious presuppositions and historical background without which the thinking and experiences of the New Testament writers cannot be understood . . . Such a knowledge enables the Christian reader to perceive the working of divine providence through long stretches of history in the preparation of a chosen people, to whom at the fulness of time God sent forth his Son.

FREDERICK B. MEYER

Read the Bible not as a newspaper, but as a letter from home. If a cluster of heavenly fruit hangs within reach, gather it. If a promise lies on the page as a blank check, cash it. If a prayer is recorded, appropriate it, and launch it as a feathered arrow from the bow of your desire. If an example of holiness gleams before you, ask God to do as much for you.

CALVIN MILLER

Our inner and private affair with Scripture means that we are regularly getting in touch with the center of ourselves, which is where we know God . . . In the quietness of self-imposed solitude, surround yourself with good books, articles, and, above all, the open Bible.   *Spirit, Word, and Story*

To see the Scriptures as divinely inspired means that God is working on both ends of scriptural inspiration. On the writer's end of the Bible, God inspires the text as adequate to human need. On the listener's end, God quickens the text in proclamation to effect inner change. I cannot countenance any sermon which proceeds from any other base than holy text.

Spirit, Word, and Story

KEITH G. MILLER

At times we find ethical trajectories in the Bible's "revealed morality"—particular guidelines or instructions for living to which God calls the faithful. At other times, ethical direction can be discerned from observing closely the life of Jesus and his modeling of love and compassion and respect and prophetic confrontation. And we can learn from the moral heroes and heroines of Scripture—those who follow after God's own heart but also are quite fallible beings, just as we are. We learn from their mistakes as well as their moral achievements.

The Word Among Us

MADELEINE AND J. LANE MILLER

The Bible itself is a concrete, picture-filled book. Even chapters which are characteristically devotional are full of phrases as vivid as the people of the East themselves are vivid.

Encyclopedia of Bible Life

We do not marvel that from nine to twelve million copies of the Bible and Scripture portions in 1,062 languages and dialects are sold per year (in the 1940s) or that men in the munitions-handling rooms of battleships shorten tedious hours by reading the Bible where they will not be interrupted; or that men without hope, on a battered life-raft sustain life by reading aloud the pages of a battered New Testament.

Encyclopedia of Bible Life

JOHN E. MITCHELL, JR.

God alone can have such knowledge concerning our character as is disclosed in the Bible. The Bible tells us things about ourselves that only God can know . . . I think that every Christian who knows this book has the feeling that it was written especially for him. He finds in it answers that fit his needs so perfectly that he has a right to say that God has spoken to him, expressly and directly.

The Christian in Business

CLAXTON MONRO

We will be taught by the Bible and fed by the Bible. But we do not believe in Christ because He is in the Bible. We believe in the Bible because Christ is in us.

ANN MONROE

At first glance, reading the Bible might seem a simple activity. But the Bible is not something we ordinarily pick up, on a free afternoon, to kill a little time. Whether we are religious or not, the Bible carries a lot of freight: the massive literary, historical, spiritual, and theological freight between its covers and an enormous amount of cultural baggage to boot. To choose to read it involves an inner gearing up, like a hawk gathering itself for a dive.

The Word

DWIGHT L. MOODY

One day I read in the tenth chapter of Romans, "Now, faith cometh by hearing, and hearing by the Word of God." I had closed my Bible and prayed for faith. I now opened my Bible and began to study, and my faith has been growing ever since.

Sin will keep you from this book. This book will keep you from sin.

I know the Bible is inspired, because it inspires me.

The Bible without the Holy Spirit is a sundial by moonlight

The Scriptures were not given to increase our knowledge but to change our lives.

ANNIE M. MORGAN

The 23rd Psalm helped me put the Word of God into reality in my life. We raised eighteen beautiful children by faith in God. This psalm helped me in my Christian growth. Times of crisis and decisions in life were made easier as a result of these verses. Recently I slipped and fell on my back. I suffered contusions. This Scripture was a mainstay in my recovery. I knew I couldn't heal and worry at the same time. The Lord is my shepherd, and I love all the words of God.   *Lamp unto My Feet*

G. CAMPBELL MORGAN

There is one sure and infallible guide to truth, and therefore, one and only one corrective for error, and that is the Word of God.

JOHN MORTIMER

Great works of literature, perhaps the greatest—the Oresteia, Hamlet, even the Bible—have been stories of mystery and crime.
                    Sunday Times (London), 4/1/1990

MALCOLM MUGGERIDGE

There's far more truth in the Bible than in the quantum theory.

GEORGE MULLER

I have read the Bible through one hundred times, and always with increasing delight. Each time it has seemed like a new book to me. Great has been the blessing from consecutive, diligent, daily study.

The vigor of our spiritual life will be in exact proportion to the place held by the Bible in our life and thoughts.

LAEL P. MURPHY

While a *Fodor's Guide* or the *Globe* travel section may be where we turn to sort out our ideas for summer escape, the Bible is the place to start when we feel lost in any other aspect of our lives. Sustaining those in our faith tradition for centuries, the Old and New Testaments seek to speak to us as well, no matter how intellectually sophisticated or technologically advanced we may be.

ANDREW MURRAY

Some read the Bible to learn and some read the Bible to hear from Heaven.

I want you to remember what a difference there is between perfection and perfectionism. The former is a Bible truth; the latter may or may not be a human perversion of that truth. I fear much that many, in their horror of perfectionism, reject perfection too.

JAMES BALL NAYLOR

King David and King Solomon
Led merry, merry lives,
With many, many lady friends
And many, many wives;
But when old age crept over them,
With many, many qualms,
King Solomon wrote the Proverbs
And King David wrote the Psalms.

David and Solomon

DAVID NEFF

It is in Scripture that God has given us clear instruction in righteousness and wisdom. He has given us wise counselors to help us apply it to our lives, and he has granted us the freedom to act within the boundaries of his will. To turn then to God and demand special guidance in decision-making is to say, "I fear you

and I don't trust the gifts you have given me. I am afraid that if I make a mistake, you will reject me and I will face spiritual ruin."
Tough Questions Christians Ask

JOHN HENRY NEWMAN

I read my Bible to know what people ought to do, and my newspaper to know what they are doing.

A Bible: Its light is like the body of Heaven in its clearness; its vastness like the bosom of the sea; its variety like scenes of nature.

NEW TESTAMENT

All Scripture is inspired by God and profitable for teaching, for reproof, for correction, for training in righteousness; that the man of God may be adequate, equipped for every good work.
2 Timothy 3:16-17

SIR ISAAC NEWTON

No sciences are better attested than the religion of the Bible.

We account the Scriptures of God to be the most sublime philosophy. I find more sure marks of authority in the Bible than in any profane history whatever.

JOHN NEWTON

I know not a better rule of reading the Scripture than to read it through from beginning to end, and, when we have finished it once, to begin it again.

The chief and grand means of edification, without which all other helps will disappoint us, are the Bible and prayer, the word of grace and the throne of grace. A frequent perusal of the Bible will give us an enlarged and comprehensive view of the whole of religion, its origin, nature, genius, and tendency, and preserve us from an over-attachment to any system of man's compilation.

MAURICE NICOLL

The central conception of Man in the Gospels is that he is an unfinished creation capable of reaching a higher level by a definite evolution which must begin by his own efforts.

ADAM NICOLSON

One can see the extraordinary phenomenon of the King James
Bible conforming both to Protestant and to pre-Protestant ideas
about the nature of Christianity. It is both clear and rich. It both
makes an exact and almost literal translation of the original and
infuses that translation with a sense of beauty and ceremony . . .
No one could fault the Translators in their meticulous attention to
the detail of the original texts, and yet in doing so, more than any
other English translators, they enshrined a high moment of
Christian meaning. *God's Secretaries*

MARK A. NOLL

No church survives as a healthy reflection of God's work which
does not honor God's written word. Yet no church speaks
responsibly to the world which does not interpret Scripture with
all the possible resources at its disposal.
The Unfettered Word

KATHLEEN NORRIS

For many years I never looked at a Bible. Now I find that it
sustains me in ways no poem or a novel could. I find no easy
answers in the Bible but only a holy simplicity.
Amazing Grace

At the end of the Revelation to John, we find justice restored,
and a God who comes to be with those who have suffered the
most in a cruel, unjust, and violent world. A God who does not
roar and strut like the ultimate dictator but who gently "wipes
away all tears from their eyes." *Amazing Grace*

SAM NUNN

There are many portions of the Bible that have guided and
sustained me through many different and difficult times in
my life. I try to use the lessons taught in the Old and New
Testaments in my professional and personal life. I believe that
as a country and as a society, we must begin to stress a return to
the basic values of tolerance and charity for one another, such
as the actions reflected in one of my favorite passages, Matthew
25:35–40. These values are tenets not only of Christianity, but
also many of the world's other religions.

DAVID F. NYGREN

If all the neglected Bibles were dusted simultaneously, we would have a record dust storm and the sun would go into eclipse for a whole week.

FLANNERY O'CONNOR

The writer whose point of view is catholic in the widest sense of the term reads nature the same way medieval commentators read Scripture. They found three levels of meaning in the literal level of the sacred text—the allegorical, in which one thing stands for another; the moral, which has to do with what should be done; and the anagogical, which has to do with the Divine life and our participation in it, the level of Grace.   *The Habit of Being*

LLOYD J. OGILVIE

God speaks through the Scriptures today to engender faith, enable adventuresome living of the abundant life, and establish the basis of obedient discipleship. The Bible, the unique Word of God, is unlimited in its resource for Christians in communicating our hope to others. It is our weapon in the battle for truth, the guide for ministry, and the irresistible force for introducing others to God.

JOHN OGREN

Preaching, teaching, music, and drama are all powerful means of conveying the riches of Scripture, but these means must be understood as secondary to actually reading the book aloud frequently and extensively. No song, drama, or sermon can speak with the same authority of Scripture itself. Neither can they be as consistently interesting and enduring as the word of God. Reading the Bible aloud may be the simplest, most powerful, and most underutilized means of telling the Christian story.
                         New Wineskins: Telling God's Story

MARVIN OLASKY

During the mid-1970s I went through an intellectual change. When I was a communist I believed that humanity's problems were external and that revolution was the solution. But Bible- and sermon-reading pushed me to see that the problem was internal and the cure was personal. God reconfigured my psychology so that the arrogance that had previously characterized me was largely gone. I remain a sinner and still have periods of self-centeredness, but ego does not control me as it used to. I no longer exalt my wisdom above God's. Reading the whole Bible helped me to confess sin. The New Testament clearly lays out the full gravity of humankind's problem and the full opportunity for redemption. *Professors Who Believe*

OLD TESTAMENT

One does not live by bread alone, but by every word that comes from the mouth of the Lord. Deuteronomy 8:1

Thy word is a lamp unto my feet, and a light unto my path.
Psalms 119:105

This book of the law must ever be on your lips; you must keep it in mind day and night so that you may diligently observe all that is written in it. Then you will prosper and be successful in all that you do. Joshua 1:8

ORIGEN (ORIGENES ADAMANTIUS)

Let us keep the Scriptures in mind and meditate upon them day and night, persevering in prayer, always on the watch. Let us beg the Lord to give us real knowledge of what we read and to show us not only how to understand it but how to put it into practice, so that we may deserve to obtain spiritual grace.

PRISCILLA J. OWENS

Give me the Bible, lamp of life immortal,
Hold up that splendor by the open grave;
Show me the light from heaven's shining portal,
Show me the glory gilding Jordan's wave.
Give me the Bible, Holy message shining;
Thy light shall guide me in the narrow way;
Precept and promise, law and love combining,
Till night shall vanish in eternal day.
"Give Me the Bible" (hymn)

RENE PACHE

The human authors of the sacred text—about 45—varied enormously. There were shepherds, kings, statesmen, scribes, priests, scholars, poets, historians, lawyers, a tax collector, a medical doctor, and unlettered fishermen along with some unnamed individuals. Still, we observe with astonishment the prodigious unity of inspiration throughout the Bible, as seen in its message and doctrine and even in its structure—yet, along with this a refreshing diversity.

The Inspiration and Authority of Scripture

The many passages referring to it in Scripture prove to us that the Bible teaching concerning the Holy Spirit is both definite and complete . . . Scripture distinctly affirms that the sacred books were not composed by men according to their fancy or their own ideas. Their authors were inspired and guided by the Spirit who alone searches and reveals the deep things of God, so that their writings afford us all the desired guarantees.

FRANK PACK

The Word of God is no lifeless, dust-covered collection of ancient chronicles and records. Whatever it contains of history, of the great acts and events of the past, of the great heroes of faith whose examples shine in the firmament of the scriptures, it continues to be our source of information concerning what God has done and what God has said to accomplish the salvation of mankind . . . It is in the Bible that he addresses us and enables us to see clearly what he would have us to do and to become.

J. I. PACKER

One of the many divine qualities of the Bible is this: it does not yield its secrets to the irreverent and censorious.

Belief in inerrancy involves an advance commitment to receive as from God all that the Bible, interpreting itself to us through the Holy Spirit in a natural and coherent way, teaches. Thus it shapes our understanding of biblical authority. So inerrantists should welcome the work of textual scholars, who are forever trying to eliminate the inauthentic and give us exactly what the biblical writers wrote, neither more nor less . . . Both these wisdoms are needed if we are to benefit fully from the written word of God.

Today, we are surrounded by people drowning in the raging
waters of hopelessness . . . God, we might say, is the lifeguard
who, in true *Baywatch* fashion, comes in person to the place
where we are drowning in order to rescue us. The Holy
Scriptures are the lifeline God throws us in order to ensure that
he and we stay connected while the rescue is in progress.

Boxed texts cannot set before us anything like the full sweep of
Scripture. Nor should we restrict our biblical diet, as some do, to
a few familiar psalms and the four Gospels. No doubt there is in
any one of these portions of Holy Writ more than we shall ever
fathom, but we are less likely to plumb their depths if we isolate
them from the rest of God's revelation. By all means let us read
and reread our favorite passages as often as we want to, but all
Scripture should be read regularly as well.   *Truth and Power*

Many today regard Scripture as man's witness to God, and
resolve its authority into the authority of the divine words to
which—more or less adequately—witness is borne. But this is
only half the truth. Scripture is also, and fundamentally, God's
witness to himself, and its authority rests ultimately on the fact
that it is his Word. Why ought we to believe biblical history, and
accept biblical teaching, and confide in Scripture promises, and
be governed by Scripture commands? Because Scripture is the
written speech of our Creator.   *God's Words*

LUIS PALAU
Scripture addresses not only many of our felt needs but also
our real needs as God diagnoses them . . . And it gives wisdom for
making right decisions.   *God Is Relevant*

At the dawn of the third millennium after the time of Jesus
Christ, it's remarkable that most Americans embrace a book
compiled nearly two hundred millennia ago from the writings of
approximately forty writers, some of whom were penning their
chapters fourteen hundred years before Christ . . . Why such
interest in reading an old book? I believe it is because it is God's
Word, filled with compelling narratives found from cover to cover
. . . The Bible tells a host of wonderful historical case studies
about real people, real problems, and, I emphatically believe, real
encounters with God.   *God Is Relevant*

MARJORIE PARKER

One can lean all day on a certain verse or passage of Scripture.
Bread from My Oven

MATTHEW PARKER

Of all the sentences pronounced by our Saviour Christ in his whole doctrine, none is more serious or more worthy to be borne in remembrance than that which he spoke openly in his gospel, saying, "Search the Scriptures, for in them ye think to have eternal life, and those they be which bear witness of me." Christ calleth . . . not only to the single reading of the Scriptures, but sendeth to the exquisite searching of them, for in them is eternal life to be found.   Preface to the *Bishop's Bible, 1568*

THEODORE PARKER

The Bible goes equally to the cottage of the peasant and the palace of the king. It is woven into literature and colors the talk of the street. The bark of the merchant cannot sail without it, and no ship of war goes to the conflict but it is there. It enters men's closets, directs their conduct, and mingles in all of the grief and cheerfulness of life.

ALICE PARMELEE

The Bible is a great river of spiritual reality rising out of Israel's remote past and continuing to flow more deeply and powerfully through succeeding centuries. It is fed by many rushing streams and mighty torrents and into it has flowed the spiritual wisdom and insight of twelve centuries. The long river of the Bible is broad and very deep, and the Spirit of God moves upon the face of its waters. Here, men that thirst come to drink of the water of life.

DOLLY PARTON

Saying the Lord's Prayer always makes me feel good. Another part of the Bible I love is the Twenty-third Psalm "The Lord is my shepherd . . . " The most important verse in the Bible to me is "Now abideth faith, hope and love." Some versions of the Bible say "charity," but it is properly translated "love." It goes on to say, "The greatest of these is love." Faith, hope and love are the three most important words in my life. I believe it is faith that helps you achieve those things you hope for, and that love is the reason for all of it. That is my "unfinished business."

Dolly: My Life and Other Unfinished Business

BLAISE PASCAL

In the Bible there is enough clarity to enlighten the Elect, and enough obscurity to humble them.

NORMAN VINCENT PEALE

The most powerful force in human nature is the spiritual-power technique taught in the Bible. Very astutely the Bible emphasizes the method by which a person can make something of himself. Faith, belief, positive thinking, faith in God, faith in other people, faith in yourself, faith in life. This is the essence of the technique that it teaches.

The Power of Positive Thinking for Young People

L. TOM PERRY

The Scriptures that are never read will never help us.

LAURENCE J. PETER

The Bible contains much that is relevant today, like Noah taking forty days to find a place to park.   *Ideas for Our Time*

EUGENE H. PETERSON

Every time the Bible is translated, you enter a culture and a language system that is unique. And the Bible is true and gets into those rhythms and those idioms and there's more truth there. The truth is kind of endless, and each culture, dialect, and language gives a new chance to express something nobody has ever done quite this way before.

Scripture is a vast tapestry of God's creating, saving, and blessing ways in this world.

A striking feature of this (biblical) writing and reading, collecting and arranging, with no one apparently in charge, the early Christians, whose lives were being changed and shaped by what they were reading, arrived at the conviction that there was, in fact, someone in charge—God's Holy Spirit was behind and in it all. In retrospect, they could see that it was not at all random or haphazard, that every word worked with every other word, and that all the separate documents worked in intricate harmony. There was nothing accidental in any of this, nothing merely circumstantial. They were bold to call what had been written "God's Word," and trusted their lives to it . . . Most of its readers since have been similarly convinced.

Matthew opens the New Testament by setting the local story of Jesus in its world historical context. He makes sure that as we read his account of the birth, life, death, and resurrection of Jesus, we see the connections with everything that has gone before. "Fulfilled" is one of Matthew's characteristic verbs: such-and-such happened "that it might be *fulfilled."*   *The Message*

The Bible ends with a flourish, vision and song, doom and deliverance, terror and triumph. The rush of color and sound, image and energy, leaves us reeling. But if we persist through the initial confusion and read on, we begin to pick up the rhythms, realize the connections, and find ourselves enlisted as participants in a multidimensional act of Christian worship . . . John's Revelation is not easy reading. John is a poet, fond of metaphor and symbol, image and allusion, passionate in his desire to bring us into the presence of Jesus, believing and adoring. But the demands he makes on our intelligence and imagination are well rewarded, for in keeping company with John, our worship of God will almost certainly deepen in urgency and joy.   *The Message*

BILL PEVLOR

Indeed, the Bible is more than just another book—the Bible is alive. It not only imparts life to the reader . . . it will live eternally. Isaiah 40:8 says, "The grass withers and the flowers fall, but the Word of our God stands forever."

JOSEPH PHELPS

As Christians, the Bible is our common authority for faith and practice. In our common Book we find models for adversaries coming together in faith and love in order to fulfill the purposes of God. Although the term "dialogue" does not appear in the Bible, we see dimensions of the work we are calling dialogue throughout its pages . . . Throughout the Old Testament, God's concern for holiness includes a primary concern with human interactions based in justice. Justice requires relationships of honor and communion between people.

More Light, Less Heat

WILLIAM LYON PHELPS

You can learn more about human nature by reading the Bible than by living in New York.   *The New York Times,* 10/19/53

I thoroughly believe in a university education for both men and women, but I believe a knowledge of the Bible without a college course is more valuable than a college course without the Bible.

Westen civilization is founded upon the Bible. Our ideas, our wisdom, our philosophy, our literature, our art, our ideals come more from the Bible than from all other books put together. It is a revelation of divinity and humanity.

Human Nature in the Bible

PHILARET, METROPOLITAN OF MOSCOW

Everyone has not only a right, but it is his bounden duty to read the Holy Scriptures in a language which he understands, and edify himself thereby.

J. B. PHILLIPS

The translator must be flexible. I feel strongly that a translator, although he must make himself as familiar as possible with New Testament Greek usage, must steadfastly refuse to be driven by the bogey of consistency. He must be guided by the context in which a word appears and by the sensibilities of modern English readers. In the story of the raising of Lazarus, for example, Martha's objection to opening the grave would be natural enough to an Eastern mind. But to put into her lips the words, "by this time he's stinking," would sound to Western ears unpleasantly out of key with the rest of that moving story. Similarly, we know that the early Christians greeted each other with "an holy kiss." Yet to

introduce such an expression into a modern English translation immediately reveals the gulf between the early Christians and ourselves, the very thing that I as a translator am trying to bridge.
The New Testament in Modern English,
Revised Student Edition (Introduction)

I have heard professing Christians of our own day speak as through the historicity of the Gospels does not matter—all that matters is the contemporary Spirit of Christ. I contend that the historicity does matter, and I do not see why we, who live nearly two thousand years later, should call into question an Event for which there were many eyewitnesses still living at the time when most of the New Testament was written. It was no "cunningly devised fable" but an historic interruption of God into human history which gave birth to a young church so sturdy that the pagan world would not stifle or destroy it.

A. T. PIERSON

For God's written Word, no substitute has ever been found . . . The humblest reader, if shut up by circumstances to this one Book, as was Bunyan, almost literally, in Bedford jail, might, without any other guide than the Bible itself, by careful, prayerful searching, come to know the Word; exploring its contents until he becomes another Apollos, mighty in the Scriptures.

ARTHUR W. PINK

God's holy Word is a light from heaven, shining here "in a dark place." Its divine rays exhibit things in their true colours, penetrating and exposing the false veneer and glamour by which many objects are cloaked.

CLARK PINNOCK

The Bible is not infallible because it says so, but because Christ says so. There is no more reliable witness to the nature of the Scriptures than the one who died and rose to be our Savior.

JOHN PIPER

When the Bible tells us that God takes pleasure in obedience, we should rejoice because that means the doctor cares whether we get well. If he took no pleasure in our doing the tasks assigned

to make us well, he would not be a God of love. So it is good
news indeed, not only that he has given us commandments for
our good, but also that he rejoices to see them done.

The Pleasures of God

When it comes to serious meditation, we have sometimes
belittled the importance of education to prepare the way for this
crucial habit. One basic and compelling reason for education—
the rigorous training of the mind—is, very simply, so that a
person can read the Bible with understanding.

JOHN POLKINGHORNE

When we read the Bible, we have to work out what we are
reading. For example, poetry is very different from prose, though
both convey truths of different kinds. Genesis 1 and 2 are not
about the scientific truth of the detail of how things happened but
about the theological truth that everything that exists does so
because of God's will that creation should be meaningful and
fruitful. When Jesus was raised from the dead, it wasn't like
someone being resuscitated, coming back to life in order to
eventually die again. He was resurrected into a new kind of
glorified life that will never end. Christians believe that it is God's
will that we, too, should share in that new life after our deaths.

CHRISTOPHER POPE

Perceived inconsistencies or inaccuracies in the words or
meanings of the Bible are the reader's misperceptions. It is a
worthwhile task to discover the resolutions of such apparent
errors, but some may be beyond present human discovery. In any
case, it is unnecessary to resolve these conflicts to be confident of
the complete truthfulness of the Bible. The believer's confidence
in the Spirit's authorship of the Bible should derive from the
internal conviction of the Holy Spirit Himself, rather than from
human authority, tradition, intuition, personal appeal, or
evidence.   *Declaration of Faith*

VERN S. POYTHRESS

The Bible indicates that we are under the authority of Jesus as
our master, who speaks to us through the Bible. Choosing which
details in Scripture we will accept makes us the master instead,
undermining our relation to Christ.

HUGH PRATHER

No story can be told about the truth of God. It can't be argued
or televised. And witnesses can't prove it exists. Yet the truth of
God brings peace instantly. There is only one unchanging truth
about anyone and everyone. None are left outside of the warm
assurance and gentle rest it offers, because God's truth is love.

Spiritual Notes to Myself

REYNOLDS PRICE

We have little sense of what constituted verbal decorum for
the various audiences who would have heard the gospels in the
years immediately after their composition. To have Mark's Jesus
turn to the leper who asks for healing and tell him, "O.K., you're
healed!" (as he does in the translation sponsored by the Jesus
Seminar) suggests Woody Allen far more nearly than the agonized
and self-doubting thaumaturge of Mark's early pages

Three Gospels

ROWLAND E. PROTHERO

The Book of Psalms contains the whole music of the heart of
man, swept by the hand of his Maker . . .a mirror in which each
man sees the motions of his own soul. They express in exquisite
words the kinship which every thoughtful human heart craves to
find with a supreme, unchanging, loving God.

The Psalms in Human Life 1904

THOM S. RAINER

It must be said without hesitation that churches that reach the
unchurched are theologically conservative. They have a high view
of Scripture. And their convictions about their beliefs are obvious.

Some readers may have been surprised by how vociferous the
formerly unchurched were about their desires for strong biblical
teaching. The evidence and data are clear. Both the formerly
unchurched and the leaders of the churches that reached them
verified the efficacy of "meaty" teaching and preaching to reach
the unchurched and to strengthen the Christians. Strategies of
recent years that sought to reach the unchurched through

"lighter," less demanding teaching and preaching not only were ineffective, they were counterproductive as well.

Surprising Insights from the Unchurched

BERNARD RAMM

Everything essential to salvation and Christian living is clearly revealed in Scripture.

SIR WILLIAM M. RAMSAY

A basic principle in the interpretation of the Bible is that one must first ask what a given Scripture was intended to mean to the people for whom it was originally written. Only then is the interpreter free to ask what meaning it has for Christians today. Failure to ask this primary question and to investigate the historical setting of Scripture has prevented many Christians from coming to a correct understanding of some parts of the Bible.

DAVID H. C. READ

The most we have a right to believe in the light of the Gospel is that life beyond the grave is richer and fuller than this one, and that it consists in a continued growth into the image of Christ—together . . . Eternal life, according to the Bible, is knowledge of God—not endless time. It is a quality of life into which we enter now, and which finds its true flowering in a totally different environment.   *The Christian Faith*

JIM REAPSOME

There are four steps in a proper encounter with the Bible: long for it eagerly; examine it intelligently; meditate in it constantly, and obey it instantly.

If we soak our minds in biblical truths, we will recall them in times of temptation, trial, and discouragement.

The Bible deals preeminently with God's plan for us, with our failure, and with God's overtures of love and grace to win us back to himself through the death and resurrection of Christ.

CLIFFORD B. REEVES

Public relations work is generally considered to be a relatively new development. Actually, the principles are as old as the ages. The ninth verse of the 14th chapter of First Corinthians reads: "Except ye utter by the tongue words easy to understand, how shall it be known what is spoken? For ye shall speak into the air." With the Bible as our authority, how can we public relations people fail?

MAX REICH

The Christian who is careless in Bible reading will be careless in Christian living.

PATRICIA H. REIFF

How do I reconcile science and Scripture? Although I certainly believe that God could have created the entire universe in six earth days six thousand years ago, it seems unlike God to confuse us with clues that argue for a much older universe. I believe that the Bible is literally true but that it uses figurative language. (When the beggar Lazarus died, he was not implanted into Abraham's bosom but was joined with Abraham in heaven.) Since God is not subject to the limitation of the speed of light, then God's time is completely irrelevant to human time. As the apostle Peter wrote, paraphrasing one of the psalms, "one day is with the Lord as a thousand years, and a thousand years as one day."

Professors Who Believe

ERMANCE REJEBIAN

Unfortunately, it would take great insight and a lifetime of study to become intimately acquainted with each one of the 150 psalms. But there is one great observation that can be made concerning them. To the people of Israel, beset throughout their history by pagan neighbors or rulers, by the scorn, tyranny, and actual violence of irreligious Israelites, the only source of help and comfort was their God, the Holy One of Israel. This is the keynote of the entire Book of Psalms, struck in the words of the 50th Psalm: "Call upon me in the day of trouble, and I will deliver thee, and thou shalt glorify me."

The Book: The Bible Studies of Ermance Rejebian

ARNOLD B. RHODES

This (Psalm 23) has sung its way into more hearts than any other part of the Bible except the Lord's Prayer . . . The tiny tot memorizes it before he can read, and the old man dies with it upon his lips. *The Layman's Bible Commentary*

CLIFF RICHARD

As far as I am concerned, the Bible is God's word to his creation, and for truth about him—and about ourselves—it is one hundred percent reliable . . . With my erratic schedule, it's difficult to set aside a regular time each day for Bible reading. Usually, I try to do some study before going to bed . . . The important thing is to come to the Bible expecting to discover something relevant, vital, and lasting.

ALAN RICHARDSON

In order to accept the teaching of the Bible about God and human destiny we do not have first to accomplish the impossible task of transforming ourselves into men of the First Century A.D. or to imagine that Aristotle and Ptolemy are nearer to the truth than Darwin and Einstein.

It cannot be too heavily stressed that in the Bible God has already come forward to meet man and that it is for man to make the response. . . There is a good sense in which men can prove God: they can trustfully accept his promise and experience his goodness for themselves, so that they do not have to accept his truth second-hand. *Religion in Contemporary Debate*

BOBBY RICHARDSON

Dick Houser, the Kansas Royals manager, had been diagnosed as having a tumor and doctors had given him maybe six months to live. I was sitting in my office and the phone rang. It was Dick and he said, "Can you encourage me from the Scriptures?" I shared with him Philippians 4. He said, "Okay, that's all I needed." In the next few months, he was a radiant Christian, sharing Christ at every opportunity. *Lamp unto My Feet*

J. M. ROBERTS

The men and women who first came to the wilderness which was all that, often, North America seemed to offer, came with minds braced to grapple with it by the religious and social order they knew at home. . . The Bible, much read by Protestant preachers, and by many Protestant laymen too, provided them with the imagery of the Chosen People, making their way through tribulation to glory, to a new Jerusalem, a city builded on a hill, in a much-quoted Puritan image.   *The Triumph of the West*

MARK D. ROBERTS

The Bible is clear. Even before you begin to seek God, God is seeking you . . . If you study all the biblical passages on seeking God, you'll find that almost every one of them assumes that seeking is something that one does *after* one has a relationship with God. Seeking is, biblically speaking, something believers do. The life of faith is not a game of finders keepers, but finders seekers.   *Searching for God in America*

A. T. ROBERTSON

The greatest proof that the Bible is inspired is that it has withstood so much bad preaching.

PAT ROBERTSON

The Bible, and the relationship that comes about through a continuous relationship with God, are the best ways of knowing His will.

JOHN ROBINSON

The holy scriptures are that divine instrument by which we are taught what to believe concerning God, ourselves, and all things, and how to please God unto eternal life.

WILL ROGERS

Moses just went up on the mountain with a letter of credit and some instructions from the Lord, and He just wrote out the Ten Commandments, and they applied to the steel men, the oil men, the bankers, the farmers, and even the United States Chamber of Commerce. And he said, "Here they are, brothers. You take 'em and live by 'em, or else."

You can't get far ridiculing a man for upholding the Bible, or even a dictionary, if it's sincere belief.

The Bible is not read more than it is because it is not in the picture section. If they could see David in his training quarters getting ready to slay Goliath with the jawbone of a Senator, people would stop and look at it.

OSCAR ROMERO

We cannot segregate God's word from the historical reality in which it is proclaimed. It would not be then God's word. It would be history, it would be a pious book, a Bible that is just a book in our library. It becomes God's Word because it vivifies, enlightens, contrasts, repudiates, praises what is going on today in this society.

THEODORE ROOSEVELT

A thorough knowledge of the Bible is worth more than a college education.

LAVINIA ROSE

The Bible chart keep in full view—
'Twill lead you safe the journey through.*

HUGH ROSS

The open door God has placed before us is the door of scientific discovery. The more scientists discover about the universe, including life, the more sharply the evidence focuses on the God of the Bible as the one who planned it, shaped it, and still holds it together, just as the Bible says. Since the Bible speaks truthfully about these matters, we can also trust its message about the purpose of all things—that people everywhere should embrace their salvation in Jesus Christ and thus form an eternal, personal relationship with Him.   *Lamp unto My Feet*

---

*Embroidered religious message featured in the design of a quilt made by Mrs. Rose of Cortlandville, New York, in the 1860s, and shown at the American Folk Art Museum in New York.

JAMES E. ROSSCUP

God has given those who seek seriously to know Him two great resource helps. These are (1) His Word, the Bible, in which He speaks to them, and (2) their word in prayer in which *they* keep in touch with Him. The two are vitally related, as Christ makes clear in John 15:7, words articulating much spiritual essence that the Bible as a whole distills. Words from God's great book are a plethora of things to help those who genuinely follow God.

EDWARD ROTHSTEIN

(Benson) Bobrick points out that the King James Bible, along with its predecessors, helped create a nation, bound by a shared set of words and meanings. We are still heirs to that language. It inspired the cadences and vocabulary of centuries of literature and poetry; even great political documents like the Declaration of Independence and the Gettysburg Address fell under its sway. Wycliffe's 14th-century biblical translation created phrases like "held his peace" and "gave up the ghost." William Tyndale's 1525 translation created words like "Passover" and "scapegoat" and may have coined the word "beautiful." Miles Coverdale's 1535 translation provided "the eleventh hour" and "tender mercies." And the King James edition digested them all and formed new varieties of poetic expression. "God is my shepherd, therefore I can lose nothing," read one 16th-century translation; the King James version replaced it with "The Lord is my shepherd; I shall not want."   *The New York Times*

JEAN-JACQUES ROUSSEAU

I must confess to you that the majesty of the Scriptures astonishes me. The holiness of the Evangelist speaks to my heart and has such striking characters of truth, and is, moreover, so perfectly inimitable, that if it had been the invention of men, the inventors would be greater than the greatest heroes.

H. H. ROWLEY

The Bible brings good news to men, the stirring message of the wonder of God's love and the redemption whereby we can be lifted to share His life and power, and enter into His purpose for the world.   *A Companion to the Bible*

DAMON RUNYON

Even the best of the Bible writers couched their stuff in a form difficult to figure out. I want my preachers to translate that into more colloquial lingo as the old-time biblical rabble-rousers used to do. They were real evangelists who went about holding up customers to great religious fervor. Some of them told a biblical story in language as simple as they told an anecdote in the street.

DR. BENJAMIN RUSH

I believe no man was ever early instructed in the truths of the Bible without having been made wiser or better by the early operation of these impressions upon his mind. Every just principle that is to be found in the writings of Voltaire is borrowed from the Bible; and the morality of Deists, which has been so much admired and praised where it existed, has been, I believe, in most cases, the effect of habits produced by early instruction in the principles of Christianity.

The interesting events and characters recorded and described in the Old and New Testaments are calculated, above all others, to seize upon all the faculties of the mind of children. The understanding, the memory, the imagination, the passion, and the moral powers are all occasionally addressed by the various incidents which are contained in those divine books, insomuch that not to be delighted with them is to be devoid of every principle of pleasure that exists in a sound mind.

JOHN RUSKIN

My mother's influence in molding my character was conspicuous. She forced me to learn daily long chapters of the Bible . . . To that discipline and patient, accurate resolve I owe not only much of my general power of taking pains but the best part of my taste for literature.

The Bible is the one book to which any thoughtful man may go with any honest question of life or destiny and find the answer of God by honest searching.

The only way to understand the difficult parts of the Bible is to read and obey the easy ones.

Everything that I have written, every greatness that has been in any thought of mine, whatever I have done in my life has been simply due to the fact that when I was a child my mother daily read with me a part of the Bible and daily made me learn a part of it by heart.

FLEMING RUTLEDGE

On the biblical stage . . . there is just one main actor and that is God. Everyone else is there at his command. Everything that happens is according to his will or permission. Nothing occurs outside his knowledge and plan. No person is an independent operator; even the great villains, like Jezebel, Haman, and Belshazzar, are in God's eye and under his judgment. He raises people up and causes them to fall. Behind, beneath, above, and before every character in the Bible is the Holy One of Israel, the God of Abraham, Isaac, and Jacob, the Almighty Creator, "in the beginning, God." We need to keep this all-encompassing fact before us.   *Help My Unbelief*

The more we know of life, the more we experience its disappointments and sorrows, the more we learn that things don't work out the way we wanted, the more the Bible has to offer us. The people of the Bible are not stained glass figures; they are like us. They are flesh and blood. They turn away from God, make deals with crooks, stab people in the back. They complain, argue, cheat, commit adultery, tell lies. They suffer; they are struck down in war, felled by disease, exploited by oppressors. Their children die, their homes are destroyed, plagues of locusts eat their crops. But here is the central fact: All of this happens in the sight of God and in the context of his faithfulness.

The Undoing of Death

LELAND RYKEN

A good Bible translation does not patronize its readers. It expects the best from them. It does not slant itself to a grade school level for the simple reason that most Bible readers are *not* grade-schoolers. The Bible deserves the quality of attention and comprehension that we devote to other kinds of reading.

The Word of God in English

The worldview of the Bible goes far in explaining the unique power of storytelling in human life. The Bible reveals that the universe in which we live is intelligible, that it has an origin, a purposeful development, and a final meaning and resolution . . . Indeed, the biblical presentation of God and man is itself a narrative, a big story told through many smaller stories that comprise the whole. If God is a storyteller, then it simply makes sense that His creatures, made in the divine image, would act in similar fashion as a matter of course, as a natural and vital activity in the expression of creaturely life. *The Christian Imagination*

Is the Bible a book known for its aphoristic flair, its vivid and memorable descriptions, its eloquence and unforgettable twists of thought, or does it possess the eminently forgettable quality of a newspaper article in which one way of stating the information is as good as another? Surely the former.

The Word of God in English

J. C. RYLE

The Bible applied to the heart by the Holy Spirit is the chief means by which men are built up and established in the faith, after their conversion.

I do not say that those who wrote copies of the original Hebrew and Greek Scriptures were incapable of making mistakes and never left out or added a word. I lay no claim to the inspiration of every word in the various versions and translations of God's word. So far as these translations and versions are faithfully and correctly done, so far they are practically of equal authority with the original Hebrew and Greek.

CHARLES C. RYRIE

Fortunately, the prophets of the Bible wrote out many of their messages. So in order to check the reliability of their predictions, we do not have to depend on hearsay. We can check the written words . . . There is no doubt about it—when we examine copies of what those ancient prophets wrote, we can safely say that we are looking at their original words.

Unlike much that passes for prophecy today, Bible prophecies in both the Old and New Testaments were delivered not as groping generalizations or mystical musings but as detailed descriptions of the future.   *The Best Is Yet to Come*

Still today the Word motivates missionary efforts, including the arduous task of reducing an unwritten language to writing and then translating and printing the Bible. Still the Word of God is being translated into many existing languages. Still its teachings are a standard for moral conduct for many people and civilizations. Still its favorite passages are called to mind in times of special needs. Still it becomes the target of attacks by those who do not accept it. Still it is used and misused to prove most any viewpoint. Still it is annotated for various and sundry reasons. All these features demonstrate its uniqueness among books, its staying power through the centuries, and its relevance for different times, peoples, and cultures.

Formatting the Word of God

CHARLES C. RYRIE and DAVID PRICE

English Bibles took a different path from other European vernacular Bibles. This is because in England, unlike most every other country, it was illegal to translate the word of God. The ban lasted some 127 years. Overcoming the political and ecclesiastical resistance to an English Bible was not an easy task. Lives were lost along the way—not only for producing English Bibles, but also for merely owning or reading them.

Let It Go Among Our People: An Illustrated
History of the English Bible

WILLIAM SAFIRE

To those interested in both worlds of governance, the secular and the spiritual, the Book of Job teaches the body politic how one upright human being can challenge any authority's abuse of power. It teaches the spiritual in us how unsuppressed dissent can strengthen the relationship between God and Man . . . Of course there is a great difference between lord and vassal in the spiritual world, and the tension between Authority and Subject in the political world. But biblical writers encouraged believers to apply the lessons of one to life in the other. Therefore, accept—for the sake of history's longest-lasting argument—the analogy of the path between God's celestial court and Job's dungheap as the earliest corridor of power. That leap of metaphoric belief will help us examine some political truisms to see if they are falsisms.

The First Dissident

J. H. SAMMIS

When we walk with the Lord
In the light of His Word
What a glory it sheds on our way!
While we do His good will
He abides with us still
And with all who will trust and obey.

"Trust and Obey" (hymn)

W. E. SANGSTER

If one believes that the Bible is, in a most special sense, the Word of God, he will count any day ill spent which does not include some time given to its reverent study. He will come to the book, not thinking first of personal enjoyment or thrill or novelty, but only of understanding it and how best he may translate its message into life. The convinced Christian approaches the book in this state of mind.   *The Secret of Radiant Life*

DOROTHY L. SAYERS

We may say that God wrote His own autobiography.

The Mind of the Maker

FRANCIS A. SCHAEFFER

The glory of the Bible is that it is enough for every age and it is enough for every person. When you consider the early chapters in Genesis on through Deuteronomy, given about 1500 B.C. to Moses, it gave truth to those people in that day. Now we come to our age, and we know a lot that those people did not know about the cosmos, all kinds of things, and those same chapters (and the rest of the Bible) are enough to give truth to us. If Christ does not come back for another 500 years, the people then will know more than we do now, and the Bible will give truth to them. So, whether it is the individual, no matter what his level of education, sophistication, etc., or whether it is the age we live in with the knowledge we have, the Bible is enough to give the answer to the questions raised by reality.   *The God Who Is There*

Because of lack of fortitude and faithfulness on the part of God's people, God's Word has many times been allowed to be bent, to conform to the surrounding, passing, changing culture of that moment, rather than stand as the inerrant Word of God judging the form of the world spirit and the surrounding culture of that moment.

LAURA SCHLESSINGER and STEWART VOGEL

The Ten Commandments are the first direct communication between a people and God. Even for Christians, who believe that salvation is not found just in obedience to God's law but also in faith in Jesus Christ, their religion demands that they put that faith into practice through the laws. God's moral laws are still binding. They are the blueprint of God's expectations upon us and His plan for a meaningful, just, loving, holy life. Each of the Ten Commandments asserts a principle, and . . . each principle is a moral focal point for thousands of real-life issues, including relating to God, family, our fellows, sex, work, charity, proper speech, and thought.

The Ten Commandments: The Significance of
God's Laws in Everyday Life

DAN SCHMIDT

People of faith—followers of Jesus—have the Bible, that book packed full as a closet. Some parts of this Bible are well known, accessible, and often perused: history, gospel, epistle. Other bits are less so, like those pesky genealogical tables. Or the Minor Prophets . . . those books wedged between the "Major" Prophets (such as Isaiah and Jeremiah) and Matthew. What if you step in and peel back the cover from them—what treasure might emerge? There are mysteries here for sure, along with rich delights. These prophets demand, and they intrigue.

Unexpected Wisdom

CHARLES M. SCHULZ

I have underlined words and sentences in one of the Bibles that has always been my study Bible, but when I look at those words and sentences now, I can't remember why they were underlined . . . My Revised Standard Version of the Bible is filled with markings, for I have gone through it word for word with study groups at least four times and, of course, I have used it on various occasions to begin speeches. I know that the underlined passages served some purpose, but here and there are verses that have no special meaning to me. It is almost as if a friend had secretly opened the book and made some markings just to tease me. What was the Spirit trying to say to me then that I no longer need to hear?   *You Don't* Look 35, *Charlie Brown*

BRIAN SCHWERTLEY

Every human relationship needs a source of authority outside itself that is transcendent, infallible, and authoritative. That is exactly what Christians have in the Bible.

SIR WALTER SCOTT

Within this ample volume lies
The mystery of mysteries.
Happiest they of human race
To whom their God has given grace,
To read, to fear, to hope, to pray,
To lift the latch, to force the way;
But better had they ne'er been born,
Who read to doubt or read to scorn.
                    The Monastery

WILLIAM SEWARD

The whole hope of human progress is suspended on the ever-growing influence of the Bible.

ANDREE SEU

Go to the Bible to meet Christ . . . He is its author, its subject matter, the doorway to its treasures, the full-throated symphony of which Adam and the prophets heard just the faintest tune.

WILLIAM SHAKESPEARE

The devil can cite Scripture for his purpose.
                    The Merchant of Venice (Act 1, Scene 3)

SAMUEL M. SHOEMAKER

Study the Bible. Here is the double record of God's search for man and man's search for God. It is a plain-spoken old Book, with unvarnished sinners and backsliding saints in it from cover to cover. Its peaks of spiritual insight and experience have never been surpassed, but it makes no excuse for human weakness nor attempt to hide it. We keep reading it because in it we keep seeing ourselves. The times, the clothes, the customs change; the people, the situations, human nature—not much!

The Bible opened up as a living record of those who tried to live in obedience to God's will. I shall never forget how it helped me to read every reference I could find to Simon Peter. He had so many weaknesses, yet God greatly used him.   *Faith at Work*

ROBERT L. SHORT

Both the parables of Jesus and the parables of *Peanuts,* to use Bonhoeffer's famous phrase, "speak in a 'secular' way about God." For one thing, they bring the explanations for the Christian faith out of the metaphysical clouds and on down to earth. In this regard, all parabolic expressions of faith are strictly in keeping with the spirit of the Bible . . Anyone who does his reading with the Bible in one hand and the daily newspaper in the other cannot be far from the Kingdom of God. And especially if he is a fan of *Peanuts* is he on the right track, as *Peanuts* is such a happy combination of these two elements: the proclamation of God's love for the world, and the world as it really is.

The Parables of Peanuts

RONALD J. SIDER

The Spirit never contradicts God's revealed word. Jesus promised that "the Counselor, the Holy Spirit, whom the Father will send in my name, will teach you all things and will remind you of everything I have said to you." The Spirit illuminates our minds so that we can more accurately grasp what Jesus said and the Scriptures teach.

CHUCK SMITH, JR.

Those who argue that the Bible must be studied strictly as literature, and not as God's revelation to us, usually have a formalist approach in mind . . . But if we disconnect the Bible from God's authorship, it is nothing more than a human creation. And if we disregard the intended effect on the reader, to open his or her eyes to God's truth, then we rob God's Word of its meaning. We can never separate the text from the God who inspired it and the readers who study it.

Epiphany: Discover the Delights of God's Word

COLIN S. SMITH

Churches are filled with many people who know stories from the Bible but do not know the story of the Bible . . . The Bible is one story. Thus it begins with two people in a beautiful garden and ends with a vast crowd in a magnificent city. All the way through it points us to Jesus Christ. He is the focal point of the whole story.   *Unlocking the Bible Story*

JOSEPH FIELDING SMITH

The theories of men changed from day to day. Much is taught new that will tomorrow be in the discard, but the word of the Lord will endure forever.

RODNEY "GIPSY" SMITH

What makes the difference is not how many times you have been through the Bible, but how many times and how thoroughly the Bible has been through you.

JOHN SMOLTZ

People say mankind is good. The Bible and life both teach us that's not so. The worst thing is to say I'm a good guy, you're a good guy. Society is my worst friend. It often keeps us from Christ . . . Baseball was God to me. It's God to most of the people here . . . (but) there's one way to God, not many highways, and I know that my hope is in Him, not in Cy Young awards.

World magazine, 8/3/2002

J. RICHARD SNEED

If a person will read three chapters every day and five chapters each Sunday, he can finish reading the entire Bible in just one year. Or, if a person desires to read the New Testament alone, and reads two chapters a day, he can finish it in less than twenty weeks. If he reads only on Sunday, completing five New Testament chapters each Sunday, he will finish it on the fifty-second Sunday. In one afternoon a person can begin with Luke's Gospel and at one sitting read the remainder of the New Testament to be thrilled forever with its moving story of power.

Your Bible Waits

JOHN SHELBY SPONG

The call of the Gospels is a call to enter the Christ experience. That is the call we need to hear if the Word of God is to speak to this generation.

R. C. SPROUL

People accept without hesitation the charge that the Bible is full of contradictions. Yet the charge is completely inaccurate and misleading. Why, then, if the charge is so inaccurate, do we hear it so often repeated? Apart from the problem of prejudice, there are other reasons why this misconception is propagated. There is a problem not only of ignorance of what the Bible says, but perhaps even more so, a problem of ignorance of the laws of logic. The word "contradiction" is used all too loosely with respect to biblical content. That there are divergencies of biblical accounts, that biblical writers describe the same things from different perspectives, is not in dispute. Whether those varied accounts are, in fact, contradictory is in dispute.

Reason to Believe

Why should we study the Bible? . . . To be sure, knowledge of God's Word does not guarantee that we will do what it says, but at least we will know what we are supposed to be doing in our quest for human fulfillment. The issue of faith is not so much whether we believe in God, but whether we believe the God we believe in.

When people say the Bible is dull, it makes me wonder why. Biblical characters are full of life. There is a unique quality of passion about them. Their lives reveal drama, pathos, lust, crime, devotion and every conceivable aspect of human existence . . . Though their life settings are different from ours, their struggles and concerns are very much like ours.   *Knowing Scripture*

If we can read the newspaper, we can read the Bible. In fact, I would venture to guess that more difficult words and concepts are expressed on the front page of a newspaper than on most pages of the Bible.

What kind of a God would reveal his love and redemption in terms so technical that only an elite corps of professional scholars could understand them? God does speak in primitive terms because he is addressing himself to primitives. At the same time, there is enough profundity contained in Scripture to keep the most astute and erudite scholars busily engaged in their theological inquiries for a lifetime.   *Knowing Scripture*

CHARLES HADDON SPURGEON

Read the Holy Scriptures every day. We quickly lose the nourishment and strength of yesterday's bread. We must feed our souls daily upon the manna God has given us . . . Read the Bible with Christ constantly in view. The whole Book is about Him. Look for Him on every page. He is there. If you fail to see Him there, you need to read that page again.

He who is but a casual reader of the Bible does not know the height, the depth, the length and breadth of the mighty meanings contained in its pages. There are certain times when I discover a new vein of thought, and I put my hand to my head and say with astonishment, "Oh, it is wonderful—I never saw this before in the Scriptures." You will find the Scriptures enlarge as you enter them. The more you study them, the less you will appear to know of them, for they widen out as we approach them.

Nobody ever outgrows the Scriptures. The Book widens and deepens with our years.

Defend the Bible? I would as soon defend a lion! Unchain it and it will defend itself.

Since God wrote it, mark its truthfulness. If I had written it, there would be worms of critics who would at once swarm on it, and would cover it with their evil spawn. Had I written it, there would be men who would pull it to pieces at once, and perhaps quite right, too. But this is the Word of God. Come, search, ye critics, and find a flaw; examine it from its Genesis to its Revelation and find an error. This is a vein of pure gold, unalloyed by quartz or any earthly substance. This is a star without a speck, a sun without a blot, a light without darkness . . . Blessed Bible, thou art all truth.   (1855 sermon)

CHARLES STANLEY

After the invention of the printing press, thousands of copies could be produced swiftly and distributed widely. The price was much lower so that more people could have a copy of the Bible. The printing press produced a "spiritual earthquake." People were hungry for the Word of God, and it became accessible to them.

I love this Book above all my earthly possessions. I have given my life so that others may love it, too. I do not take this subject lightly. I literally base everything I am now and all my future on this Book.   *The Glorious Journey*

Living by faith requires that we become familiar with God's promises to us. The Bible is filled with promises to believers. Nothing is more encouraging or nurturing to our faith than reviewing God's promises. Every morning when I awake I review a list of promises that I have assembled. I rehearse in my mind His promises regarding my foregiveness, my protection, my relationship with Him, and the future inheritance He is preparing for all His children. I have also made it a habit to claim certain promises for my children.   *The Glorious Journey*

HENRY STANLEY

During my attack of African fever, I took up the Bible to while away tedious hours. I read Job, and then Psalms. The Bible, with its noble and simple language, I continued to read with a higher and truer understanding than I had ever before conceived. Its powerful verses had a different meaning, a more penetrating influence, in the silence of the wilds. I came to feel a strange glow while absorbed in its pages, and a charm particularly appropriate to the deep melancholy of African scenery. When I laid down the book, the mind commenced to feed upon what memory suggested . . . Alone in my tent, I flung myself on my knees, and

poured out my soul utterly in secret prayer to Him from whom I
had been so long estranged; to Him who had led me mysteriously
into Africa, there to reveal Himself, and His will.

In Darkest Africa

DOUGLAS V. STEERE

How many times one has laid the Bible aside in favor of what
seemed more real and compelling . . . only to be driven back to it
again by the great hunger to let the measured dignity and beauty
of its language stir in him an emotion like that which comes in
listening to classical music or in seeing a finely proportioned
building.   *Prayer and Worship*

JEANNE STEIG

Our forebears (thanks to good King James)
Talked funny. They had oddish names.
They fell in love, succumbed to lust,
And trampled strangers in the dust.
They suffered flood and fire and drought.
A few of them remained devout.
Their lives were jolly, vapid, grim,
According to Jehovah's whim.
How little things have changed since then!
Whose fault that is, God knows. Amen.
The Old Testament Made Easy

A. M. STIBBS

If the Bible is "the most valuable thing which this world
affords," it is surely wrong to use it carelessly and casually, to
presume to know what it teaches without first taking great pains
to discover exactly what it does teach.

Understanding God's Word

JOHN STOTT

We must allow the Word of God to confront us, to disturb our
security, to undermine our complacency, and to overthrow our
patterns of thought and behavior.

The chief reason why the Christian believes in the divine
origin of the Bible is that Jesus Christ himself taught it.

The dual authorship of Scripture is an important truth to be carefully guarded. On the one hand, God spoke, revealing the truth and preserving the human authors from error, yet without violating their personality. On the other hand, men spoke, using their own faculties freely, yet without distorting the divine message. Their words were truly their own words. But they were (and still are) also God's words, so that what Scripture says, God says.

The particularity of each New Testament author was in no way smothered by the unique process of inspiration. On the contrary, the Holy Spirit first prepared and then used their individuality of upbringing, experience, temperament and personality in order to convey through each some distinctive and appropriate truth.

It was Jesus Christ himself in the Sermon on the Mount who told us to be bird-watchers. "Behold the fowls of the air" is how the King James' Version renders his command . . . The Bible tells us that birds have lessons to teach us as well. As a matter of fact, Scripture bids us go beyond birds and include in our interest everything God has made. "Great are the works of the Lord, studied by all who delight in them." Since the works of the Lord refer to his works of both creation and redemption, it seems to me that nature study and Bible study go together. Many Christians have a good doctrine of redemption, but need a better doctrine of creation. We ought to pursue at least one aspect of natural history.

The Birds, Our Teachers: Essays in Orni-Theology

LEE STROBEL

God's astounding claims about you and me are sprinkled throughout the pages of Scripture. There are assertions about how we can grow in virtue, relate to others with authenticity, earn a living with integrity, and make a difference even in the midst of a culture that's unraveling at the seams. When I come across one of these nuggets, I can't help but shake my head in wonder . . . If we take them seriously and open ourselves to God's activity, we can discover new insights into who we are and new principles as to how we can live with courage and conviction. In fact, it's no exaggeration to say that God's claims can change the entire trajectory of your life. At least, that's what happened to me.

God's Outrageous Claims

DAVID SUCHET

From somewhere I got this desire to read the Bible again.
That's the most important part of my conversion. I started with
the Acts of the Apostles and then moved to Paul, letters—
Romans and Corinthians. And it was only after that that I came to
the Gospels. In the New Testament I suddenly discovered the
way that life should be followed.

These wonderful stories that are found in the Old Testament
and the New, they're glorious. I don't find them dusty, I find
them full of humanity, full of reality, full of drama.

EMMANUEL SUHARD

We advise all who feel hemmed in by a closed and stifling
world to open the Old and New Testaments. They will there find
vistas which will liberate them, and the excellent food of the only
true God.   *The Church Today*

J. CARTER SWAIM

The real influence of the Bible cannot be measured; it is
reckoned only in terms of hearts that have been lifted up,
decisions that have been changed, the men and women who, in
response to its impervious demands, have done justice and loved
kindness and walked humbly with God.   *The Book God Made*

LEONARD SWEET

Every time I open my *New English Bible,* I invoke two prayers.
First, a prayer of thanks to William Tyndale, the biblical scholar,
who gave his life that you and I can do something we take for
granted: read the Scriptures in our own language. Second, a
prayer offering my life as a Third Testament to be deployed and
distributed in any way God sees fit.   *Soul Salsa*

I take my study Bible everywhere. I write in it, mark it up,
underline passages, and generally make it beautiful with rain, tear,
and coffee stains and dog-eared pages. It's been rebound in
leather twice, and the gold lettering on the brown binding is
almost invisible. It's almost ready for me to turn over to my son
Thane. On the day Thane was born, I dedicated this Bible to him.
For the past nine years, I've been underlining passages for him,

writing notes to him in the margins, and inserting prayers for him in various places throughout the text. I will give this Bible to him after I have read him the chapter you are now reading. He won't fully understand its significance, or what I've inscribed to him, until he's much older. But it's perhaps the best gift I'll ever give him . . . It's one of the favorite things I do in life: make my kids a part of my devotional life.   *Soul Salsa*

CHARLES W. SWINDOLL
His Book has the answers. Scripture never leaves us with a bewildered look on our faces, wondering about the issues of life. It says, "This is the way it is. That is the way it is not to be. This is the way to walk; do not walk there." It tells us straight. It provides the kind of solid foundation you and I need.
Growing Deep in the Christian Life

It is my privilege to introduce you to a man of enormous integrity who modeled continual forgiveness. His name is Joseph. Unless I miss my guess, you will never forget this man. But why should we be surprised? His biography is found in the single most astounding book ever written—the Bible. No life recorded there is either unimportant or forgettable.
Joseph: A Man of Integrity and Forgiveness

Reading sweeps the cobwebs away; it increases our power of concentration; it makes us more interesting to be around, and it strengthens our ability to glean truth from God's Word.

In order for old defeating thoughts to be invaded, conquered, and replaced by new, vigorous ones, a process of reconstruction must transpire. The best place I know to begin the process of mental cleansing is with the all-important discipline of memorizing Scripture. I realize it doesn't sound very sophisticated or intellectual, but God's Book is full of powerful ammunition.   *Living Above the Level of Mediocrity*

ISAAC TAYLOR
The deathless book has survived three great dangers: the negligence of its friends; the false systems built upon it; the warfare of those who have hated it.

KENNETH N. TAYLOR

Who but God could make an unending universe, sized by billions of light years? And who could dream of knowing such a God personally? I am one who believes this, and have based my life on the Bible as God's message to mankind. But how to manage Bible-reading when it is in such an ancient language? How to crack the shell of the coconut and find the milk and meat? That is why I spent 16 years translating the Bible into living English.

WILLIAM MACKERGO TAYLOR

The man of one book is always formidable, but when that book is the Bible he is irresistible.

SIR JOHN M. TEMPLETON

The Bible speaks often about the meaning of love. In the Sermon on the Mount, we are told to love our enemies. We are told to love those who hate us. We are told to turn the other cheek. Some people scoff at this advice and call it impractical. But, in fact, it's extremely practical. There is really no other way to lead a truly successful life.

When I was a small boy growing up in Winchester, Tennessee, Sunday school was an important part of my life. It was there that I began to see the magical power of spiritual conversation. I learned that when God talks to us, His means of communication is the Bible. The great lessons of Jesus are narrated for our edification and from Genesis to Revelation, light is shed on the mysteries of spiritual existence.

Riches for the Mind and Spirit

CORRIE TEN BOOM

If you try to analyze the Bible as a book of science or even as a book of theology, you cannot be nourished by it. Like chocolate, it is to be eaten and enjoyed, not picked apart bit by bit.

Tramp for the Lord

MERRILL C. TENNEY

The Bible is a book of personal interest and relevance. Almost every page has some precept, word of comfort or counsel, or example of spiritual aspiration and conduct that is applicable to contemporary life. Even a casual perusal of its pages will yield truth that is understandable and immediately helpful in personal needs.   *The Bible Almanac*

GARY THOMAS

There can be great benefit in reading the same passages of Scripture over and over until you know them by heart. Imagine the power of reading a psalm at age eighty that you read daily in your thirties. Rituals can tie our years together with the common thread of faith . . . In my early teens I started the practice of reading a chapter of the Bible first thing in the morning and last thing in the evening—my first and last conscious activity would be God's Word. I've heard of another Christian who places his Bible on his shoes at night. Before he can get dressed the next morning, he'll need to read the Scriptures.   *Sacred Pathways*

The Bible is replete with verses calling us to reach out to the disenfranchised of our society. Deuteronomy tells us that God defends the cause of the orphan, widow, and alien. A portion of the Israelites' tithes was to be set aside for these three groups. We are told to take an active role in defending the cause of the poor. This means our spiritual obligation isn't fulfilled simply by *not doing harm,* but only by *actively getting involved* to confront and challenge injustice . . . The book of Proverbs suggests that God's willingness to hear our prayers is contingent upon our willingness to hear the cry of the poor. If we stop up our ears to the cry of the poor, God stops up his ears to our own prayers of petition.
                                                             Authentic Faith

JOHN W. THOMASON, JR.

The thing is, that the Bible, whether you consider it as a collection of fables, transmitted through the golden mists of an elder time, or as a system of ethics, or as a profession of faith, is the most convincing and comprehensive record of human experience and aspiration that exists in our world.
                                                           American Mercury

JAMES THORPE

Rarely has fame ever been so well placed as that which surrounds the Gutenberg Bible. This noble book, which appeared about 1455, has long been taken to represent the invention of printing in the western world. In that role, it symbolizes one of the small handful of the greatest human accomplishments of all time. It can be considered along with such great ancient achievements as writing and numeration, along with such modern achievements as the steam engine and the use of electricity.

The Gutenberg Bible: Landmark of Learning

W. J. TOMS

Be careful how you live. You may be the only Bible some person ever reads.   *Detroit News*

SERGIO TORRES

In Latin America, a liberative reading of the Bible has its roots in the practice of the poor working in the organization of basic ecclesial communities. It is not just reading passages that speak about oppression or liberation. The whole Bible is seen as a project with a liberation message.

R. A. TORREY

Every type of destruction that human philosophy, human science, human reason, human art, human cunning, human force, and human brutality could bring to bear against a book has been brought to bear against this book, and yet the Bible stands absolutely unshaken today. At times, almost all the wise and great of the earth have been pitted against the Bible, and only an obscure few for it. Yet it has stood.

When you read a verse in the Bible, ask yourself: What does this verse mean? Then ask: What does it mean for me? When that is answered, ask yourself again: Is that all it means? And do not leave it until you are quite sure that is all it means for the present.

God's Word is pure and sure, in spite of the devil, in spite of your fear, in spite of everything.

A verse must be read often, and re-read and read again before the wondrous message of love and power that God has put into it begins to appear. Words must be turned over and over in the mind before their full force and beauty takes possession of us. One must look a long time at the great masterpieces of art to appreciate their beauty and understand their meaning, and so one must look a long time at the great verses of the Bible to appreciate their beauty and understand their meaning.

PAUL TOURNIER

Can we count on direct inspiration from God? Yes, I believe so. I am always at a loss to understand those Christians who deny this. The Bible is full of examples, from Abraham's call to leave his homeland, Moses' call before the burning bush, the signs in the Heaven and the law's reception on Sinai, the calls to all the prophets wherein God told them what they were to do and say, all the way to the Gospel and the apostolic writings. There we see the calm certainty of Jesus who is led by his Father; Joseph and Paul who are warned by God through dreams. There is, finally, the experience of believers all through the ages including our own days.   *To Resist or to Surrender?*

There are plenty of gloomy Christians, who delight in the contemplation of the Passion, for whom Christianity means essentially sacrifice, renunciation, and pain. They do not find themselves altogether at ease in the triumphant joy of Easter because they feel that the Cross is no longer being taken seriously if it is looked upon only as a stage in the road to the Resurrection. Other preachers, I am glad to say, stress the incomparable power of the Gospel as a source of life, of victories, and of fulfillment . . . There is something to restore the courage of those neurotics who always insist on turning to the severe and pessimistic parts of the Bible.   *A Place for You*

BRITT TOWERY

Whatever it takes in time and energy, find time to relax and give daily Bible-reading a chance. Read with an eager mind and an open heart. The Bible can make bad days good and good days better.   *Brownwood* (Texas) *Bulletin*

A. W. TOZER

I believe that much of our religious unbelief is due to a wrong conception of God and a wrong feeling for the Scriptures of Truth. A silent God began suddenly to speak in a book and when the book was finished lapsed into silence again . . . The facts are that God is not silent, has never been silent. It is the nature of God to speak

MARY M. TRAMMELL and WILLIAM DAWLEY

For Wycliffe (in the 14th century), the Bible was the only legitimate power governing humanity. "Holy Scripture is the preeminent authority for every Christian," he wrote, "and the rule of faith and of all human perfection." *Any* sincere Christian, he argued—not just priests—can preach the gospel. *Any* Christian can understand the Bible, or God's law . . . With an understanding of God's Word, the humblest Christian could be as fully empowered as the most exalted church official, Wycliffe felt.

The Reforming Power of the Scriptures

PHYLLIS TRIBLE

The Bible is not a sanitized book. It does not have a single point of view. It comes to us full of conflicts and contradictions and problems . . . We see behind it and in front of it all these conflicted ways of looking at human life. And biblical people don't agree with one another. To me, this is one of the great blessings of the Bible. It is an authentic document precisely because of that, among other reasons. It can speak authentically to human existence out of its conflicted nature.

Genesis: A Living Conversation

BARBARA TUCHMAN

The work that reached fruition in the (King James Version) Bible of 1611 really began with Tyndale in 1525, but his was by no means the first translation into the English vernacular. All the earlier ones, however, had predated the invention of printing and were self-limited by the difficulty of producing copies in longhand. Once printing was available, the floodwaters were loosed, and the vernacular Bible could no longer be kept from the

people, for as fast as the church authorities could buy them up or
burn them, more copies could be printed.

Bible and Sword: England and Palestine
From the Bronze Age to Balfour

TAD TULEJA

In the Bible, what is the root of all evil? Not money, as is often
supposed, but the *love* of money. Paul made the famous but
generally misquoted observation in his first epistle to Timothy:
"For the love of money is the root of all evil: which while some
coveted after, they have erred from the faith and pierced
themselves through with many sorrows." . . . Paul's teachers in
Tarsus were the most rigorous of all world despisers, those
curmudgeonly iconoclasts the Cynics. The grand old man of their
tradition, Diogenes, said, "The love of money is the marketplace
of every evil," three centuries before Paul was born.

A. DOUGLAS TUSHINGHAM

The Dead Sea Scrolls cast a new light on the elements of
Judaism that influenced Christian development. They also reveal
the hitherto mysterious Essenes, whose spiritual struggle swells
out of the past like a mighty hymn. Khirbat Qumran, high on its
blighted terrace, is now a dead ruin in a dead world; nothing
grows in the bitter marl; nothing stirs among the ancient stones . . .
But here, a long time ago, men strove to find God. And the
record they left of their endeavors gives us a better understanding
of the religious climate into which Jesus was born.

Everyday Life in Bible Times

MARK TWAIN

If I were going to construct a God I would furnish Him with
some ways and qualities and characteristics which (the Bible)
lacks. He would spend some of His eternities in trying to forgive
Himself for making man unhappy when He could have made him
happy with the same effort, and He would spend the rest of His
eternities studying astronomy.

Mark Twain's Notebook

Most people are bothered by those passages in Scripture which they cannot understand; but as for me, I always noticed that the passages in Scripture which trouble me most are those which I do understand.

WILLIAM TYNDALE

(Deuteronomy) is a book worthy to be read in day and night and never to be out of hands. For it is the most excellent of all the books of Moses. It is easy also and light and a very pure gospel, a preaching of faith and love: deducing the love to God out of faith, and the love of a man's neighbour out of the love of God.

Let it not make thee despair, neither let it discourage thee, O reader, that it is forbidden thee in pain of life and goods, or that it is made breaking of the king's peace, or treason unto his highness, to read the Word of this soul's health—for if God be on our side, what matter maketh it who be against us, be they bishops, cardinals, popes.

A passage from one of Tyndale's tracts (1536)

M. F. UNGER

Authority resides in God's inspired Word (the Bible) interpreted by God's Spirit operating through Spirit-taught human agents.

What a tremendous treasure the Word of God is and what an indescribable blessing to all who study and receive its great soul-transforming truth and heart and life. *Unger's Bible Handbook*

JAMES J. VANCE

The Bible breaks at dawn with God's voice saying: "Let there be light." It sets at dusk with God's truth proclaiming: "Let there be life." Between the two speak all voices that can breathe a prayer, plead a need, confess a sin, utter a warning, sob a sorrow, or sigh a penitent's tear . . . Between the two are the stories of nations, the acclaim of heroes, the fall of empires, the rise of kingdoms, the decline of dynasties, the tramp of armies, the crack and clash of civilizations, and the coming of him who is "the bright and morning star."   *Bible Vistas*

DICK VAN DYKE

Quite logically, children relate Bible allusions to the world they live in. If they don't have an answer, one soon comes bubbling up from their imagination. One boy, when asked why there are no longer burnt offerings to God, suggested, "Air pollution." Another, answering a question, described the "multitude that loafs and fishes."

HENRY VAN DYKE

Born in the East and clothed in Oriental form and imagery, the Bible walks the ways of all the world with familiar feet and enters land after land to find its own everywhere. It has learned to speak in hundreds of languages to the heart of man. Children listen to its stories with wonder and delight, and wise men ponder them as parables of life. The wicked and the proud tremble at its warnings, but to the wounded and penitent it has a mother's voice. It has woven itself into our dearest dreams, so that Love, Friendship, Sympathy, Devotion, Memory, Hope, put on the beautiful garments of its treasured speech. No man is poor or desolate who has this treasure for his own.
Companionable Books

The Bible does not profess to make men omniscient, but simply to tell them enough to make them happy and good, if they will believe it and live up to it.

HENDRIK WILLEM VAN LOON

This book has been a most faithful companion of man for several generations. You can never be thoroughly educated without knowing these stories. Besides, at one time or another in your lives, you may badly need the wisdom that lies hidden within these ancient chronicles.

GENE EDWARD VEITH, JR.

The Word of God itself sets forth a worldview. The Bible speaks not just of ethereal "spiritual" truths. Rather, it reveals truths about the nature of existence that speak to every dimension of life.

BURTON VISOTZKY

The Bible has too often been used as a wedge to drive people apart . . . (But) the communal study of the Bible can continue to provide us with a means of clarifying our ideas about the world around us and for linking them historically to a long-standing tradition. In a community of readers a conversation takes place. The give-and-take of interpretation creates an extra voice in the room, the sound of Reading the Book . . . Every group, every person has something unique to offer in the interpretation of the Bible—all we need to do is learn how to listen.

Genesis: A Living Conversation

VOLTAIRE

If God did not exist, it would be necessary to invent him . . . If we would destroy the Christian religion, we must first of all destroy man's belief in the Bible.

WALL STREET JOURNAL

From the early pilgrims to the civil-rights movement, American leaders interpreted their actions through the religious understandings and imagery of the Bible. Start with John Winthrop's vision of "a city upon a hill," one of Ronald Reagan's favorite metaphors. Or Abraham Lincoln's allusion to the "house divided," which he found in the Gospel of Mark. Not to mention Martin Luther King, who in his last speech spoke of "going up to the mountaintop." In that same speech, Dr. King went on to say that he might not make it into the Promised Land with his people, a remark drained of all its power absent a familiarity with the story of Exodus.

"Gospel Truth" (editorial), 11/12/99

LAURA WALTON

I do believe the Bible is the word of God. Everything in there that God said he would do, he is going to do . . . But, I think it speaks to special situations. If we are going for healing, you are going for one thing, and I another. I'm not sure if he intended for all of us to get the same measure. Two people could have two different interpretations, and God could be speaking through both. The Bible is an enigma. It takes a lot of depth and understanding.

Quoted by Ann Monroe in *The Word*

JOHN WANAMAKER

I have of course made large purchases of property in my time, involving millions of dollars. But it was as a boy in the country, at the age of 11 years, that I made my greatest purchase in the little mission Sunday School. I bought a small red-leather Bible for $2.75, which I paid for in small installments. Looking back over my life, I see that little red book was the foundation on which my life has been built and has made possible all that has counted in my life. I know now that it was the greatest investment and the most important and far-reaching purchase I ever made.

BENJAMIN B. WARFIELD

The verities of our faith remain historically proven true to us— so bountiful has God been in his fostering care—even had we no Bible; and through those verities, salvation. But to what uncertainties and doubts would we be the prey!—and to what errors, constantly begetting worse errors exposed!—to what refuges, all of them refuges of lies, driven! . . . Let us bless God, then, for His inspired word! And may he grant that we may always cherish, love, and venerate it, and conform all our life and thinking to it! So we may find safety for our feet, and peaceful security for our souls.

The Inspiration and Authority of the Bible

ANNA B. WARNER

Jesus loves me! This I know,
    For the Bible tells me so.
Little ones to him belong;
    They are weak but He is strong

Yes, Jesus loves me!
The Bible tells me so.

Jesus loves me! He who died
    Heaven's gate to open wide;
He will wash away my sin,
    Let His little child come in.

"Jesus Loves Me"

RICK WARREN

God has not left us in the dark to wonder and guess. He has clearly revealed his purposes for our lives through the Bible. It is our Owner's Manual, explaining why we are alive, how life works, what to avoid, and what to expect in the future. It explains what no self-help or philosophy book could know.

The Purpose-Driven Life

I am amazed at how some Bible teachers are able to take the most exciting book in the world and bore people to tears with it. I believe it is a *sin* to bore people with the Bible. When God's Word is taught in an uninteresting way, people don't just think the pastor is boring, they think *God* is boring! We slander God's character if we preach in an uninspiring style or tone. The message is too important to share it with a "take-it-or-leave-it" attitude.

The Purpose-Driven Church

A way to establish a friendship with God is by thinking about his Word during your day. This is called meditation, and the Bible repeatedly urges us to meditate on who God is, what he has done, and what he has said. It is impossible to be God's friend apart from knowing what he says. You can't love God unless you know him, and you can't know him without knowing his Word. The Bible says God "revealed himself to Samuel through his word." God still uses the same method today.

The Purpose-Driven Life

BOOKER T. WASHINGTON

Perhaps the most valuable thing I got out of my second year (at Hampton University) was an understanding of the use and value of the Bible . . . Before this I never cared a great deal about it, but now I learned to love to read the Bible, not only for the spiritual help it gives, but on account of it as literature.

Up from Slavery

GEORGE WASHINGTON

It is impossible to rightly govern the world without God and the Bible.

DAVID WATSON

As I spent time chewing over the endless assurances and promises to be found in the Bible, so my faith in the living God grew stronger and held me safe in his hands. God's word to us, especially his word spoken by his Spirit through the Bible, is the very ingredient that feeds our faith. If we feed our souls regularly on God's word, several times each day, we should become robust spiritually just as we feed on ordinary food several times each day, and become robust physically. Nothing is more important than hearing and obeying the word of God.   *Fear No Evil*

ISAAC WATTS

Dear Lord, this Book of thine
Informs me where to go
For grace to pardon all my sin,
And makes me holy, too.
                    "Praise to God for Learning to Read"

How glad the heathens would have been
That worship idols, wood, and stone
If they the book of God had seen,
Of Jesus and his gospel known.
                            "Praise for the Gospel"

The stars that in their courses roll
Have much instruction given,
But thy good Word informs my soul
How I may climb to Heaven.
                        "The Excellency of the Bible"

Thy Word is everlasting truth;
How pure is every page!
That holy book shall guide our youth
And well support our age.
            "How Shall the Young Secure Their Hearts?"

LESLIE D. WEATHERHEAD

We judge the Bible by Jesus, not Jesus by the Bible, yet it is from the Bible we get what we believe to be a true picture of him

. . . We have a certain picture of Jesus made up from the four Gospels and from other evidence we can collect from the authentic experiences of men. If there is something that does not harmonize with that picture, we put it to one side and say, "It cannot be true, or else there must be light upon it that explains it in some other way." I think that is a sound rule to adopt.

When the Lamp Flickers

It is one thing to be told that the Bible has authority because it is divinely inspired, and another thing to feel one's heart leap out and grasp its truth.

DANIEL WEBSTER

I believe that the Bible is to be understood and received in the plain and obvious meaning of its passages, since I cannot persuade myself that a book intended for the instruction and conversion of the whole world should cover its true meaning in such mystery and doubt that none but critics and philosophers can discover it.

The Bible is a book of faith, and a book of doctrine, and a book of morals, and a book of religion, of special revelation from God. But it is also a book which teaches man his own individual responsibility, his own dignity, and his equity with his fellow-man.

I have read through the entire Bible many times. I now make it my practice to go through it once a year. It is the book of all others for lawyers as well as ministers. I pity the person that cannot find in it a rich supply of thought and of rules for his or her conduct. It fits a person for life. It prepares them for death.

MICHAEL and LIBBY WEED

It is too bad that well-meaning people have tried to make the Bible look solemn (solid black covers) or even dainty (white covers), so that it never looks interesting or alive. The truth is that the Bible is as alive as the people you see every day. The Bible pulls no punches when it describes human activities. It doesn't try to make man appear better or worse than he really is.

Bible Handbook

RENITA J. WEEMS

When we read Scripture, we're also in conversation with those ancient people who experienced God and left us something so that we might also be in conversation with Him. We're in conversation with God. We're in conversation with our neighbors. And we're in conversation with this ancient community which has so lovingly bequeathed to us these stories.

Genesis: A Living Conversation

G. S. WEGENER

In the Bible the believing Christian finds the Word of God. But the doubter, too, even the unbeliever, must acknowledge that the Bible has left its mark on the history of mankind as no other book has done, and has exercised a decisive influence on the Western world. Its story is part of the fabric of our civilization. Its importance transcends the boundaries of sect and schism.

6000 Years of the Bible

H. G. WELLS

Throughout the first two centuries after Christ, the Christian religion spread throughout the Roman Empire, weaving together an ever-growing multitude of converts into a new community of ideas and will. The attitude of the emperors varied between hostility and toleration. There were attempts to suppress this new faith in both the second and third centuries, and finally in 303 and the following year a great persecution under the Emperor Diocletian. The considerable accumulations of church property were seized. All Bibles and religious writings were confiscated and destroyed. Christians were put out of the protection of the law and many executed. The destruction of the books is particularly notable. It shows how the power of the written word in holding together the new faith was understood by the authorities.

An Illustrated Short History of the World

JOHN WESLEY

I want to know one thing, the way to Heaven—how to land safe on that happy shore. God Himself has condescended to teach the way. For this very end he came from Heaven. He has written it down in a book. Give me that book! At any price, give me the book of God! I have it; here is knowledge enough for me. Let me be *homo unius libre*—"a man of one book."

Try all things by the written word, and let all bow down before it. You are in danger of fanaticism every hour, if you depart ever so little from Scripture; yea, or from the plain, literal meaning of a text, taken in connection with the context.

My ground is the Bible . . . I follow it in all things, both great and small.   *The Journal of John Wesley,* 6/5/1766

At some rare times, when I have been in great distress of soul or in utter uncertainty how to act in an important case which required a speedy determination, after using all other means that occurred, I have cast lots, or opened the Bible. And by this means I have been relieved from that distress, or directed in that uncertainty.   *Collected Works* (Volume 5)

BROOKE FOSS WESTCOTT

Blessed Lord, by whose providence all holy scriptures were written and preserved for our instruction, give us grace to study them this and every day with patience and love. Strengthen our souls with the fullness of their divine teaching. Keep us from all pride and irreverence. Guide us in the deep things of thy heavenly wisdom, and of thy great mercy lead us by thy Word unto everlasting life; through Jesus Christ our Lord and Saviour.
          The Complete Book of Christian Prayer

LAURIE WHALEY

If you look at the New Testament and the life of Christ, he was coming to people where they were. He wasn't high and mighty. Jesus himself was a part of culture, and he understood using culture to communicate his message.

MICHAEL WHELEN

The Bible is thoroughly immersed in time even as it is timeless. The faithful disciple who wants to read the Bible with an open mind and heart, intent on hearing the Word, must experience himself or herself as part of the drama that the Bible is. Abraham Heschel writes that "the Bible is not a book to be read but a drama in which we participate." The Bible will not be a source of life for me if it remains simply an object of academic or aesthetic interest, or a collection of rules and moral norms, or a factual record of what has happened and what will happen. I must experience what is written there as intimately expressive of my own life.

Living Strings: An Introduction to Biblical Spirituality

The Bible *exposes* rather than *imposes*. It is an unveiling, an uncovering, a bringing to light and setting free of what is already there, at least potentially. The Bible helps us see "what is," to distinguish reality from irreality. The Bible reveals God as God really is, people as people really are, events as events really are, things as things really are—if we have the ears and eyes with which to hear and see.

Living Strings: An Introduction to Biblical Spirituality

JAMES EMERY WHITE

The worldview of the Bible is profound. If we are made by a designer, then we are not here by chance. Life is not a series of random developments. We were created for a reason. There is intentionality about each and every one of us. We are not accidents. We were meant to be.   *A Purposeful Life*

REGGIE WHITE

The Bible is more than just a book to me. The Bible is my life. It is the basis for everything I do. I like the way Tunch Ilkin put it. Tunch was a Pro Bowl lineman for the Pittsburgh Steelers before finishing his career alongside me at the Packers. Tunch said, "The Steelers had a playbook with 150 plays. If we mastered them, we could win. God has a playbook, too. It's called the Bible. Everything we need to know is in God's playbook." The football analogy is a good one. The Bible is our playbook for life. Its game plan details how we can lead a rich, rewarding life. It offers answers to questions about family and faith and career fulfillment, in times of trouble or triumph. This playbook reshapes our lives, if we let it.   *God's Play Book: The Bible's Game Plan for Life*

WILLIAM P. WHITE

The Bible is a harp with a thousand strings. Play on one to the exclusion of its relationship to the others, and you will develop discord. Play on all of them, keeping them in their places in the divine scale, and you will hear heavenly music all the time.

GEORGE WHITEFIELD

I began to read the holy Scriptures upon my knees, laying aside all other books, and praying over, if possible, every line and word. This proved meat indeed and drink indeed to my soul. I daily received fresh life, light, and power from above.

WALT WHITMAN

How many ages and generations have brooded and wept and agonized over this book! What untellable joys and ecstacies, what support to martyrs at the stake, from it! To what myriads has it been the shore and rock of safety—the refuge from the driving tempest and wreck! Translated in all languages, how it has united this diverse world! Of its thousands there is not a verse, not a word, but is thick-studded with human emotion.

JOHN GREENLEAF WHITTIER

We search the world for truth; we cull
　　The good, the pure, the beautiful
From graven stone and written scroll
　　From all old flower beds of the soul,
And, weary seekers of the best,
　　We come back laden from our quest,
To find that all the sages said
　　Is in the book our mothers read.

"Miriam"

ROBERT S. WICKS

One of our ablest New Testament scholars points out that where Paul used these words, "the wrath of God," he never says that God is angry. He speaks of "the wrath" as though it were some kind of impersonal process, like the regular working out of consequences which men bring on themselves. Augustine said that it was never necessary for God to break in on this system of consequences and do something extra and arbitrary in the way of correction.   *The Edge of Wisdom*

KATHY WIDENHOUSE

If we truly believe that the Bible is divinely inspired and that it instructs us in righteous living and equips us for every good work, then we should be eager to delve deep into its pages.

As we read the Bible we may find we have to face some hard truths about ourselves and our inner motives. Is that worthwhile? Said the ancient Greek philosopher Plato, "The life which is unexamined is not worth living." . . . There is a priceless treasure within your reach right now. Get it off the shelf and read it today.
Signs of the Times

WILLIAM WILBERFORCE

We can scarcely indeed look into any part of the sacred volume without meeting abundant proofs that it is the religion of the Affections which God particularly requires . . . Joy . . . is enjoined on us as our bounden duty and commended to us as our acceptable worship . . . A cold, unfeeling heart is represented as highly criminal.

OSCAR WILDE

Endless repetition, in and out of season, has spoiled for us the freshness, the naivete, the simple romantic charm of the Gospels. We hear them read far too often and far too badly, and all repetition is anti-spiritual. When one returns to the Greek, it is like going into a garden of lilies out of some narrow and dark house.   *De Profundis*

H. ORTON WILEY

Spiritual men and women—those filled with the Holy Spirit— are not unduly concerned with either higher or lower criticism. They have a broader and more substantial basis for their faith. It rests with their risen Lord, the glorified Christ. They know the Bible is true . . . because they are acquainted with its Author. The Spirit which inspired the Word dwells within them and witnesses to its truth.   *Christian Theology*

JIM WILHOIT and LELAND RYKEN

It is our use of Bible knowledge, not the mere possession of Bible facts, that produces growth toward godliness. To know who composed the Book of Ruth or where Moab is or what a kinsman-redeemer was will not by itself direct our lives. Knowing God's providence is at work in the daily routine will. Of course, such knowledge emerges from specific details, but an effective teacher weaves them into life-changing concepts.

Effective Bible Teaching

DALLAS WILLARD

The Bible is, after all, God's gift to the world through his Church, not to the scholars. It comes through the life of his people and nourishes that life. Its purpose is practical, not academic. An intelligent, careful, intensive but straightforward reading—that is, one not governed by obscure and faddish theories or by a mindless orthodoxy—is what it requires to direct us into life in God's kingdom. Any other approach to the Bible, I believe, conflicts with the picture of the God that, all agree, emerges from Jesus and his tradition.

The Divine Conspiracy

As a pastor, teacher, and counselor I have repeatedly seen the transformation of inner and outer life that comes simply from memorization and meditation upon Scripture. Personally, I would never undertake to pastor a church or guide a program of Christian education that did not involve a continuous program of memorization of the choicest passages of Scripture for people of all ages.   *The Spirit of the Disciplines*

Still today the Old Testament book of Psalms gives great power for faith and life. This is simply because it preserves a conceptually rich language about God and our relationships to him. If you bury yourself in Psalms, you emerge knowing God and understanding life.   *The Divine Conspiracy*

While the biblical teachings do not speak of eliminating poverty, they *always* insist that the needy are to be cared for, that the poor are not to be taken advantage of but defended and given opportunity, and that they are to be taken into consideration in all

aspects of life. In the Old Testament manifold provisions for the
poor are made and repeatedly emphasized. The New Testament
goes so far as to state that pure and undefiled religion essentially
involves our "looking after orphans and widows in their distress,"
they being the poorest of the poor under usual circumstances.

The Spirit of the Disciplines

ROGER WILLIAMS

We find not in the Gospel that Christ hath anywhere provided
for the uniformity of churches, but only for their unity.

WILLIAM H. WILLIMON

The Bible does not address all contemporary human questions,
but perhaps the Bible wants to rearrange our questions, to entice
us away from our merely contemporary infatuations, to take us
places we would not have gone without the prodding of the Bible.

WESLEY K. WILLMER

The Bible is not a book of rules. This disappoints some people
who are looking for exact guidelines by which to live, while others
are glad since it means they can justify living any way they want.
Both of these groups have missed the heart of the matter, which
is Christ. The Christian is someone who has found riches that
boggle the imagination. To know Christ and to live a life of
obedience to Him is what truly matters to the fully committed
believer.   *God and Your Stuff*

WESLEY K. WILLMER and J. DAVID SCHMIDT

The Bible is their source of guidance. Where secular leaders
turn to business publications like the Wall Street Journal or
Harvard Business Review, the parachurch leader turns to the
Bible. The overwhelming majority of parachurch leaders have a
Bible on or near their desks, and are likely to turn to it in times of
need. Many parachurch leaders do not need any lessons in the
importance of seeking answers in scripture.

The Prospering Parachurch

A significant segment of parachurch donors view the Bible as
the guide to all of life and take seriously its instruction about
possessions. Martin Luther said there are three conversions for a

Christian—head, heart, and pocketbook. Jesus evidently felt this, too. Seventeen of the thirty-eight parables focus on possessions.

The Prospering Parachurch

WOODROW WILSON

A man has found himself when he has found his relation to the rest of the universe, and here is the Book in which those relations are set forth.

When you have read the Bible, you will know it is the Word of God because you will have found in it the key to your own heart, your own happiness, and your own duty . . . I am sorry for the men who do not read the Bible every day. I wonder why they deprive themselves of its strength and of the pleasure. It is one of the most singular books in the world, for every time you open it, some old text that you have read a score of times suddenly beams with a new meaning. There is no other book I know of, of which this is true—no other book that yields its meaning so personally, that seems to fit itself so intimately to the very spirit that is seeking its guidance.

I ask of every man and woman in this audience that from this night on they will realize that part of the destiny of America lies in their daily perusal of this great book of revelations—that if they would see America free and pure, they will make their own spirits free and pure by this baptism of the Holy Scripture.

Conclusion of a public address in 1911

OPRAH WINFREY

I read the Bible all the time. It just calms me, gives me peace.

Oprah Winfrey Speaks

LAUREN F. WINNER

The Bible is a book for minimalists. The Book of Ruth is a spare short story, four chapters, ninety-five verses in all. It opens with the biblical equivalent of "It was a dark and stormy night." The first six verses, prelude and background rolled into one, tell us over and over that all is not well . . . I am just barely grammar-school age in Christian years, and what you learn in grammar school is how to read. The Book of Ruth is not a bad primer.

Girl Meets God: On the Path to a Spiritual Life

ROBERT L. WISE

For twenty centuries the Holy Bible and Christian tradition have been the beacon lights along the shore, leading us on through the dark and foggy nights of confusion. Scripture describes itself as a "lamp unto our feet." No source could be more helpful and reassuring to us in finding spiritual direction.

Spiritual Abundance

JOHN WITHERSPOON

The character of a Christian must be taken from Holy Scriptures—the unerring standard.

KAROL JOSEF WOJTYLA (POPE JOHN PAUL II)

God speaks of himself to each and every person. He says that he is forgiveness. Only in the world of the Gospels do we encounter forgiveness. It is maybe difficult to find a text which can speak to us better about God in this aspect. How realistic the parable of the prodigal son is! And this is not a literary realism but an existential one. The Gospels are not a description of God. In them, God *is*.

It is truly a unique book. It has by now been translated into almost every language in the world and even into various dialects, but it loses nothing of its initial freshness and even a certain Semitic flavor. This regional flavor, which is derived from the fact that Jesus taught in Aramaic and lived in Palestine, in no way diminishes its universality. Its unique content strikes and affects people everywhere.   *The Way to Christ: Spiritual Exercises*

KENNETH L. WOODWARD

No one, of course, denies that both the Hebrew and the Christian Scriptures—like the God who rules the biblical heavens—exhibit an overarching androcentric outlook. Few women are mentioned by name, fewer yet get their stories told. The promise of feminist biblical scholarship is that it can alter this imbalance by interpreting the Bible from the perspectives of women's experiences. The danger is that feminist ideology will overreach the text.   *Newsweek*, 12/8/2003

REBECCA ABST WRIGHT

Does God know what is going on in the world today? If God knows, does God care? If God knows and cares, does God become involved? Such questions are as current as daily news broadcasts and as old as the story of the Israelite slaves in Egypt. Many thoughtful people wonder about God's presence and concern today. Some folk are afraid that such questions indicate a lack of strong faith, but the Bible is clear that neither God nor Jesus ever scolds anyone for asking honest questions.

New International Lesson Annual, 1999–2000

JOHN WYCLIFFE

This Bible is for the Government of the People, by the People, and for the People.

(Preface to the Wycliffe translation* of the Bible, 1384)

PHILIP YANCEY

The New Testament presents the realm of the Spirit as the culmination of God's work on earth, and as I compare it to what went before, I catch a glimpse why. An Israelite in the Old Testament approached God with fear and trembling, through an elaborate series of rituals under the auspices of professional priests. Jesus's disciples had a much more personal connection. Even so, they seemed to grasp only a portion of what he said, and until the end badly misconstrued his mission. The Holy Spirit, though, "personalizes" God's presence in a way uniquely tailored to my own soul.   *Christianity Today,* 10/25/99

If the Old Testament's overwhelming lesson about God is that he is personal and intimate, its overwhelming lesson about human beings is that we matter. What we say, how we behave, even what we think and feel—these things have an enormous effect upon God. They have, in fact, cosmic implications.

The Bible Jesus Read

---

*Nicholas of Hereford, an ardent follower of John Wycliffe, is often named as the chief translator of this word-for-word translation from Latin, the first complete English Bible. Soon after Wycliffe's death an idiomatic, literary version of the Wycliffe translation was written that is said to owe much to Lollard scholar John Purvey.

DAVID YOUNT

A path is needed through the Bible because it is both easy and hard to read. Easy because its language is so straightforward, difficult because the book is such a jumble of seemingly unrelated bits of literature . . . Reading and quoting the Bible is no substitute for acting on what God reveals there. The two great commandments are to love God and to love one's neighbor. All the rest is footnote.

Growing in Faith: A Guide for the Reluctant Christian

RAVI ZACHARIAS

Just as the Word of God is definitive in explaining the human heart, that same Word must connect our lives through turbulent times—times past and times to come. The Word was the instrument Jesus used to counter evil in His own wilderness experience. As Satan taunted Jesus and tried to persuade Him to compromise the greatest good for a seemingly innocent moment of self-glorifying power, Jesus reponded to every distortion of the good with the simple words, "Be gone. It is written." This confidence in God's Word not only instructs us in our battles against wickedness but puts into perspective the short-lived emotional impact of even the greatest victories. Only the written Word transcends every experience, good and bad.

Deliver Us from Evil

Throughout history the Word of God has remained firm. It rises up to outlive its pallbearers.

BEN D. ZEVIN

The Bible is timeless. Man's adoration of the Holy Scriptures is reflected in the works of artists of every age and in every field of endeavor. In all the arts, fine and applied, there has ever been a continual striving to interpret the Bible's inspiration through art and craftsmanship.

"The Bible Through the Ages," address to the
Rowfant Club of Cleveland, Ohio

Until quite recently, as time is measured, it was dangerous to have anything at all to do with publishing the Bible. Heresy might lurk in the phrasing of a marginal gloss or, worse, in a typographical error inadvertently left uncorrected in the published book. The biographies of those connected with the early history of the English Bible—printers, translators, sponsors—are rare which do not end suddenly in martyrdom at the stake or tell of long periods spent in the prisons of the Lancastrian or Tudor Kings.

"The Bible Through the Ages," address to the
Rowfant Club of Cleveland, Ohio

ZIG ZIGLAR

The Bible is crystal clear on what we must do to spend eternity in heaven with Christ . . . The good news is there is nothing you can do that is bad enough to keep you out of heaven; the bad news is there is nothing you can do that is good enough to get you into heaven. The best news: It is not what you do, but what He did on the cross, that guarantees your eternity.

Zig: The Autobiography

In my daily Bible reading, I express my praise to God and the Lord reveals to me His daily provision. On my walk and in speaking the Scriptures aloud, I express to the Lord where I am in my grieving, and He, in turn, provides for me the insight, joy, and help that I need to be healed and made stronger in my faith. My trust grows daily. And that truly seems to be the way God has designed our spiritual growth . . . Our healing from grief to a very great extent lies in our daily communication with God.

Confessions of a Grieving Christian

ROY B. ZUCK

No book other than the Bible has ever given precise predictions of future events (prophecies) hundreds of years in advance, predictions that were fulfilled exactly. Far from vague generalities or general guesses, the prophecies in Scripture contain explicit details which no human could possibly devise on his own. Imagine trying to come up with the name, ancestry, birthplace, and kind of death for a person who would be born in 2800. That would be humanly impossible! Only God could make such predictions and see them carried out perfectly. But that is exactly what we have in the Bible. Jesus' identity, name, birthplace, triumphal entry, betrayal, suffering, death, and

burial—all were foretold in the Old Testament seven hundred
years before He was born.

ULRICH ZWINGLI

Our view of the matter is this: that we should hold the Word of
God in the highest possible esteem . . . and we should give to it a
trust which we cannot give to any other word. For the Word of
God is certain and can never fail. It is clear, and will never leave
us in darkness. It teaches its own truth. It arises and irradiates the
soul of man with full salvation and grace.

The Certainty or Power of the Word of God

Brief Notes on Authors

A selective list of authors expressing thoughts on
the Word of God in this anthology of quotations
about the Bible and Bible-reading.

ADAMS, JOHN QUINCY (1767–1848) Sixth president of
the United States of America. Served in the Senate, as minister to
Great Britain, and as secretary of state, helping to formulate the
Monroe Doctrine. Son of John Adams, the new republic's second
president.

AKBAR, NA'IM (b. 1944) American clinical psychologist.
Changed his name from Luther B. Weems Jr. upon joining
Nation of Islam in 1971. He was awarded a Ph.D. from the
University of Michigan. Akbar established his private consultancy
and a publishing company, Mind Productions, in the late 1980s.

ALBRIGHT, WILLIAM FOXWELL (1891–1971) American
biblical scholar and educator. Born in Chile to missionary parents,
Albright earned his Ph.D. at Johns Hopkins University and
launched in Jerusalem a career that encompassed Semitic
philology, archaeology, and ancient languages. He returned to
Hopkins in 1929, and taught there for nearly 30 years. His
career's highlight arrived when he confirmed the Dead Sea
Scrolls' authenticity in 1948.

ALLISON, WICK (contemporary) American journalist. He
is publisher and editor-in-chief of a Dallas magazine titled *D*, one
of the nation's most successful periodicals of its type. In an
extensive publishing career, Allison has owned several other
magazines including *Art and Antiques* and *Sport*.

ALTER, ROBERT (contemporary) American university
professor. Since 1967, Dr. Alter has taught at the University of
California at Berkeley, where he is professor of Hebrew and

comparative literature. He has twice been a Guggenheim fellow and has been also a senior fellow of the National Endowment for the Humanities. His books include *The World of Biblical Literature.*

ANDERS, MAX (b. 1947) American author and former megachurch pastor whose writing seeks to bridge the gap between scholars and readers unfamiliar with theology. Anders also is editor of the *Holman New Testament Commentary.* With Bruce Wilkinson, he was co-founder of the popular Walk Thru the Bible Ministries. His book titles include *30 Days to Understanding the Bible, The New Christian's Handbook, The Good Life,* and *What You Need to Know,* the latter a ten-volume series on basic biblical teachings.

ANDERSON, PAUL M. (contemporary) American biochemist and educator. Dr. Anderson joined the faculty in the new school of medicine at the University of Minnesota at Duluth in 1971 and later served as head of its biochemistry department for 14 years. He has been a member of the *Journal of Biological Chemistry's* editorial board and received a Fulbright scholarship to India.

ARMOUR, MICHAEL C. (contemporary) American executive coach, Church of Christ minister, retired U.S. Navy captain (naval intelligence), and author. He was dean of Pepperdine University before becoming president of Columbia Christian College (now Cascade College). Editions of Dr. Armour's *Newcomer's Guide to the Bible* have been published in Russian and other languages.

ARNDT, WILLIAM FREDERICK (1880–1957) American Lutheran pastor who joined the faculty of St. Paul's College and Concordia Seminary. Joined William Gingrich of Albright College in producing *A Greek-English Lexicon of the New Testament and other Early Christian Literature,* translating and adapting Walter Bauer's Greek-German lexicon.

ARNOLD, MATTHEW (1822–1888) English poet, best remembered for *Dover Beach.* He worked 35 years as inspector of schools and wrote well-regarded books on religion and other topics.

ARTHUR, KAY (contemporary) American evangelist. Founder of Precept Inductive Bible Courses, beginning with a class of 250 in Atlanta, Georgia, a nondenominational Bible study ministry that during two decades has taught hundreds of thousands of men and women in more than 85 countries. She is the author of *How to Study Your Bible,* and other books.

ATKINS, GAIUS GLENN (1868–1956) American clergyman, pastor of Congregational churches.

AUGUSTINE, SAINT (354–430) Bishop of Hippo; greatest of the Latin fathers of the early Christian movement. A leading philosopher and church advocate.

BACH, JOHANN SEBASTIAN (1685–1750) German organist and composer, who wrote an enormous quantity of church, vocal, and instrumental music. Bach dedicated many of his compositions "to the glory of God."

BANDO, SAL (contemporary) American baseball player, league executive, and businessman. Bando, who played college ball for Arizona State, was a major leaguer for eleven seasons with the Oakland Athletics (a key player in the team's World Series championships in 1972, 1973, and 1974) and five with Milwaukee's Brewers. Bando is a business and civic leader in Milwaukee, where he also served eight years as a senior vice president in the Brewers organization. He was chairman of National Bible week, November 23–30, 2003.

BARCLAY, WILLIAM (1907–1978) Scottish preacher, scholar, and prolific writer of books on biblical subjects. In 1963, joined faculty of Glasgow University to become professor of divinity and biblical criticism.

BARNES, ALBERT (1798–1870) American theologian and Presbyterian minister who supported social reforms including the campaign against slavery. He wrote the eleven-volume *Notes Explanatory and Practical on the New Testament* and other popular biblical commentaries.

BARNES, WILLIAM (1801–1886) English poet, schoolmaster, and priest, noted for poetry reflecting the rural life of southwestern England. His first poems were published in the Dorset *County Chronicle.*

BARROW, WILLIE (contemporary) African-American minister and social activist. Field organizer for Dr. Martin Luther King during major civil rights marches and demonstrations of the 1950s and 1960s. Later, she took a key role in Operation Push by becoming an aide to the Rev. Jesse Jackson.

BARTH, KARL (1886–1968) Swiss theologian and writer who criticized the liberal theology of the 19th Century. He reaffirmed the basic principles of the Reformation, traveled extensively to foster ecumenism, and vigorously opposed the rise of the Nazi movement in Germany.

BARTON, BRUCE (1886–1967) American advertising executive and author. Barton worked as a publicist and magazine editor until 1919, when he co-founded the BBDO advertising agency. Heading it until 1961, he built the agency into an industry leader; he created the character of "Betty Crocker" in one of BBDO's famous campaigns. Barton was most widely known as author of best-selling guides to personal success and his famed 1925 book *The Man Nobody Knows,* which depicted Jesus Christ as a successful salesman, publicist, and role model for modern businessmen.

BEECHER, HENRY WARD (1813–1887) American preacher, editor, writer, orator, and reformer. Accepted call in 1847 to Brooklyn's Plymouth Church, where his sermons won a huge following. He attacked slavery and advocated women's suffrage and free trade. After three years as editor of *The Independent,* Beecher founded in 1870 a nondenominational periodical, *The Christian Union.*

BENSEN, D. R. (contemporary) Bensen's limerick "The Tower of Babel," based on Genesis 11:1–9, appeared in his book of limericks, which was published in 1986 and features illustrations by Albrecht Dürer. The book's introduction by Isaac Asimov contends that Don Bensen one day overheard Lucifer chuckling to himself about a limerick he'd composed, and thereupon got the idea of rewriting Bible stories in the five-line form of light verse. Bensen's objective, he added, was to portray Bible incidents accurately while involving some play on words, startling thoughts, and odd rhyme. The book's subtitle: *Old Testament Stories Re-Versed.*

BENSON, ROBERT (contemporary) American writer. Benson is the author of *Between the Dreaming and the Coming True, Living Prayer, The Game,* and other works.

BETHUNE, MARY McLEOD (1875–1955) American educator, the daughter of slaves, named as a special adviser to President Franklin D. Roosevelt on problems of minority groups. An 1895 graduate of Moody Bible Institute, she established a school for girls and later became president of Bethune-Cookman College. Gained fame as "the teacher who tamed the Ku Klux Klan" in a 1920 confrontation.

BILLINGS, JOSH, pen name of American writer Henry Wheeler Shaw (1818–1885). For years he lived as an explorer, coal miner, farmer, and auctioneer. He began writing and lecturing in 1860, using rural dialect for his humorous sketches and homespun philosophies. They won wide popularity during the 1870s, published in Billings' *Farmer's Allminax.*

BOBRICK, BENSON (b. 1947) American poet and scholar. Bobrick, who lives and teaches in Vermont, is the author of several distinguished works of history including *Angel in the Whirlwind: The Triumph of the American Revolution.*

BOETTNER, LORAINE (1901–1990) American professor and author of theological works. A graduate of Princeton Seminary, he received honorary doctorates in divinity and literature. His works include *A Harmony of the Gospels* and *The Millennium.*

BOICE, JAMES MONTGOMERY (1938–2000) American minister and author. He was pastor of Philadelphia's Tenth Presbyterian Church and teacher for the Bible Study Hour radio program for more than three decades.

BOLTON, MARTHA (contemporary) American humorist. A staff writer for comedian Bob Hope for more than a dozen years, Ms. Bolton authored 23 books of humor beginning with *A Funny Thing Happened to Me on My Way Through the Bible.* In addition to her work for Bob Hope, she has also written for Phyllis Diller, Mark Lowry, and Ann Jillian and has been the "Cafeteria Lady" columnist for *Brio,* a magazine for teenage girls.

BONHOEFFER, DIETRICH (1906–1945) German Lutheran minister and theologian who worked covertly for the anti-Nazi resistance movement in World War II. He was imprisoned in 1943 and executed after being linked to an attempt to assassinate Adolf Hitler.

BOORSTIN, DANIEL (b. 1914) American historian, author, educator, and editor. Boorstin was Librarian of Congress from 1975 to 1987 and emeritus thereafter.

BOSWELL, WILLIAM D. (1877–1961) American Baptist pastor, a former ranch hand, who preached between 5,000 and 6,000 sermons during his 58-year ministry in Texas.

BOYCE, JAMES PETIGRU (1827–1888) American theologian and educator. Member of the Southern Baptist Theological Seminary faculty.

BREWER, DAVID JOSIAH (1837–1910) Associate justice of the U.S. Supreme Court from 1889 until his death, having served earlier as a justice of the Kansas supreme court and a federal circuit court. Brewer was born in Smyrna, Turkey, the son of American missionaries.

BROADUS, JOHN ALBERT (1827–1895) American minister, professor, and author who was president of Southern Baptist Theological Seminary in the early 1890's. During the Civil War, he served for a time as chaplain in Robert E. Lee's army.

BROOKS, PHILLIPS (1835–1893) American preacher and bishop of the Episcopal Church, known for his oratorical skills and imposing presence. He was the author of many works and, for Sunday school children, composed the Christmas carol "O Little Town of Bethlehem."

BRUCE, FREDERICK FYVIE (1910–1991) Scottish author, editor, and professor, known as "the dean of evangelical scholars" at the University of Manchester. At Aberdeen University and Cambridge he was a distinguished scholar before taking a faculty post at Sheffield University. A world-renowned expert on the Old and New Testaments, he wrote *History of the Bible in English, Hard Sayings of the Bible,* and other works.

BUCHANAN, ROBERT (1841–1901), English poet and novelist who used the pseudonym Thomas Maitland when he wrote an article for *Contemporary Review* attacking Rossetti and other pre-Raphaelites.

BUCK, PEARL (1892–1973) American author, the daughter of a missionary couple, who lived in China most of the first forty years of her life. From childhood she spoke both English and Chinese. She graduated in 1914 from Randolph-Macon Woman's College in Virginia. Her second novel, *The Good Earth,* won the Pulitzer Prize in 1935. Ms. Buck received the Nobel Prize in literature in 1938. Besides novels, she wrote short stories, biography, poetry, children's literature, drama, and translations from Chinese.

BUCKINGHAM, JAMES WILLIAM "JAMIE" (1932–1992) American author, writer or ghostwriter of 47 Christian books that sold more than 34 million copies. Buckingham was a popular speaker in the charismatic movement and a lifelong supporter of Bible translators in the mission field.

BUCKLEY, WILLIAM F., JR. (b. 1925) American social and political commentator. He became a public figure when his first book was published—*God and Man at Yale,* on the place of faith in people's lives—and has since authored more than 35 other books. Buckley founded the monthly magazine *National Review* and hosted a long-running TV program, *Firing Line.*

BUECHNER, FREDERICK (b. 1926) American author, a Pulitzer Prize winner for his historical fiction. Buechner's other works include biblical fiction and satire as well as theological and inspirational writing. Among his titles are *Whistling in the Dark* and *The Alphabet of Grace.*

BUNYAN, JOHN (1628–1688) English author and preacher, best known for writing one of England's most widely read books, *The Pilgrim's Progress,* an allegory published in 1678. Bunyan was imprisoned for 12 years for holding religious services which did not conform to practices of the Church of England.

BUTLER, SAMUEL (1835–1902) English novelist and satirist. Butler's novels included *Erewhon,* a utopian story, and *The Way of All Flesh,* a satire of family life.

BUTTRICK, GEORGE ARTHUR (1892–1980) American minister, author, and professor at Harvard University, Chicago Theological Seminary, and Garrett Theological Seminary. For twenty-seven years, Buttrick was pastor of the Madison Avenue Presbyterian Church in New York City. He was born in England, leaving for America after World War I service as a military chaplain.

CAHILL, THOMAS (contemporary) American scholar and author, formerly director of religious publishing at Doubleday before retiring to write full-time. For six years, he was a North American correspondent for the *Times of London.* Cahill is well known for his best-selling "Hinges of History" book series.

CALVIN, JOHN (1509–1564) Swiss theologian, a Protestant, who founded Calvinism and promoted a rigorous doctrine of predestination. In 1536, Calvin became professor of divinity and minister of the church in Geneva. He emphasized an omnipotent God and salvation by God's grace alone.

CALVOCORESSI, PETER (b. 1912) English publisher and author, a partner at The Hogarth Press and later chief executive of Penguin Books. He was chairman of the London Library and Open University Educational Enterprises and served on the council of the International Institute for Strategic Studies.

CAMPBELL, ALEXANDER (1788–1866) American frontier preacher, born in Ireland of Scottish lineage, who led Protestant followers in what became known as the Restoration movement, advocating a return to scriptural simplicity in organization and doctrine. He edited the *Millennial Harbinger,* and in 1840 founded Bethany College in Virginia, becoming its president.

CAMPBELL, STAN (contemporary) American youth minister and writer. Campbell is the author of the eight-book "BibleLog" series and more than twenty other books for young Christians.

CARD, MICHAEL (contemporary) American songwriter-musician who has recorded more than twenty albums, including *Joy for the Journey* and *Soul Anchor.* He has also authored

Scribbling in the Sand and other books. Card's song "El Shaddai" was recognized by the National Endowment for the Arts and the Recording Industry Association as one of the 365 finest songs of the 20th Century.

CARLYLE, THOMAS (1795–1881) Scottish historian and essayist. He began a teaching career but abandoned it to move to London and begin writing a history of the French revolution. This work, published in 1837, and his subsequent books attracted broad interest. In 1865 he was named rector of Edinburgh University.

CARTER, JIMMY (b. 1924) Thirty-ninth president of the United States, after serving as governor of Georgia. Negotiated the Camp David peace agreement between Israel and Egypt.

CARVER, GEORGE WASHINGTON (1860–1943) American researcher and developer of markets for farm products. After earning a master's degree from Iowa State Agricultural College in 1895, Carver headed the agriculture department at Tuskegee Institute in Alabama. By developing some 300 marketable products from peanuts and more than 100 from sweet potatoes, he became a hero to Southern farmers.

CHADWICK, SAMUEL (1860–1932) English clergyman and author who served as principal of Cliff College, Sheffield. Chadwick ministered at Oxford Place Chapel for a decade, beginning in 1894. His writings include *The Way to Pentecost* and many collected sermons.

CHAMBERS, OSWALD (1874–1917) Scottish theologian, teacher, and author of the Christian classic *My Utmost for His Highest*, a title with millions of copies in print. In 1911, Chambers founded the Bible Training College at Clapham, London. During World War I he ministered as a YMCA chaplain to Australian and New Zealand troops, dying in Egypt after surgery for a ruptured appendix. Most of his books were published posthumously.

CHANNING, WILLIAM ELLERY (1780–1842) American minister in Boston called "the apostle of Unitarianism." He led a movement opposed to Calvinists and influenced Thoreau, Emerson, and other New England writers.

CHARLES, RAY (1930–2004) Professional name of Ray Robinson, American singer, songwriter, and musician born in Georgia and raised in Florida. Completely blind by age of seven. Studied piano, saxophone and clarinet at Saint Augustine School of the Blind and Deaf. Won fame as recording artist in the 1950s and formed a big band in the 1960s. Awarded National Medal of Arts in 1992.

CHESTERTON, GILBERT K. (1874–1936) English free-lance journalist and author, a convert to Roman Catholicism in 1922. Writer of *Orthodoxy* and other works on theology and philosophy. After converting to Catholicism, he wrote his celebrated Father Brown series of detective novels wherein the priest proves adept at both sleuthing and sermonizing.

CLIBURN, VAN (b. 1934) American classical pianist. In 1958, at age twenty-three, Cliburn won the inaugural Tchaikovsky International Piano Competition held in Moscow. He embarked on an ambitious recording and performing career. Cliburn retired from the stage in 1978, but resumed limited concert appearances in 1989. Named in his honor by its founders, the Van Cliburn International Piano Competition is held quadrennially in Fort Worth, Texas.

COLERIDGE, SAMUEL TAYLOR (1772–1834) English poet and author of the famed "Rime of the Ancient Mariner." Collaborated with William Wordsworth on an important collection of English Romantic verse, *Lyrical Ballads.*

COLSON, CHARLES W. (b. 1931) American lay minister and writer. Began career as a Washington attorney; special counsel to President Nixon in 1969-72. In 1976, after the Watergate scandal, he founded Prison Fellowship Ministries to reach prisoners with the gospel and provide for their families' needs. Colson was awarded Templeton Prize for Progress in Religion in 1993. His books include an autobiography, *Born Again,* and *How Now Shall We Live?* He is the host of *BreakPoint,* a syndicated daily radio broadcast.

COOK, JOSEPH (1838–1901) American Congregationalist social reformer and syndicated newspaper writer who gained international renown as a lecturer and popular spokesman for Protestantism in the 1870s.

COWPER, WILLIAM (1731–1800) English poet and writer of hymns including "God Moves in a Mysterious Way" and "Oh! For a Closer Walk With God." Regarded as a forerunner of Romantic poets Wordsworth, Burns, and Coleridge.

CRANMER, THOMAS (1489–1556) English reformer and archbishop of Canterbury. He was a translator of the Bishop's Bible, which preceded the King James Version. Cranmer also was the primary author of the Anglican *Book of Common Prayer*, giving the prayer book its stately and rhythmical language. A friend and supporter of Henry VIII, Cranmer opposed a return to Catholicism. After accession by Queen Mary, he was convicted of treason by a papal commission in 1555, condemned for heresy, and burned at the stake.

CRISWELL, WALLIE AMOS (1909–2002) American minister, pastor of the First Baptist Church of Dallas from 1944 to 1991. Under his leadership the church grew to more than 25,000 members. Founder of Criswell College and radio station KCBI, Criswell was noted for the firm fundamentalist views as expressed in his 1969 book, *Why I Preach That the Bible Is Literally True*.

DANIELL, DAVID (contemporary) British author and educator. Daniell is emeritus professor of English at University College, London, where he has been director of Shakespeare studies. He is the author of many articles and books on Shakespeare. Yale University Press published several of his works including *The Bible in English* and *William Tyndale: A Biography*.

DANTE ALIGHIERI (1265–1321) Italian poet whose masterpiece, *The Divine Comedy,* describes a pilgrim's progress from damnation in Hell, through Purgatory, and eventually to heavenly bliss in Paradise.

DAVIES, ROBERTSON (1913–1995) Canadian man of letters; author of novels, essays and plays. He was a young actor with the Old Vic Company in England, publisher of the *Peterborough* (Ontario) *Examiner,* and a university professor and first master of Massey College at the University of Toronto. Davies's novels include *Tempest-Tost* and *A Mixture of Frailties*.

DOBSON, JAMES (b. 1936) American author and international radio broadcaster. Dr. Dobson is founder and president of Focus on the Family, a nonprofit evangelistic organization based in Colorado Springs, Colorado. His radio broadcasts are heard on more than 2,000 stations worldwide.

DOCKERY, DAVID (b. 1952) American theologian. Dockery formerly was dean of the Southern Baptist Seminary at Louisville, Kentucky. He is editor of the *New American Commentary.*

DOUGLASS, FREDERICK (1817–1895) American abolitionist, orator, and journalist. An ex-slave, Douglass edited four newspapers and lectured widely in the United States and abroad.

DRYDEN, JOHN (1631–1700) English dramatist and poet who dominated the London literary scene of his time. His works included a theatrical comedy, *Marriage-a-la-Mode.* Dryden was England's poet laureate from 1668 to 1688.

EDDY, MARY BAKER (1821–1910) American writer and founder of the Church of Christ, Scientist. Recovering from a serious injury in 1866, Mary Baker Eddy began to formulate the ideas that would lead her to found the church she chartered in Boston in 1889. She explained her beliefs, including healing by faith, in *Science and Health,* published in 1875.

EDINGTON, ANDREW "ANDY" (1914–1998) American educator. Edington was named president emeritus of Schreiner College (now Schreiner University) in Kerrville, Texas, after serving 21 years as its active president. A Christian layman whose specialty was teaching the Bible, Edington's career included years as a college football coach, athletic director, Navy ship captain, and foundation president.

EDWARDS, JONATHAN (1703–1758) Puritan theologian in colonial America who led the Great Awakening of the 1740s. For five years, Edwards prayed fervently that God would bring revival to his congregation in Northampton—prayers that were answered in the Great Awakening.

ELLINGTON, EDWARD K. "DUKE" (1899–1974) American composer, pianist, and jazz orchestra leader. Influenced by ragtime pianists, Ellington began to play professionally at seventeen and became one of the most eminent jazz artists of his time. Late in his life he wrote *In the Beginning: God* as "religious jazz," performed in 1968 at New York City, London, and churches in West Germany.

EMERSON, RALPH WALDO (1803–1882) American clergyman, poet, essayist, and a noted 19th Century literary figure. Pastor of the Old North Church in Boston, a Unitarian congregation, from 1829 to 1832. His Transcendental philosophy hailed the virtues of serenity, self-reliance, and optimism.

ERASMUS, DESIDERIUS (1466–1536) Dutch scholar. Erasmus, a leading figure of the Humanist Renaissance in northern Europe, lectured at Oxford and Cambridge universities. While editing the Greek New Testament, he influenced the pronunciation of biblical Greek that is still widely accepted. Erasmus also wrote satires against corruption in the medieval church.

EVANS, ANTHONY T. "TONY" (contemporary) American minister and writer. Dr. Evans, a leading spokesman for biblical racial reconciliation, is senior pastor of Oak Cliff Bible Fellowship in Dallas and president of The Urban Alternative, a parachurch ministry. His books include *The Kingdom Agenda* and *The Perfect Christian.*

FARADAY, MICHAEL (1791–1867) English physicist and discoverer of the principles of the electric motor and dynamo. Many electrical engineers regard Faraday as the "father" of their profession. As a teenager he was an errand boy for two bookbinders, his intense interest in science aroused by books at his workplace.

FARRAR, FREDERIC WILLIAM (1831–1903) English clergyman, theological writer, and expert philologist. Became canon of Westminster Cathedral in 1876 and dean of Canterbury in 1895. Wrote *Eric, or Little by Little,* a sentimental novel of school life that went into thirty-six editions.

FAULKNER, WILLIAM (1897–1962) American author ranking as the preeminent figure of the Southern literary renaissance in the 20th century. In the 1950s, he received two Pulitzer Prizes along with numerous additional awards, honored more than any other American writer during the decade.

FEILER, BRUCE (contemporary) American author. Feiler, a free-lance writer for *The New Yorker, Condé Nast Traveler,* and other magazines, is a frequent contributor to the broadcasts of National Public Radio's *All Things Considered* program. He has written several award-winning books including *Walking the Bible: A Journey by Land Through the Five Books of Moses* (2001), the story of an inspiring and rigorous personal journey covering 10,000 miles by foot, jeep, rowboat, and camel.

FIELDS, W. C., stage name of William Claude Dukenfield (1880–1946), American vaudeville and motion picture actor and comedian. Starred in films including *David Copperfield* and *My Little Chickadee.*

FOX, GEORGE (1624–1691) English preacher and founder of the Society of Friends, commonly called the Quakers. He emphasized a God-given light of inspiration as a source of authority and revelation. Fox traveled to North America for missionary efforts.

FRANKLIN, BENJAMIN (1706–1790) American philosopher, scientist, statesman, and printer in Philadelphia. Published *Poor Richard's Almanack;* helped found University of Pennsylvania; invented the lightning rod and bifocal spectacles. Franklin also was a signer of the Declaration of Independence and served as the U.S. government's minister to England and later France.

FRAZIER, IAN (contemporary) American writer of books and essays. After graduating in 1977 from Harvard University, where he wrote for the *Lampoon,* Frazier became a member of *The New Yorker* staff, continuing later as a contributor while writing also for *Harper's* and *Atlantic Monthly.* In 1997 he won the first Thurber Prize for American Humor. His books include *Coyote V. Acme, On the Rez,* and *Lamentations of the Father.*

FREUD, SIGMUND (1856–1939) Austrian neurologist and founder of psychoanalysis. Developed theories based on repressed and forgotten memories. Dr. Freud examined infantile sexuality and dreams, and popularized his concept of the id, ego, and superego.

GABOR, ZSA ZSA (b. 1918) Budapest-born American film actress who married nine times. Best-known as a whimsical TV celebrity who made a career of joking about her love of men, jewelry, and furs. Her screen credits include *Moulin Rouge* (1951) and *Queen of Outer Space* (1958). She is the mother of Francesca Hilton, her daughter with hotel magnate Conrad Hilton.

GAEBELEIN, FRANK E. (1899–1983) American educator and editor. Dr. Gaebelein was the first headmaster of Stony Brook School on Long Island, where he served 41 years. He was an associate editor of *Christianity Today,* a longtime member of the American Tract Society's board, the editor of the *New Scofield Reference Bible,* and chairman of the New International Version style committee. He served also as general editor of the *Expositor's Bible Commentary.*

GALLUP, GEORGE, JR. (contemporary) American public opinion analyst. Gallup is cochairman of The Gallup Organization and chairman of the George H. Gallup International Institute. He holds a degree from Princeton University's department of religion and serves on the board of Trinity Episcopal School for Ministry.

GARDNER, JOHN WILLIAM (1912–2002) American public official. Previously president of the Carnegie Foundation for the Advancement of Teaching, he served in President Lyndon Johnson's cabinet as Secretary of Health, Education, and Welfare. He founded Common Cause, a nonpartisan citizens' lobby, and was its chairman from 1970 to 1977.

GARRETT, LEROY (b. 1918) American philosophy professor, author, lecturer, and historian of the religious movement led by Alexander Campbell and Barton Stone on the American frontier. Dr. Garrett was editor and publisher of a Christian journal, *Restoration Review,* for forty years.

GERSMEHL, PHILIP J. (contemporary) American professor of geography. After receiving a doctorate from the University of Georgia, Gersmehl taught at Concordia Teachers College until 1975 and since then has been a member of the University of Minnesota faculty. He has written extensively about agricultural resources and on other subjects relating to geographic education.

GIBBS, JOE (contemporary) American football coach and businessman. Gibbs began his coaching career in 1964 at San Diego State University and in 1992 became one of the winningest coaches in National Football League history when his Washington Redskins won the Super Bowl by defeating the Buffalo Bills.

GOETHE, JOHANN WOLFGANG VON (1749–1832) German poet, essayist, and dramatist. Goethe, the greatest figure of the German Romantic period, contributed to the *Sturm und Drang* movement. He combined his philosophical and religious thought in a masterpiece, *Faust,* the work of a lifetime.

GOMES, PETER J. (b. 1942) American professor and minister. Gomes served as director of freshman studies at Tuskegee Institute before returning to Boston, his birthplace, in 1970. He was appointed Plummer Professor of Christian Morals at Harvard in 1974, the same year he began his ministry at the university's Memorial Church.

GONZALEZ, JUSTO L. (contemporary) American historian, theologian, and writer. He attended United Seminary in Cuba, where he later taught for eight years, and was the youngest person to be awarded a Ph.D. in church history at Yale. Dr. Gonzales also taught at two Georgia institutions, Emory University and the Interdenominational Theological Center. He is the author of the three-volume *History of Christian Thought* and other works.

GRAHAM, BILLY (b. 1918) American worldwide evangelist. Ordained by a Southern Baptist church, Graham gained renown with his Los Angeles gospel meetings in 1949. Since then, he has preached to more than 210 million people through various meetings, reaching hundreds of millions more through TV and other global media. He founded in 1950 the Billy Graham Evangelistic Association, which headquarters in Minneapolis. His writings include an autobiography, *Just As I Am,* and many theological and devotional books.

GRANT, ULYSSES S. (1822–1885) American military leader and president. The general, an Ohio native, was Abraham Lincoln's choice in 1864 as commander of the Union armies in the Civil War. After the war, Grant was easily elected to two terms in the White House.

GREELEY, HORACE (1811–1872) American journalist and politician, influential in molding thought in northern states. Founder of the *New York Tribune.* Republican candidate for President in 1872.

GREENAWAY, BRIAN (contemporary) British biker, president of the U.K. chapter of a notorious motorcycle club. Before finding Christian faith in prison, Greenaway was violent, full of hate, and deeply into drugs, as detailed in *Hell's Angel,* his autobiography written with Brian Kellock.

GRIMKE, ANGELINA (1805–1879) American campaigner for civil liberties and women's suffrage. As a teenage girl in Philadelphia, she joined the Society of Friends (Quakers). Later, Angelina and her sister Sarah published antislavery pamphlets and became pioneers in the struggle for women's rights. She married Theodore Weld, another antislavery crusader, and they opened schools at locations in New Jersey and New York.

GROUNDS, VERNON C. (b. 1914) American educator and author. Dr. Grounds is chancellor of Denver Seminary and teaches in areas of ethics and counseling. He joined the fledgling seminary as dean in 1951 and became its second president in 1955, a position he held until 1979.

GUINNESS, OS (b. 1941) American writer and public speaker. Born in China, where his parents were medical missionaries, he was educated in England and graduated with a doctorate from Oxford. Since 1985 he has lived in the Washington, D.C., area, where he is a senior fellow at The Trinity Forum. He has written or edited more than twenty books, including *The Call, Time for Truth,* and *Long Journey Home.*

HALLEY, HENRY H. (1874–1965) American preacher and biblical scholar. Author of *Halley's Bible Handbook,* "designed as a handy manual for the average Bible reader," with more than one million copies in print.

HEINE, HEINRICH (1797–1856) German lyric poet whose international literary reputation and influence developed from the 1827 publication of *Buch der Lieder (Book of Songs).* He became a controversial figure with critical and satirical writings that prompted censorship.

HELLO, ERNEST (1828–1885) French critic. At a young age, Hello edited and published a newspaper of his own, *Le Crois,* for two years. Afterward, he wrote extensively for other publications. Historians believe his best work is found in a series of philosophical and critical essays.

HENRY, CARL F. H. (1913–2003) American theologian, journalist, and leader of the evangelical movement. In 1955, at the urging of Billy Graham, Henry founded *Christianity Today* magazine and was its editor until 1968. He was lecturer-at-large for World Vision International for 12 years and served on the board of Prison Fellowship Ministries from 1981 to 1998.

HENRY, PATRICK (1736–1799) American statesman, lawyer, and champion of religious liberty. A dynamic orator and popular leader, he served five terms as governor of his native Virginia.

HERBERT, GEORGE (1593–1633) Welsh Anglican priest and metaphysical poet, described as a master of metrical form and versecraft. He was elected to Parliament in 1625, but became a priest in 1630 and spent the rest of his life as rector in Bemerton, where he preached and wrote poetry. He also wrote *A Priest to the Temple,* a popular manual for country parsons reprinted more than a dozen times in sixty years.

HERSHISER, OREL LEONARD IV (b. 1958) American professional baseball player and coach. Pitcher with Los Angeles Dodgers and Cleveland Indians. Cy Young Award winner and Most Valuable Player of 1988 World Series, playing for Dodgers. Resumed career in 1991 following radical shoulder reconstruction. Retired from pitching in 2000 after 510 major league appearances and joined the staff of the Texas Rangers' team manager.

HESTON, CHARLTON (contemporary) American actor whose career included starring performances in many biblical stories. Heston's interest in the Bible was piqued in 1954, when Cecil B. DeMille cast him in the role of Moses for the film epic *The Ten Commandments.* In 1992 the actor was featured in a four-part TV series, *Charlton Heston Presents the Bible,* later adapted for videotape, CD-ROM, and a book.

HEWITT, HUGH (contemporary) American broadcast journalist who served for six years in the Reagan Administration in a variety of posts, including White House assistant counsel. He is the host of a syndicated radio program and is a professor on the faculty of Chapman University Law School in Orange, California. For notable work in public television, he won two Emmy awards.

HODGE, CHARLES (1797–1878) American professor at Princeton University, a faculty pioneer who taught students at Princeton from 1822 to1878. He became the leading Presbyterian theologian of the 19th century. Hodge wrote extensively including the three-volume *Systematic Theology* considered his masterpiece.

HOLMES, OLIVER WENDELL, SR. (1809–1894) American physician and author. Dr. Holmes wrote notable poems including "Old Ironsides" and "The Chambered Nautilus," as well as novels, essays, and light, witty verse. His son, Oliver Wendell Holmes, Jr., served as a Supreme Court justice for thirty years.

HOOK, SIDNEY (1902–1989) American philosopher and professor. Dr. Hook for more than two decades headed the philosophy department at New York University. Originally a Marxist, he later was disenchanted with Marxism and became active in anti-Communist causes.

HOOVER, J. EDGAR (1895–1972). American criminologist. Director of the Federal Bureau of Investigation from 1924 to 1972.

HULETT, LOUISA "SUE" (contemporary) American professor and author. Dr. Hulett is professor and chair of political science at Knox College, where she received the Distinguished Teaching Award in 1994. Earlier, she taught at state universities in Illinois, Nebraska, and California. She received her doctorate in international relations from the University of Southern California.

HUXLEY, THOMAS (1825–1895) English biologist. Foremost advocate in England of Charles Darwin's theory of evolution.

HYBELS, BILL (b. 1952) American evangelical pastor, pioneer of the seeker-sensitive worship service. In 1975, at age 23, he founded Willow Creek Community Church and led it to megachurch growth in a suburb northwest of Chicago. His books on Christian living include *Becoming a Contagious Christian.*

JAKES, T. D. (b. 1957) American preacher, evangelist, and author. He began his ministry in 1979, founding a small storefront church in Montgomery, West Virginia. By the beginning of the 21st century, Bishop Jakes was pastor of The Potter's House, an interracial charismatic congregation at Dallas and one of the nation's fastest-growing megachurches.

JENKINS, PHILIP (b. 1952) American educator and author. Distinguished Professor of History and Religious Studies at Penn State University. Besides *The Next Christendom* (2002), his published works include *Hidden Gospels* and *Mystics and Messiahs.*

JEROME, SAINT (340-420) One of the four Doctors of the Church given official recognition in the Middle Ages. As a theologian, he was a prolific writer and an expert on Hebrew and Greek. In 386 he went to a monastery at Bethlehem in Palestine, where he devoted himself to study and writing. Jerome's translation of the Bible into Latin became widely accepted as the *Latin Vulgate.* His other writing included works on church history.

JOHN PAUL II, POPE—see Wojtyla, Karol Josef.

JOHNSON, AUDREY WETHERELL (1907–1984) English Bible scholar, missionary to China, and founder of Bible Study Fellowship International. Educated in France, Miss Johnson traveled to China in 1936 to join the China Inland Mission, teaching the Bible to Chinese students in Chinese. She was interned during Japanese occupation and experienced the strain of living in China under a Communist regime. Beginning in 1952 in the U.S. as a study group of five women led by Miss Johnson, Bible Study Fellowship has grown into a worldwide organization of more than 300 groups studying God's Word.

JOHNSON, PAUL (contemporary) English historian and journalist. Among his books are *A History of the Jews, The Birth of the Modern, Intellectuals,* and *Modern Times.* He is a frequent contributor to leading newspapers and magazines in the United States and England.

JONES, TIMOTHY (contemporary) American author, editor, and speaker specializing in the spiritual life. Jones was the managing editor of Ballantine Books' former Christian division, Moorings, and an editor of *Christianity Today* for six years, after eight years of pastoral ministry. His published books include *The Art of Prayer, Awake My Soul,* and (with coauthor George Gallup, Jr.) *The Next American Spirituality* and *The Saints Among Us.*

KAGAWA, TOYOHIKO (1888–1960) Japanese anti-poverty crusader. After attending Presbyterian College in Tokyo and Princeton University in the U.S., Kagawa devoted much of his life to social reforms. He organized unions among farmers and workers in shipyards and factories; established credit unions, hospitals, schools, and churches; founded an anti-war league; and lectured on Christian principles.

KANT, IMMANUEL (1724–1804) German philosopher who developed categories of consciousness and their ethical and aesthetic consequences. Kant held that morality requires a belief in God but that the nature of God is unknowable.

KANTZER, KENNETH S. (contemporary) American journalist and theologian. In 1978, while editor of *Christianity Today,* joined forces with other evangelical leaders at the first "summit" session of the International Council on Biblical Inerrancy, a group that held its final congress nine years later. Kantzer became professor of biblical and systematic theology at Trinity Divinity School in Illinois.

KELLER, HELEN (1880–1968) American lecturer who worked on behalf of the blind at home and abroad. She was deprived of sight, hearing, and the ability to speak before the age of two, yet overcame her physical handicaps and graduated *cum laude* from Radcliffe College in 1904. The author of several articles and books, she lectured in more than twenty-five countries.

KELLER, WERNER (b. 1909) German writer, a leading journalist covering archaeology and other scientific fields. His writing of *The Bible as History* in 1955 grew out of the fascination that developed as he discovered work by archaeologists and historians corroborated biblical accounts he had previously dismissed as "pious tales." Dr. Joachim Rehok collaborated with him in writing the revised 1978 edition.

KIERKEGAARD, SOREN (1813–1855) Danish philosopher and religious thinker, regarded as the father of Existentialism.

KILBY, CLYDE S. (contemporary) American professor and writer. An authority on the life and works of C. S. Lewis, Kilby is curator of the Lewis Collection at Wheaton College and is co-author of *C. S. Lewis: Images of His World.*

KNOX, JOHN (1514–1572) Scottish spokesman for the Reformation of the Church of Scotland, becoming its foremost leader and an influence for both moral and democratic principles. After Mary Tudor, a Roman Catholic, became England's queen, Knox ministered to a congregation of English exiles in Geneva. He returned to Scotland in 1559.

KNOX, RONALD (1888–1957) British author and historian who served as Roman Catholic chaplain to Oxford University from 1926 to 1939.

KNUTH, DONALD (contemporary) American computer scientist, mathematician, professor, and author. Dr. Knuth is professor emeritus of The Art of Computer Programming at Stanford University, where he became a professor in 1968. His software systems are used extensively by book publishers throughout the world. He holds honorary doctorates from 16 colleges and universities in America and from nine foreign universities.

KRAYBILL, J. NELSON (contemporary) American educator, theologian, and writer. Kraybill, a former pastor, is president of Associated Mennonite Biblical Seminary at Elkhart, Indiana. His works include *On the Pilgrims' Way* and *Imperial Cult and Commerce in John's Apocalypse.*

KREEFT, PETER (contemporary) American professor, author, and lecturer. Dr. Kreeft teaches courses in philosophy at Boston College and frequently speaks at national and international conferences. He is the author of more than 40 books including *Fundamentals of the Faith, Prayer: The Great Conversation,* and *Three Philosophies of Life.*

KRISTOF, NICHOLAS D. (contemporary) American journalist. A member of the *New York Times* staff, he has served as *Times* bureau chief in Hong Kong, Beijing, and Tokyo. Kristof and his wife, Sheryl WuDunn, also a staff member, shared a Pulitzer Prize in 1990 for the *Times* coverage of the Tiananmen Square democracy movement in China and its suppression. They are the authors of *China Wakes: The Struggle for the Soul of a Rising Power.*

KUSHNER, HAROLD (b. 1935) American rabbi of Temple Israel at Natick, Massachusetts, and author of the 1981 best-seller, *When Bad Things Happen to Good People.*

LAHAYE, TIM (contemporary) American author, minister, and lecturer Dr. LaHaye is coauthor with Jerry B. Jenkins of the best-selling "Left Behind" series of Christian novels. He formerly was pastor of a San Diego church for 25 years. He has written more than 50 nonfiction books with combined sales of some thirteen million copies. Dr. LaHaye often speaks at Bible prophecy conferences in the U.S. and Canada.

LANDRY, TOM (1924–2000) American football coach who led the Dallas Cowboys to five Super Bowl appearances, two Super Bowl titles, and twenty consecutive winning seasons. His regular season record was 270 wins, 178 losses, and six ties. Landry was active in the Fellowship for Christian Athletes.

LATHBURY, MARY ARTEMISIA (1841–1913) American writer, widely known for her songs and hymns composed especially for the religious programs at Chatauqua, New York, including "Break Thou the Bread of Life" and "Day Is Dying in the West."

LAUBACH, FRANK CHARLES (1884–1970) American Congregationalist missionary and worldwide literacy advocate. Dr. Laubach entered missionary service in the Philippine Islands in 1915. On the island of Mindanao in 1929 he began a literacy work with underprivileged people, using the approach "Each One Teach One," which became known as the Laubach Method as the movement spread to other countries.

LEE, ROBERT E. (1807–1870) American soldier, hero of the Confederacy. A West Point graduate, he served with distinction in the Mexican War. When the Civil War broke out, Lee resigned his commission and joined the Southern forces, becoming famous as he led the army to a series of victories. He finally surrendered to General Ulysses Grant after the Gettysburg battle. After the war, General Lee became president of Washington College, later named Washington and Lee University.

LEE, UMPHREY (1893–1958) American Methodist preacher, college administrator, and scholar. Lee became pastor of Highland Park Methodist Church in Dallas in 1923 and taught theology at Southern Methodist University. After two years as a dean at Vanderbilt University, he was named president of SMU in 1939, a post he held until becoming chancellor in 1954.

L'ENGLE, MADELEINE (b. 1920) American writer and leader of writing workshops. Author of more than 40 books, crossing literary genres and writing for readers of all ages. Her first book, *A Wrinkle in Time,* was published in 1962 and won the Newbery Medal, the highest honor for children's writing in America.

LEWIS, CLIVE STAPLES (1898–1963) English professor, literary critic, author, and influential Christian thinker. During his distinguished academic career teaching at Oxford and Cambridge, Lewis seized every opportunity to proclaim and defend essentials of Christianity in lectures, essays, and radio broadcasts. Besides *Mere Christianity* and other works of apologetics, Lewis wrote *The Chronicles of Narnia* and popular science-fiction allegories.

LIGHTFOOT, NEIL R. (contemporary) American educator. Dr. Lightfoot is Frank Pack Distinguished Professor of New Testament at Abilene Christian University and is the author of several books, including *Everyone's Guide to Hebrews.*

LINCOLN, ABRAHAM (1809–1864) Sixteenth president of the United States, lawyer, statesman. Lincoln preserved the Union during the American Civil War; his Emancipation Proclamation of 1863 freed all slaves in the rebellious states. Many scholars regard him as America's most religious president, citing notably his second inaugural address in 1864. Tragically, he was assassinated before he could oversee the South's reconstruction.

LIVINGSTONE, DAVID (1813–1873) Scottish missionary, physician, and explorer of African continent. Authored *Missionary Travels and Researches in South Africa,* which became a best-seller in Britain in 1857. Died during an expedition seeking the source of the Nile River, and was buried in Westminster Abbey in 1874.

LLOYD-JONES, MARTYN (1899–1981) English evangelical minister, who preached at Westminster Chapel in London from 1938 to 1968. A strong defender of biblical authority, Lloyd-Jones was the author of multi-volume commentaries on Romans and Ephesians. His other titles include *Heirs of Salvation, Authentic Christianity,* and *Why Does God Allow War?*

LOCKE, JOHN (1862–1704) English philosopher who was a lecturer at Oxford University with views that exerted great influence on American and English political thought. His most famous work is *An Essay Concerning Human Understanding,* described as an inquiry into the nature of knowledge.

LOCKYER, HERBERT (1886–1984) Scholar, author, and pastor. Popular in America, England, and Scotland, he made a lasting impact by producing an impressive number of volumes of comprehensive indexes for various biblical categories. Lockyer compiled and wrote the *All the _____ of the Bible* (titles about men, women, apostles, miracles, parables, promises, etc.) as well as *All the Teachings of Jesus.*

LONGMAN, TREMPER III (contemporary) American professor and writer. Dr. Longman is chairman of the religious studies department at Westmont College, joining its faculty in 1998 after teaching for eighteen years at Westminster Theological School. He is the author of *Reading the Bible with Heart and Mind* and other works.

LOTZ, ANNE GRAHAM (contemporary) American parachurch leader. The second of Billy and Ruth Graham's five children, Ms. Lotz is president of AnGel Ministries and an international speaker at universities, seminaries, conferences, and churches. She is the author of *The Vision of His Glory.*

LUCADO, MAX (contemporary) American preacher and writer. He is minister of a San Antonio megachurch, Oak Hills Church of Christ, and the host of a daily radio program broadcast by more than 180 stations. Lucado's many books, selling more than eighteen million copies, include *When God Whispers Your Name, Traveling Light,* and *Next Door Savior.*

LUCE, HENRY (1898–1967) American editor and publisher. The son of a Presbyterian missionary in China, Luce and a Yale classmate cofounded *Time* with the news magazine's issue of March 3, 1923. Luce became editor-in-chief of *Time* and sole head of Time Inc. in 1929, later founding *Fortune, Life, Sports Illustrated,* and other periodicals.

LUNDIN, ROGER (contemporary) American professor and writer. Lundin is professor of English at Wheaton College, and is the author of *The Culture of Interpretation* and a biography of Emily Dickinson in The Library of Religious Biography series.

LUTHER, MARTIN (1483–1546) German religious reformer and leader of the Protestant Reformation. Opposed the sale of indulgences. Luther posted his "95 theses" on the door of the Wittenberg castle church in 1517.

MACARTHUR, GEN. DOUGLAS (1880–1964) American army general commanding Allied forces in the southwest Pacific in World War II. By 1945 his forces liberated the Philippines on the way to invading Japan. He accepted the Japanese surrender in Tokyo Bay, then led the occupation forces in the reconstruction of Japan. Because of a dispute over military strategy he was relieved by President Truman of his command of United Nations forces during the Korean War, MacArthur having publicly advocated invasion of China.

MACARTHUR, JOHN (b. 1939) American pastor, author, and educator. MacArthur is president of The Master's College and Seminary. He has been a featured speaker with the radio program "Grace to You" since becoming pastor of Grace Community Church in Sun Valley, California, in 1969. Dr. MacArthur produced the *MacArthur Study Bible* and has written more than six dozen books that have been distributed worldwide.

MACARTNEY, CLARENCE EDWARD (1879–1957) American fundamentalist preacher, a Presbyterian, and author of fifty-seven books. Macartney was a popular lecturer at home and abroad.

MACAULEY, THOMAS BABBINGTON (1800–1859) English historian who initially pursued a political career before achieving fame as a distinguished writer.

MACDONALD, GEORGE (1824–1905) Scottish minister who turned novelist and poet. MacDonald's stories—reflecting his love of fantasy and his vision of Christ's righteousness—are said to have significantly influenced later writers including C. S. Lewis and J. R. R. Tolkien.

MACDONALD, JAMES (b. 1960) American minister, author, and radio broadcaster. Founding pastor of Harvest Bible Chapel in the Chicago area, MacDonald is heard daily on the *Walk in the Word* program broadcast by more than 500 stations, and also via *Lighten Up,* a one-minute radio feature syndicated to more than one thousand stations.

MARSHALL, PETER (1902–1949) American Presbyterian minister, born in Scotland. Chaplain of the U.S. Senate. Best known for several books of his sermons including *Mr. Jones, Meet the Master,* and *Joe Doe, Disciple,* published posthumously.

McCHEYNE, ROBERT MURRAY (1813–1843) Scottish minister and hymn writer. The Edinburgh native held pastorates at Larbert, near Falkirk, and at Dundee. McCheyne wielded wide influence during his short lifetime, and afterward was even more powerful through his writing. Edited by Andrew Bonar, McCheyne's *Memoirs and Remains* exceeded one hundred English editions.

McCOSH, JAMES (1811–1894) Scottish educator, a philosopher and advocate of a lively evangelical faith. McCosh taught logic and metaphysics at a Belfast university for sixteen years, then was appointed in 1868 as president of the New Jersey college which soon evolved into Princeton University.

McDOWELL, JOSH (b. 1939) American parachurch evangelist, lecturer, and author or co-author of more than seventy books, including *Evidence That Demands a Verdict* and *Beyond Belief to Convictions.* In 1964, he began his speaking ministry when he joined the Campus Crusade for Christ. Since then, he has spoken on the campuses of more than seven hundred colleges and universities worldwide.

McGAVRAN, DONALD (b. 1897) American missionary to India for three decades with the Disciples of Christ. Founded Oregon-based Institute of Church Growth in 1961, and four years later became founding dean of Fuller Theological Seminary's mission school and church growth program.

McINTOSH, DOUG (contemporary) American clergyman and author. Dr. McIntosh is senior pastor of the Cornerstone Bible Church in Lilburn, Georgia. His books include *Life's Greatest Journey* and *The War Within You.*

MEAD, FRANK S. (1898–1982) American preacher, teacher, author, and editor. An ordained Methodist minister, Mead edited *Tarbell's Teachers Guide,* a widely used Sunday school annual, for many years. His books included *Twelve Decisive Battles of Christianity* and *The Handbook of Denominations.*

MERTON, THOMAS (1915–1968) American spiritual writer and poet. He was born in Prades, France, of an American mother and a New Zealander father. A Trappist monk for twenty-seven years, Merton gave insight into his early life at the monastery in his journal published as *The Sign of Jonas,* followed by *New Seeds of Contemplation,* reflecting his devotional world and mature ecumenical outlook, and *Raids on the Unspeakable,* a book of essays and meditations.

METZGER, BRUCE M. (contemporary) American educator, writer, and linguistic expert. A Princeton Theological School professor, Metzger is the author or editor of more than 35 books. He served as general editor of the *Readers Digest Condensed Bible* and headed the translation committee for the New Revised Standard Version of the Bible.

MEYER, FREDERICK B. (1847–1929) English Baptist pastor, writer, and evangelistic speaker. On one of his twelve trips to the United States, Meyer preached one hundred times, visiting thirteen cities during a tour of 3,500 miles.

MILLER, CALVIN (b. 1936) American professor at Beeson Divinity School in Birmingham, Alabama. He is well-known as an author, poet, artist, and public speaker. Miller, who was a pastor for three decades, is the author of more than forty books including *The Singer Trilogy: The Mythic Retelling of the Story of the New Testament.* Also among his works are *The Empowered Communicator* and *Spirit, Word and Story.*

MONROE, ANN (contemporary) American journalist. A former *Wall Street Journal* staff reporter, Ms. Monroe is a contributing writer at *Mother Jones* magazine and a freelance writer for other periodicals. She is the author of *The Word: Imagining the Gospel in Modern America.*

MOODY, DWIGHT L. (1837–1899) American evangelist and urban revivalist. He quit a successful business to pursue missionary work, and in 1875 spoke to at least 1.5 million in London. Moody led a strongly evangelical Young Men's Christian Association at Chicago, where the Moody Bible Institute was later founded.

MORGAN, G. CAMPBELL (1863–1947) English expository preacher widely known in both Great Britain and North America. Morgan served twice as pastor of London's Westminster Chapel.

MUGGERIDGE, MALCOLM (1903–1990) English author, journalist, and broadcaster. He produced documentary programs for the BBC and for four years was editor of *Punch* magazine. In his *Confessions of a Twentieth Century Pilgrim,* Muggeridge recounted his journey to Christian faith in an age of disbelief. His many books include *Something Beautiful for God,* which introduced Mother Teresa to the West, and *Jesus Rediscovered.*

MULLER, GEORGE (1805–1898) English preacher and philanthropist. A native of Germany, Muller became a naturalized British subject and resolved to engage in missionary work. In 1832, after two years as minister for a congregation at Teignmouth, he moved to Bristol and devoted himself to the care of orphan children—a few at first, but eventually the number increased to 2,000. Financial support for the orphanage was voluntarily contributed, mainly resulting from wide circulation of Muller's narrative, *The Lord's Dealings With George Muller.*

MURRAY, ANDREW (1828–1917) South African pastor and author. Murray actively led congregations in farming communities until he reached the age of seventy-eight, when he began devoting full time to his manuscripts. His devotional books include *The Practice of God's Presence* and *with Christ in the School of Prayer.*

NAYLOR, JAMES BALL (1860–1945) Physician, poet, and historical novelist from Malta, Ohio.

NEWMAN, JOHN HENRY (1801–1890) English churchman, teacher, and author. Newman played a leading role in the Oxford Movement which tried to bring the Church of

England and the Roman Catholic Church closer together. In 1843, he resigned his post at St. Mary's Church in Oxford and preached his last Anglican sermon. Received into the Catholic church two years later, he became the first rector of Dublin's Catholic university. Pope Leo XIII named Newman a cardinal-deacon in 1879.

NEWTON, SIR ISAAC (1642–1727) English mathematician-physicist and author. Formulated three fundamental laws of motion, leading to the law of gravitation. He invented the methods of mathematical calculus and expanded human understanding of light and color. The *Principia,* his monumental work published in 1687, established the mathematical method by which modern scientists try to understand and explain the laws of nature.

NEWTON, JOHN (1725–1807) English sailor who became a clergyman and hymn writer. After being ordained, Newton collaborated with William Cowper on *Olney Hymns* in 1779. He wrote "Amazing Grace" and "How Sweet the Name of Jesus Sounds."

NICOLSON, ADAM (contemporary) English publisher and travel writer. Nicolson is the author of many books including *Sea Room* and *God's Secretaries.*

NOLL, MARK A. (contemporary) American educator, historian, and writer. Noll is McManis Professor of Christian Thought and professor of history at Wheaton College and has been a visiting professor at Harvard Divinity School. He has written extensively on the modern history of Christianity in North America.

NORRIS, KATHLEEN (b. 1947) American writer. A recipient of grants from the Bush and Guggenheim foundations, she is an award-winning poet and author of best-selling books including *Amazing Grace* and *The Cloister Walk.* She is unrelated to prolific novelist Kathleen Thompson Norris (1880–1960).

NUNN, SAM (b. 1938) American lawyer and legislator. After serving in the Georgia House of Representatives in 1958-72, Nunn won election to the U.S. Senate. A conservative Democrat, he was one of the Senate's most powerful members from 1972 until his retirement in 1997, particularly while serving as chairman of the Armed Services committee. In 2001 he became head of Nuclear Threat Initiative, an organization devoted to controlling the proliferation of nuclear arms. He has also taught at Georgia Tech university and has served on several corporate boards.

O'CONNOR, (MARY) FLANNERY (1925–1964), American Catholic author, who excelled at short fiction sensitive to the deep South and its cultural and religious conventions. Literary critics observe that she consistently found supernatural grace operating in the midst of degradation and horror.

OGILVIE, LLOYD (contemporary) American minister, author, and chaplain of the U.S. Senate from 1995 to 2003. Before going to Washington to become the Senate's sixty-first chaplain, Dr. Ogilvie hosted a television ministry and led Hollywood Presbyterian Church in California for more than twenty years.

OLASKY, MARVIN (contemporary) American magazine editor and university professor. Olasky, the editor of *World,* a newsmagazine written from a Christian perspective, is also an author of books of history and cultural analysis and taught journalism at the University of Texas. He has written extensively for periodicals including *National Review, The Weekly Standard, Policy Review,* and *The Wall Street Journal.* Olasky received an A.B. degree from Yale and a Ph.D. from the University of Michigan.

PACKER, JAMES INNELL (b. 1926) Canadian theology professor, lecturer, and writer. Packer was born in England and educated at Oxford, where he received a Ph.D. degree in 1954. He joined the faculty of Regent College, Vancouver, in 1979. Packer's books include *Knowing God* and *Never Beyond Hope.* He is a frequent contributor to *Christianity Today.*

PALAU, LUIS (b. 1934) American global evangelist, born in Buenos Aires and raised in England. He was hailed as the new "Billy Graham of Latin America" in 1970 when 106,000 attended his Mexico City crusade. His Luis Palau Evangelistic Association, now based in Oregon, has organized hundreds of crusades and festivals in 95 countries. Palau has proclaimed the gospel to more than twelve million in stadiums and concert halls and hundreds of millions by radio and television. He is the author of several books on spirituality and the Christian life.

PARKER, THEODORE (1810–1860) American Unitarian minister and social reformer, active in the Transcendentalist movement. Parker spent much of his ministry at Boston's 18th Congregational Church.

PARTON, DOLLY (b. 1946) American singer-songwriter, born in an impoverished mountain area of Tennessee, who rose to become a major force in country music. Successful as a recording artist and film actress, she established Dollywood as a theme park in Pigeon Forge, Tennessee, creating jobs and funding an educational foundation serving the area.

PASCAL, BLAISE (1623–1662) French mathematician, physicist, and philosopher. Developed the modern theory of probability. One of his discoveries became the basis for modern hydraulics. Later in life, while visiting his sister in a convent, Pascal began to seek God and found him in a dramatic mystical experience. Afterward, he declared that perfect knowledge comes only through Christian revelation.

PEALE, NORMAN VINCENT (1898–1993) American minister and writer noted for his buoyant faith in God and his belief in the powers of faith and positive thinking. At age thirty-four, Peale was named pastor of the Marble Collegiate Reformed Church in New York. He used radio, television, and newspapers to take his message to millions across the nation.

PETERSON, EUGENE H. (b. 1932) American evangelical minister and writer, widely known for *The Message,* his paraphrase of the Bible in contemporary English. A contributing editor at *Leadership Journal,* Peterson was pastor of Christ Our King Presbyterian Church in Bel Air, Maryland, for twenty-nine years. He has taught spiritual theology at Regent College.

PHELPS, JOSEPH (contemporary) American Baptist pastor who helped found Church of the Savior in Austin, Texas, in 1985. He was an Austin newspaper columnist for eight years. In 1997, Phelps moved to Louisville, Kentucky, as pastor of the Highland Baptist Church. He has written about open dialogue as an effective tool to avoid conflicts and confrontations.

PHELPS, WILLIAM LYON (1865–1943) American scholar, critic, and syndicated newspaper columnist. For forty-one years, Phelps was a member of the English department at Yale

University, where students voted him Yale's most inspiring professor and thronged to his classes.

PHILLIPS, J. B. (1906–1982) English writer prominent in the mid-twentieth century. His *New Testament in Modern English* was aimed at making the Bible understandable, based on his view that its meaning was inspired rather than its words. Phillips also wrote *Your God Is Too Small,* which addressed prevailing inadequate views of God, and *Ring of Truth: A Translator's Testimony.*

PIERSON, ARTHUR TAPPAN (1837–1911) American minister and writer. After leading Presbyterian churches in Waterford, N.Y., and Detroit, Pierson pastored the Bethany Tabernacle in Philadelphia from 1883 to 1889. He authored more than fifty books, and for 25 years was editor of *The Missionary Review of the World.* After his death, the Pierson Bible College in Seoul, Korea, was established in his honor.

PHILARET, METROPOLITAN OF MOSCOW (1782–1867) Russian theologian and church leader.

PINK, ARTHUR WALKINGTON (1886–1952) English clergyman who preached in the United States and Australia as well as his homeland. Pink wrote and published *Studies in the Scriptures,* a widely circulated magazine devoted to biblical exposition.

PINNOCK, CLARK (b. 1940) Canadian professor, editor, and writer. Pinnock teaches at McMaster Divinity College in Ontario. He is the author of *A Wideness in God's Mercy, Grace Unlimited, Flame of Love,* and *Unbounded Love: A New Theology for the 20th Century.* He edited *Searching for an Adequate God* and *The Openness of God.*

PIPER, JOHN (contemporary) American theologian and author. Dr. Piper has been the senior pastor of Bethlehem Baptist Church in Minneapolis since 1980. More than 250,000 volumes of his books have been sold, including *Desiring God, Future Grace,* and *The Roots of Endurance.*

POLKINGHORNE, SIR JOHN (b. 1930) English mathematical physicist and Anglican priest, a leading figure in the search for interface between science and religion. Received in

2002 the annual Templeton Prize for Progress Toward Research
or Discoveries about Spiritual Realities, the world's best-known
religion prize. In 1979, Polkinghorne resigned a prestigious post
at Cambridge University to pursue theological studies. He is the
author of *Science and Christian Belief* and *Faith, Science and
Understanding*.

POYTHRESS, VERN SHERIDEN (contemporary)
American author and polymath, professor of New Testament
Interpretation at Westminster Theological Seminary. Poythress
received a bachelor's degree from Cal Tech, later earning a Ph.D
in mathematics from Harvard and a theology doctorate from the
University of Stellenbosch in South Africa.

RAINER, THOM S. (b. 1955) American minister and
founding dean of Southern Baptist Theological Seminary's Billy
Graham School of Evangelism. He is the author of *Surprising
Insights From the Unchurched* and other books on the keys to
church growth.

RAMSAY, SIR WILLIAM M. (1851–1939) Scottish
archaeologist and biblical scholar. Professor at Oxford University
and the University of Aberdeen.

REAPSOME, JAMES (contemporary) American writer and
editor who also has pastored churches in Illinois and
Pennsylvania. Reapsome was editor of *Evangelical Missions
Quarterly* from 1964 to 1997 and *World Pulse* from 1992 to 1997,
subsequently becoming editor-at-large for both publications.
Earlier, he was managing editor of *Christianity Today* and editor
of *The Sunday School Times*. He was also chaplain and assistant
professor of religion at Malone College.

REIFF, PATRICIA H. (contemporary) American scientist
and educator. Dr. Reiff is professor and department chairman of
space physics and astronomy at Rice University, where she
received her Ph.D. degree. She has served on advisory
committees for the National Science Foundation, NASA, and
National Academy of Science, and has been Rice's representative
for the Universities Space Research Association.

RICHARD, CLIFF (b. 1940) British rock-and-roll singer
whose career was launched in 1958 when his first record, "Move
It," reached number two on the charts. Reached stardom during

the Beatles era and made public his Christian conversion at a Billy Graham crusade. During a long-lasting career in pop music, Richard gave testimony to his faith at his concerts, lent support to evangelistic campaigns, and raised more than a million pounds for the Tear Fund and other charities seeking to alleviate Third World poverty.

RICHARDSON, BOBBY (b. 1936) American professional baseball star. Richardson played second base on seven pennant-winning teams of the New York Yankees and won five consecutive Gold Glove awards (1961–1965). He was respected as a competitor and as a clean-living, God-fearing gentleman. After retiring from the Yankees in 1966, he coached college teams.

ROGERS, WILL (1879–1935) American humorist, actor, and newspaper columnist. A veteran of vaudeville, Rogers acted in many motion pictures and wrote a series of books with such titles as *The Cowboy Philosopher on Prohibition* and *The Illiterate Digest*. Beginning in 1926, he wrote a highly popular syndicated newspaper column.

ROMERO, OSCAR (1917–1980) Roman Catholic archbishop of El Salvador's capital city, San Salvador. He was cut down by a sniper's bullet while celebrating holy communion on March 24, 1980, at the Divine Providence Cancer Hospital. For three years, Archbishop Romero had regularly received threats from both the right and left wings of El Salvador during a guerilla-style civil war. Romero, an outspoken foe of social injustice, had been nominated in 1979 for the Nobel Peace Prize.

ROOSEVELT, THEODORE (1856–1919) Twenty-sixth president of the U.S. He was elected governor of New York in 1898, and became William McKinley's GOP running mate in 1900, succeeding him to the presidency when McKinley was assassinated in 1901. Afterward, "T. R." won a full elective term in 1904, but failed in his 1912 bid to return to the White House, running on the Progressive Party ticket but losing to Woodrow Wilson.

ROSS, HUGH (b. 1945) American astrophysicist. Ross, evangelical coordinator at Sierra Madre Congregational Church, is leader of the Reasons to Believe ministry. He is opposed to evolution, and uses scientific data about the history of the universe, the theory of relativity, and the biblical story of creation as apologetic tools. Books by Ross include *The Creator and the Cosmos, The Fingerprint of God,* and *The Genesis Question.*

ROSSCUP, JAMES E. (contemporary) American seminary professor and writer. He is professor of Bible exposition at The Master's Seminary, joining its faculty in 1987 after serving twenty-two years as chairman of the department of Bible exposition at Talbot Theological Seminary. He is the author of *Abiding in Christ, Commentaries for Bible Expositors,* and other theological works. An Arizona native, he also has written western novels.

ROUSSEAU, JEAN-JACQUES (1712–1778) Swiss-French philosopher and practical theorist. His autobiography was published posthumously in 1782.

RUNYON, DAMON (1880–1946) American journalist and author. Runyon joined the staff of the *New York American* after writing for newspapers in Denver and San Francisco. His popular short stories featured breezy prose about gamblers, underworld characters, cops, cab drivers, and other urban types; the stage and film musical *Guys and Dolls* was based on his story "The Idyll of Miss Sarah Brown." He coauthored with Howard Lindsay the 1935 Broadway play *A Slight Case of Murder.* His works include *Runyon a la Carte* and *Trials and Tribulations.*

RUSH, DR. BENJAMIN (1745–1813) American physician, patriot, and signer of the Declaration of Independence.

RUSKIN, JOHN (1819–1900) English writer, art critic, and scholar of widely varied interests. Ruskin took up the cause of economic and social reform as an outgrowth of his conviction that good art was created as the result of education, morality, religious faith, and good social conditions. Ruskin championed the Gothic Revival movement in architecture and decorative arts, and during the Victorian period inflenced public taste in the arts. He also influenced public opinion about economic issues and working conditions.

RUTLEDGE, FLEMING (contemporary) American preacher and author. An Episcopal parish priest for twenty-two years in New York City and its suburbs, Ms. Rutledge now is engaged in a nationwide ministry of preaching and teaching. Her collections of sermons, published as *The Bible and the New York Times* and *Help My Unbelief,* have been best sellers.

RYKEN, LELAND (contemporary) American professor and author. Dr. Ryken is professor of English at Wheaton College, where he has taught since 1968. He has written more than twenty books, including *The Bible as Literature* and *Realms of Gold: The Classics in Christian Perspective*.

RYLE, J. C. (1816–1900) English historian, author, and evangelical bishop in the Anglican communion. Ryle was Bishop of Liverpool from 1880 to 1900. His books include *Holiness, Knots Untied,* and *Lights From Old Times.*

RYRIE, CHARLES CALDWELL (b. 1925) American educator and editor, and biblical scholar. For many years he served as dean of doctoral studies and a professor at Dallas Theological School. Dr. Ryrie, editor of the *Ryrie Study Bible,* is known internationally for his writings on premillennial theology and for his collection of rare Bibles. His books include *The Bible of the Middle Way, The Grace of God,* and *Neo-Orthodoxy.*

SAFIRE, WILLIAM (b. 1929) American newspaper columnist. A speechwriter for President Richard M. Nixon, Safire joined the *New York Times* staff in 1973, becoming a widely syndicated editorial columnist. He also writes a Sunday column, "On Language," for the *New York Times Magazine.*

SAYERS, DOROTHY (1893–1957) English writer and one of the first women to receive an Oxford degree. She profited so greatly from her popular detective novels that she was able to devote her later years to her religious convictions. Ms. Sayers's radio dramatization of the life of Christ, "The Man Born to Be King," was broadcast in twelve episodes by the BBC.

SCHAEFFER, FRANCIS A. (1912–1984) American evangelical missionary, lecturer, and author. With Edith, his wife, Dr. Schaeffer founded L'Abri, an international study center and caring community in the Swiss Alps, in 1955, later adding branches in England, Sweden, the Netherlands and the United States. He was the author of 24 books including *True Spirituality, He Is There and He Is Not Silent,* and *Art and the Bible.*

SCHLESSINGER, LAURA C. (contemporary) American marriage, family, and child counselor, radio personality, and author. Dr. Schlessinger's radio talk show is syndicated to about

300 stations with twelve million listeners. She formerly taught at the University of Southern California and Pepperdine University.

SCHMIDT, DAN (contemporary) American minister and writer. The pastor of an international church near San Jose, Costa Rica, Schmidt is the author of two books, *Follow the Leader* and *Unexpected Wisdom,* along with articles for newspapers and magazines.

SCHULZ, CHARLES (1922–2000) American cartoonist, creator of *Peanuts,* internationally syndicated and one of the most successful newspaper comic strips of the twentieth century.

SEWARD, WILLIAM (1801–1872) American statesman and U.S. secretary of state who negotiated the purchase of Alaska from Russia.

SHOEMAKER, SAMUEL M. (1893–1963) American Episcopal priest. As rector of Calvary Episcopal Church in New York, Smith established the Calvary House mission and aided the founders of Alcoholics Anonymous in formulating their "Twelve Steps" program.

SHORT, ROBERT L. (contemporary) American minister, writer, and lecturer. Short has given color-slide lectures for more than three decades on the theological implications of Charles Schulz's syndicated comic strip, *Peanuts.* The author of *Short Meditations on the Bible and Peanuts,* he established Robert Short's Visual Programs in "Christianity Without Gloom or Doom."

SIDER, RONALD J. (contemporary) American seminary professor and author. Sider, the president of Evangelicals for Social Action, teaches at Eastern Baptist Theological Seminary in Philadelphia.

SMITH, CHUCK, JR. (contemporary) American pastor and author. Smith is senior pastor of Capo Beach Calvary Chapel in Capistrano Beach, California. He has written *Epiphany,* a book about Bible study; *Living Water;* and *Charisma vs. Charismania.*

SMITH, RODNEY "GIPSY" (1860–1947) English evangelist. Smith enlisted in William Booth's Christian mission as a young preacher, establishing his own gospel ministry in the mid 1880s. In later years he made about fifty trips to the United

States, conducting evangelistic services in assembly halls and churches.

SMOLTZ, JOHN (b. 1967) American professional baseball player. Smoltz, who had played for the Detroit Tigers' Eastern League farm club, was traded in 1987 to the Atlanta Braves. He became a superb big-game pitcher for the Braves, leading the National League in wins in 1996—receiving the Cy Young Award—and by the end of the Nineties had collected more post-season wins than any pitcher previously. In September 2002, Smoltz became the seventh pitcher in baseball history to record fifty saves in a season.

SPROUL, ROBERT CHARLES (b. 1939) American theologian and author of more than forty books. Dr. Sproul, a member of the Knox Seminary faculty, is the founder and chairman of Orlando-based Ligonier Ministries, a teaching ministry. Among other activities, Ligonier produces *Renewing Your Mind* as a national radio program featuring Dr. Sproul and sponsors several seminars each year.

SPURGEON, CHARLES HADDON (1834–1892) English preacher who became pastor of London's Park Street Chapel at the age of twenty, and soon was using the 7,000-seat Surrey Gardens Music Hall to accommodate the crowds. In 1861, the huge Metropolitan Tabernacle was built for his use. He established an orphanage in 1869.

STANLEY, CHARLES (b. 1933) American preacher, teacher, and author. Stanley, a former president of the Southern Baptist Convention, has been pastor of the First Baptist Church in Atlanta, Georgia, since 1971. His book titles include *The Wonderful Spirit-Filled Life, How to Listen to God,* and *Finding Peace.* He has also written the *In Touch* series of Bible studies.

STANLEY, SIR HENRY MORTON (1841–1904) Anglo-American journalist and explorer, best-known for his expedition into central Africa to find missionary David Livingstone. The expedition was financed by James Gordon Bennett, publisher of the *New York Herald.* Stanley reached Livingstone in November 1871, greeting him with the words, "Dr. Livingstone, I presume." Stanley published several books, including *Through the Dark Continent.*

STOTT, JOHN (b. 1925) English minister and evangelical leader. He is president of the London Institute for Christianity and directs the John Stott Ministries, which trains pastors in third world countries. Ordained in 1945, Stott has served in various capacities at London's All Souls Church. He was appointed Chaplain to the Queen in 1959 and designated as an Extra Chaplain in 1991. He has written several New Testament commentaries and many books, including *Basic Christianity, The Incomparable Christ,* and *The Contemporary Christian.*

STROBEL, LEE (b.1952) American pastor, journalist, and author. A self-described spiritual skeptic before 1981, Strobel became teaching pastor at Willow Creek Community Church in suburban Chicago after his conversion to Christianity. He was an award-winning newsman for thirteen years at the *Chicago Tribune* and other newspapers. He is the best-selling writer of *The Case for Christ* and other books.

SUCHET, DAVID (b.1946) British stage, television, and film actor. Suchet is known to millions for his TV-series role as Belgian detective Hercule Poirot, a popular character in Agatha Christie mysteries. Along with many other fictional roles, Suchet also appeared in theatrical performances as Sigmund Freud and Edward Teller.

SWEET, LEONARD (b. 1947) American pastor, professor, and author. President of United Theological Seminary before being appointed as the E. Stanley Jones professor of evangelism at Drew University in Madison, New Jersey. Offering a unique blend of evangelicalism and postmodern concepts, his books including *Soul Tsunami* and *Soul Salsa* have been best-sellers.

SWINDOLL, CHARLES W. "CHUCK" (b. 1934) American minister and author. The chancellor (formerly president) of Dallas Theological Seminary, Swindoll is pastor of Fellowship Bible Church and host of *Insight for Living* broadcasts. His books include the *Great Lives from God's Word* series and many best-selling titles.

TAYLOR, KENNETH NATHANIEL (b.1917) American publishing executive. In 1954, riding the commuter train to his job with Moody Press in Chicago, Taylor began paraphrasing the New Testament into modern English. After it was self-published in 1962, Billy Graham used a paperback edition as a television premium, catapulting the book to national prominence. Taylor and his wife, Margaret, founded Tyndale House Publishers, and in 1972 *Publishers Weekly* reported *The Living Bible* was America's best-selling book. Taylor served as president and chief executive of the publishing company until 1984.

TEMPLETON, SIR JOHN MARKS (contemporary) American-born British citizen John Marks Templeton, a resident of the Bahamas. Described by *The New York Times Magazine* as "dean of global investing," he sold his mutual funds company in 1992. Since retiring from the financial world, he has devoted time to philanthropic work through the Templeton Foundation. He is the author or editor of numerous books including *Worldwide Laws of Life* and *The Humble Approach*. For more than three decades he has funded the annual Templeton Prize for Progress in Religion.

TEN BOOM, CORRIE (1892–1983), Dutch evangelical author and Nazi death camp survivor. During World War II, her family became leaders in the Underground, hiding Jews who were fleeing the terrors of the Nazis. She shared her testimony about wartime experiences in *The Hiding Place*, widely distributed as a book and motion picture. In 1946 she began many years of itinerant preaching in more than 60 countries, writing many books.

THOMAS, GARY L. (contemporary) American author, speaker, and seminary teacher. His books include *Seeking the Face of God* and *Authentic Faith*. Thomas is a member of the adjunct faculty at Western Seminary in Portland, Oregon.

TORRES, SERGIO G. (contemporary) Chilean priest. Father Torres teaches systematic theology at the Alfonsin Institute of Pastoral Theology in Santiago, Chile. He has been active in the Ecumenical Association of Third World Theologians, an organization formed in 1976.

TORREY, REUBEN ARCHER "R. A." (1856–1928) American evangelist and Congregational minister. After pastoring churches in Ohio and Minnesota, Torrey headed Moody's Chicago Training Institute and led a worldwide evangelistic ministry, preaching to more than 15 million persons in eleven countries in 1902–1905. He was named dean of the Bible Institute of Los Angeles in 1912. A prolific writer, he wrote or edited forty books.

TOURNIER, PAUL (1909–1986) Swiss physician who developed ideas about helping patients through insights of psychology and Christian faith. Tournier's books about his experiences of holistic medicine in practice have sold millions of copies in 16 languages.

TOZER, AIDEN WILSON (1897–1963) American minister of the Christian and Missionary Alliance, and author of about thirty books. He was pastor of the Southside Alliance Church in Chicago for more than three decades and also led churches in Ohio, West Virginia, and Ontario.

TRIBLE, PHYLLIS (contemporary) American educator and theologian. Since 1979, Dr. Trible has taught at Union Theological Seminary, where she is the Baldwin Professor of Sacred Literature. She has also taught at Wake Forest University and the Andover Newton Theological School. She has written extensively in the fields of biblical literature and literary criticism.

TUCHMAN, BARBARA (1912–1989) American historian and author. She covered the Spanish Civil War for the magazine *The Nation* in the 1930s, and in 1963 won a Pulitzer Prize for *The Guns of August,* her history of the beginnings of World War I. Another of her many history books brought Ms. Tuchman a Pulitzer Prize in 1972.

TWAIN, MARK, pen name of Samuel Langhorne Clemens (1835–1910), a major figure in American literature. Twain worked as a printer's apprentice, a journalist, a riverboat pilot, and, briefly, a soldier. After editing a newspaper, he made writing his chief occupation and soon acquired a reputation as a humorous author and lecturer specializing in tall tales and accounts of travel and adventure. His novels (including *The Adventures of Huckleberry Finn*), stories, and essays earned him international fame and popularity.

TYNDALE, WILLIAM (c.1495–1536) English Bible translator and Protestant martyr. After being prevented by authorities in England from publishing an English version of the Bible, Tyndale arranged for printing of the New Testament in Germany. He was condemned for heresy and burned at the stake. Later, the King James Version of the Bible was based on Tyndale's translation.

UNGER, MERRILL F. (1909–1980) American evangelical theologian and Bible reference authority. Unger wrote frequently on the operation of the Holy Spirit in the dispensationalist system. *Unger's Bible Handbook* and *Unger's Concise Bible Dictionary* are popular reference works.

VAN DYKE, HENRY (1852–1933) American minister, author, educator, and diplomat. Van Dyke was appointed by President Woodrow Wilson as ambassador to both the Netherlands and Luxembourg, serving from 1913 to 1916. Earlier, he was pastor of the famed Brick Presbyterian Church in New York City and chaired the committee which produced *The Book of Common Worship of the Presbyterian Church.* For eight years, he taught English literature courses at Princeton University.

VAN LOON, HENDRIK WILLEM (1882–1944) Dutch-born American historian. Emigrating to the U.S. in 1903, he became a history teacher and journalist. In 1922, Van Loon's illustrated *Story of Mankind* was published as a best seller, followed by a number of popular histories.

VEITH, GENE EDWARD (contemporary) American teacher, editor, and author. He is professor of English at Concordia University-Wisconsin and cultural editor of *World* magazine. Veith's books include *State of the Arts, Postmodern Times,* and *A Christian Guide to Contemporary Thought.*

VISOTZKY, BURTON L. (contemporary) American rabbi and educator. Since being ordained in 1977, Rabbi Visotzky has served on the faculty of the Jewish Theological Seminary of America, holding the Nathan and Janet Appleman Chair in Midrash and Interreligious Studies. He is adjunct professor of biblical studies at Union Theological Seminary. He is the author of four scholarly books and many articles and reviews.

VOLTAIRE, pseudonym of Francois-Marie Arouet (1694–1778), a French author noted for his wit, satire, and critical capacity. With his pen, he crusaded against tyranny and cruelty in public life. Voltaire, who affirmed the deity, wrote extensively on philosophical and moral problems.

WANAMAKER, JOHN (1838–1922) American urban retailing pioneer and Christian philanthropist. In 1858, he founded Philadelphia's Bethany Sabbath School and became secretary of the city's new YMCA chapter—organizations which flourished under his continued leadership.

WARFIELD, BENJAMIN B. (1851–1921) American theologian. Warfield began his teaching career after a year's ministry at Baltimore's First Presbyterian Church, 1877–1878. As a professor of theology at Princeton Theological Seminary, he wrote for academic journals and contributed to encyclopedias and periodicals. From 1890 to 1903, Warfield edited *The Princeton Review*.

WARNER, ANNA B. (1827–1915) Four stanzas of "Jesus Loves Me" appeared in the novel *Say and Seal*, which Anna Warner and her sister, Susan, wrote in 1860. The sisters, who lived near West Point, New York, wrote more than 70 books. They taught a Sunday school Bible class in their home for West Point cadets. In 1861, William Bradbury composed the tune to which "Jesus Loves Me" has been sung ever since.

WARREN, RICHARD "RICK" (b. 1954) American evangelical pastor of Saddleback Church in California, one of America's largest and best-known congregations with 15,000 weekly attendees. Warren, who founded the church in 1982, conducts an annual Purpose-Driven Ministries conference and is regarded as a mentor by many American pastors, *Christianity Today* avers. His best-selling books include both *The Purpose-Driven Church* and *The Purpose-Driven Life*.

WASHINGTON, BOOKER T. (1856–1950) American educator, founder and first president of Tuskegee Institute in Alabama. Washington gained a national reputation from his acclaimed "Atlanta Address" in 1895 and his subsequent autobiography, *Up From Slavery*, published in 1901. He used his influence to encourage African-American self-reliance in agriculture, commerce, and industry.

WASHINGTON, GEORGE (1732–1799) American general and first president of the United States. He was commander in chief of the Continental Army during the American revolution, and permanently shaped the character of the U.S. presidency with precedents he established.

WEBSTER, DANIEL (1782–1852) American statesman and orator, noted especially for his constitutional speeches. Webster served as senator from Massachusetts from 1827 to 1841. He opposed the Mexican War and supported Henry Clay's compromise measures on slavery.

WEEMS, RENITA J. (contemporary) American writer, minister and professor. Dr. Weems, wife of a Baptist pastor, received two graduate degrees from Princeton Theological Seminary and has taught at Vanderbilt University Divinity School. She has been an ordained elder in the African Methodist Episcopal Church since 1984. Her published works include *Just a Sister Away* and *Battered Love,* the latter a volume on marriage, sex, and gender imagery in prophetic literature.

WELLS, HERBERT GEORGE (1866–1946) English novelist, journalist, popular historian, and sociologist exerting powerful influence on Britain's movement toward change in society, religious beliefs, and morals in the early years of the 20th century.

WESLEY, JOHN (1703–1791) English theologian, evangelist, and founder of Methodism. Experiencing an evangelical conversion at London in 1738, Wesley began a life-long itinerant ministry in which he preached more than 40,000 sermons and traveled widely. The Methodist movement launched by Wesley spread to the colonies in North America in the 1760s.

WHELEN, MICHAEL (contemporary) Australian Marist priest and lecturer who has served as president of the Catholic Theological Union in Sydney, Australia. He received his doctorate in philosophy at the Institute of Formative Spirituality at Pittsburgh's Duquesne University.

WHITEFIELD, GEORGE (1714–1770) English evangelist and revivalist. His tours of Great Britain and America inspired the founding of colleges.

WHITTIER, JOHN GREENLEAF (1807–1892) American writer of poetry and hymns, best known for his pastoral New England poetry. His books include *Legends of New England of Prose and Verse.* Whittier was so closely connected with his faith that he was called the "Quaker Poet."

WILBERFORCE, WILLIAM (1759–1833) English statesman, an evangelical Christian serving in the House of Commons, leader of a long, relentless, and ultimately successful battle against the African slave trade. Wilberforce also became a philanthropist who supported public literacy and social reforms.

WILDE, OSCAR (1854–1900) Irish-born novelist, dramatist, and poet. Leader of an aesthetic movement advocating "art for art's sake." Near the end of his life he was tried and found guilty of homosexual practices and served more than two years in prison. Wilde's works include *The Importance of Being Earnest* and *The Ballad of Reading Gaol.*

WILLARD, DALLAS (contemporary) American theologian, scholar, and writer. Willard is a philosophy professor at the University of California and has held visiting appointments at UCLA and the University of Colorado. He is the author of *Renovation of the Heart, The Spirit of the Disciplines,* and other books.

WILLIMON, WILLIAM H. (contemporary) American minister, lecturer, educator, and author. Dr. Willimon, formerly pastor of Methodist churches in Georgia and North Carolina, is dean of Duke University Chapel, preaching and directing the program of campus ministry. He is the author of fifty books and serves on the editorial boards of six periodicals. A Baylor University survey selected him as one of the "twelve most effective preachers in the English-speaking world."

WILLMER, WESLEY K. (contemporary) Professor and vice president of university advancement at Biola University, La Mirada, California.

WILSON, WOODROW (1856–1924) Twenty-eighth president of the U.S. Elected in 1912 after previously serving as governor of New Jersey and, earlier, president of Princeton University.

WINFREY, OPRAH (b. 1954) American television personality, actress, and entrepreneur. In college, won the title of Miss Tennessee. Began her career as a news reporter for radio station WVOL, Nashville, in 1971. Since then, while presiding over daytime talk TV and becoming the world's richest female entertainer, she has won more than two dozen Emmy awards.

WINNER, LAUREN F. (contemporary) American freelance writer, editor, and scholar. Ms. Winner, a contributing editor of *Christianity Today*, formerly was book editor for *Beliefnet*. She is the author of *Girl Meets God* and *Mudhouse Sabbath*.

WOJTYLA, KAROL JOSEF (b. 1920) Polish priest elevated in 1978 as Pope John Paul II of the Roman Catholic faith. First non-Italian pope in 456 years and history's first Slavic pope. Previously professor of moral theology, archbishop of Krakow, and cardinal. He helped pry loose the tight grip of the Soviet bloc on eastern Europe. In October 2003, Catholics from around the world gathered in Rome to celebrate his twenty-fifth anniversary, saluting the intellectual vigor and engaging personal warmth he brought to the Vatican.

WYCLIFFE, JOHN (c.1330–1384) English theologian and religious reformer. Wycliffe preached the supreme authority of the Scriptures. He led the fourteenth-century movement to see that the Scriptures were translated into English and were made available to everyone.

YANCEY, PHILIP (contemporary) American author and journalist. A featured columnist with *Christianity Today* magazine, Yancey has written twelve award-winning books, including four selling more than one million copies each. His works include *What's So Amazing About Grace?* and *Rumors of Another World: What on Earth Are We Missing?*

ZACHARIAS, RAVI (b. 1946) American global evangelist, born in Madras, India. A graduate of Ontario Bible College, Zacharias journeyed to preach in South Vietnam and Cambodia. After teaching at Alliance Theological Seminary, he established U.S.-based Ravi Zacharias International Ministries, Inc., in 1984, with offices in Canada and India as well. He has authored ten books including *The Lotus and the Cross* and *Light in the Shadow of Jihad*.

ZEVIN, BENJAMIN DAVID (1901–1984) American book publishing executive Ten years after joining Cleveland-based World Publishing Company in 1935, Zevin became president of the publicly-held corporation. By 1940, World was the nation's largest publisher of Bibles and dictionaries.

ZIGLAR, ZIG (contemporary) American motivational speaker and author. Ziglar, chairman of Dallas-based Zig Ziglar Corp., travels the world to deliver a message of hope, humor, and enthusiasm. His many books include *See You at the Top*, *Something to Smile About*, and *Confessions of a Happy Christian*.

ZUCK, ROY (b. 1928) American teacher, writer and editor. Formerly a professor at Dallas Theological Seminary, he was editor of the journal *Bibliotheca Sacra* and co-edited the *Bible Knowledge Commentary* with John Walvoord, the seminary's president. Among Dr. Zuck's other works are *Teaching as Paul Taught* and the *Dictionary of the Occult and the New Age*.

ZWINGLI, ULRICH (1484–1531) Swiss preacher and theologian. A participant in the 1529 council at Marburg, Germany, which united Protestant leaders for the first time, Zwingli was the clear-headed evangelical who became the spokesman for the Swiss Reformation movement.

A CATALOG OF SELECTED
DOVER BOOKS
IN ALL FIELDS OF INTEREST

A CATALOG OF SELECTED DOVER
BOOKS IN ALL FIELDS OF INTEREST

CONCERNING THE SPIRITUAL IN ART, Wassily Kandinsky. Pioneering work by father of abstract art. Thoughts on color theory, nature of art. Analysis of earlier masters. 12 illustrations. 80pp. of text. 5⅜ x 8½. 23411-8

ANIMALS: 1,419 Copyright-Free Illustrations of Mammals, Birds, Fish, Insects, etc., Jim Harter (ed.). Clear wood engravings present, in extremely lifelike poses, over 1,000 species of animals. One of the most extensive pictorial sourcebooks of its kind. Captions. Index. 284pp. 9 x 12. 23766-4

CELTIC ART: The Methods of Construction, George Bain. Simple geometric techniques for making Celtic interlacements, spirals, Kells-type initials, animals, humans, etc. Over 500 illustrations. 160pp. 9 x 12. (Available in U.S. only.) 22923-8

AN ATLAS OF ANATOMY FOR ARTISTS, Fritz Schider. Most thorough reference work on art anatomy in the world. Hundreds of illustrations, including selections from works by Vesalius, Leonardo, Goya, Ingres, Michelangelo, others. 593 illustrations. 192pp. 7⅛ x 10¼. 20241-0

CELTIC HAND STROKE-BY-STROKE (Irish Half-Uncial from "The Book of Kells"): An Arthur Baker Calligraphy Manual, Arthur Baker. Complete guide to creating each letter of the alphabet in distinctive Celtic manner. Covers hand position, strokes, pens, inks, paper, more. Illustrated. 48pp. 8¼ x 11. 24336-2

EASY ORIGAMI, John Montroll. Charming collection of 32 projects (hat, cup, pelican, piano, swan, many more) specially designed for the novice origami hobbyist. Clearly illustrated easy-to-follow instructions insure that even beginning papercrafters will achieve successful results. 48pp. 8¼ x 11. 27298-2

THE COMPLETE BOOK OF BIRDHOUSE CONSTRUCTION FOR WOODWORKERS, Scott D. Campbell. Detailed instructions, illustrations, tables. Also data on bird habitat and instinct patterns. Bibliography. 3 tables. 63 illustrations in 15 figures. 48pp. 5¼ x 8½. 24407-5

BLOOMINGDALE'S ILLUSTRATED 1886 CATALOG: Fashions, Dry Goods and Housewares, Bloomingdale Brothers. Famed merchants' extremely rare catalog depicting about 1,700 products: clothing, housewares, firearms, dry goods, jewelry, more. Invaluable for dating, identifying vintage items. Also, copyright-free graphics for artists, designers. Co-published with Henry Ford Museum & Greenfield Village. 160pp. 8¼ x 11. 25780-0

HISTORIC COSTUME IN PICTURES, Braun & Schneider. Over 1,450 costumed figures in clearly detailed engravings–from dawn of civilization to end of 19th century. Captions. Many folk costumes. 256pp. 8⅜ x 11¾. 23150-X

STICKLEY CRAFTSMAN FURNITURE CATALOGS, Gustav Stickley and L. & J. G. Stickley. Beautiful, functional furniture in two authentic catalogs from 1910. 594 illustrations, including 277 photos, show settles, rockers, armchairs, reclining chairs, bookcases, desks, tables. 183pp. 6½ x 9¼.   23838-5

AMERICAN LOCOMOTIVES IN HISTORIC PHOTOGRAPHS: 1858 to 1949, Ron Ziel (ed.). A rare collection of 126 meticulously detailed official photographs, called "builder portraits," of American locomotives that majestically chronicle the rise of steam locomotive power in America. Introduction. Detailed captions. xi+ 129pp. 9 x 12.   27393-8

AMERICA'S LIGHTHOUSES: An Illustrated History, Francis Ross Holland, Jr. Delightfully written, profusely illustrated fact-filled survey of over 200 American light-houses since 1716. History, anecdotes, technological advances, more. 240pp. 8 x 10¾.
25576-X

TOWARDS A NEW ARCHITECTURE, Le Corbusier. Pioneering manifesto by founder of "International School." Technical and aesthetic theories, views of industry, eco-nomics, relation of form to function, "mass-production split" and much more. Profusely illustrated. 320pp. 6⅛ x 9¼. (Available in U.S. only.)   25023-7

HOW THE OTHER HALF LIVES, Jacob Riis. Famous journalistic record, expos-ing poverty and degradation of New York slums around 1900, by major social reformer. 100 striking and influential photographs. 233pp. 10 x 7⅞.   22012-5

FRUIT KEY AND TWIG KEY TO TREES AND SHRUBS, William M. Harlow. One of the handiest and most widely used identification aids. Fruit key covers 120 deciduous and evergreen species; twig key 160 deciduous species. Easily used. Over 300 photographs. 126pp. 5⅜ x 8½.   20511-8

COMMON BIRD SONGS, Dr. Donald J. Borror. Songs of 60 most common U.S. birds: robins, sparrows, cardinals, bluejays, finches, more–arranged in order of increasing complexity. Up to 9 variations of songs of each species.
Cassette and manual 99911-4

ORCHIDS AS HOUSE PLANTS, Rebecca Tyson Northen. Grow cattleyas and many other kinds of orchids–in a window, in a case, or under artificial light. 63 illus-trations. 148pp. 5⅜ x 8½.   23261-1

MONSTER MAZES, Dave Phillips. Masterful mazes at four levels of difficulty. Avoid deadly perils and evil creatures to find magical treasures. Solutions for all 32 exciting illustrated puzzles. 48pp. 8¼ x 11.   26005-4

MOZART'S DON GIOVANNI (DOVER OPERA LIBRETTO SERIES), Wolfgang Amadeus Mozart. Introduced and translated by Ellen H. Bleiler. Standard Italian libretto, with complete English translation. Convenient and thoroughly portable–an ideal companion for reading along with a recording or the performance itself. Introduction. List of characters. Plot summary. 121pp. 5¼ x 8½.   24944-1

TECHNICAL MANUAL AND DICTIONARY OF CLASSICAL BALLET, Gail Grant. Defines, explains, comments on steps, movements, poses and concepts. 15-page pictorial section. Basic book for student, viewer. 127pp. 5⅜ x 8½.   21843-0

THE CLARINET AND CLARINET PLAYING, David Pino. Lively, comprehensive work features suggestions about technique, musicianship, and musical interpretation, as well as guidelines for teaching, making your own reeds, and preparing for public performance. Includes an intriguing look at clarinet history. "A godsend," *The Clarinet*, Journal of the International Clarinet Society. Appendixes. 7 illus. 320pp. $5\frac{3}{8}$ x $8\frac{1}{2}$. 40270-3

HOLLYWOOD GLAMOR PORTRAITS, John Kobal (ed.). 145 photos from 1926-49. Harlow, Gable, Bogart, Bacall; 94 stars in all. Full background on photographers, technical aspects. 160pp. $8\frac{3}{8}$ x $11\frac{1}{4}$. 23352-9

THE ANNOTATED CASEY AT THE BAT: A Collection of Ballads about the Mighty Casey/Third, Revised Edition, Martin Gardner (ed.). Amusing sequels and parodies of one of America's best-loved poems: Casey's Revenge, Why Casey Whiffed, Casey's Sister at the Bat, others. 256pp. $5\frac{3}{8}$ x $8\frac{1}{2}$. 28598-7

THE RAVEN AND OTHER FAVORITE POEMS, Edgar Allan Poe. Over 40 of the author's most memorable poems: "The Bells," "Ulalume," "Israfel," "To Helen," "The Conqueror Worm," "Eldorado," "Annabel Lee," many more. Alphabetic lists of titles and first lines. 64pp. $5\frac{3}{16}$ x $8\frac{1}{4}$. 26685-0

PERSONAL MEMOIRS OF U. S. GRANT, Ulysses Simpson Grant. Intelligent, deeply moving firsthand account of Civil War campaigns, considered by many the finest military memoirs ever written. Includes letters, historic photographs, maps and more. 528pp. $6\frac{1}{8}$ x $9\frac{1}{4}$. 28587-1

ANCIENT EGYPTIAN MATERIALS AND INDUSTRIES, A. Lucas and J. Harris. Fascinating, comprehensive, thoroughly documented text describes this ancient civilization's vast resources and the processes that incorporated them in daily life, including the use of animal products, building materials, cosmetics, perfumes and incense, fibers, glazed ware, glass and its manufacture, materials used in the mummification process, and much more. 544pp. $6\frac{1}{8}$ x $9\frac{1}{4}$. (Available in U.S. only.) 40446-3

RUSSIAN STORIES/RUSSKIE RASSKAZY: A Dual-Language Book, edited by Gleb Struve. Twelve tales by such masters as Chekhov, Tolstoy, Dostoevsky, Pushkin, others. Excellent word-for-word English translations on facing pages, plus teaching and study aids, Russian/English vocabulary, biographical/critical introductions, more. 416pp. $5\frac{3}{8}$ x $8\frac{1}{2}$. 26244-8

PHILADELPHIA THEN AND NOW: 60 Sites Photographed in the Past and Present, Kenneth Finkel and Susan Oyama. Rare photographs of City Hall, Logan Square, Independence Hall, Betsy Ross House, other landmarks juxtaposed with contemporary views. Captures changing face of historic city. Introduction. Captions. 128pp. $8\frac{1}{4}$ x 11. 25790-8

AIA ARCHITECTURAL GUIDE TO NASSAU AND SUFFOLK COUNTIES, LONG ISLAND, The American Institute of Architects, Long Island Chapter, and the Society for the Preservation of Long Island Antiquities. Comprehensive, well-researched and generously illustrated volume brings to life over three centuries of Long Island's great architectural heritage. More than 240 photographs with authoritative, extensively detailed captions. 176pp. $8\frac{1}{4}$ x 11. 26946-9

NORTH AMERICAN INDIAN LIFE: Customs and Traditions of 23 Tribes, Elsie Clews Parsons (ed.). 27 fictionalized essays by noted anthropologists examine religion, customs, government, additional facets of life among the Winnebago, Crow, Zuni, Eskimo, other tribes. 480pp. $6\frac{1}{8}$ x $9\frac{1}{4}$. 27377-6

FRANK LLOYD WRIGHT'S DANA HOUSE, Donald Hoffmann. Pictorial essay of residential masterpiece with over 160 interior and exterior photos, plans, elevations, sketches and studies. 128pp. 9¼ x 10¾.   29120-0

THE MALE AND FEMALE FIGURE IN MOTION: 60 Classic Photographic Sequences, Eadweard Muybridge. 60 true-action photographs of men and women walking, running, climbing, bending, turning, etc., reproduced from rare 19th-century masterpiece. vi + 121pp. 9 x 12.   24745-7

1001 QUESTIONS ANSWERED ABOUT THE SEASHORE, N. J. Berrill and Jacquelyn Berrill. Queries answered about dolphins, sea snails, sponges, starfish, fishes, shore birds, many others. Covers appearance, breeding, growth, feeding, much more. 305pp. 5¼ x 8¼.   23366-9

ATTRACTING BIRDS TO YOUR YARD, William J. Weber. Easy-to-follow guide offers advice on how to attract the greatest diversity of birds: birdhouses, feeders, water and waterers, much more. 96pp. 5³⁄₁₆ x 8¼.   28927-3

MEDICINAL AND OTHER USES OF NORTH AMERICAN PLANTS: A Historical Survey with Special Reference to the Eastern Indian Tribes, Charlotte Erichsen-Brown. Chronological historical citations document 500 years of usage of plants, trees, shrubs native to eastern Canada, northeastern U.S. Also complete identifying information. 343 illustrations. 544pp. 6½ x 9¼.   25951-X

STORYBOOK MAZES, Dave Phillips. 23 stories and mazes on two-page spreads: Wizard of Oz, Treasure Island, Robin Hood, etc. Solutions. 64pp. 8¼ x 11. 23628-5

AMERICAN NEGRO SONGS: 230 Folk Songs and Spirituals, Religious and Secular, John W. Work. This authoritative study traces the African influences of songs sung and played by black Americans at work, in church, and as entertainment. The author discusses the lyric significance of such songs as "Swing Low, Sweet Chariot," "John Henry," and others and offers the words and music for 230 songs. Bibliography. Index of Song Titles. 272pp. 6½ x 9¼.   40271-1

MOVIE-STAR PORTRAITS OF THE FORTIES, John Kobal (ed.). 163 glamor, studio photos of 106 stars of the 1940s: Rita Hayworth, Ava Gardner, Marlon Brando, Clark Gable, many more. 176pp. 8⅜ x 11¼.   23546-7

BENCHLEY LOST AND FOUND, Robert Benchley. Finest humor from early 30s, about pet peeves, child psychologists, post office and others. Mostly unavailable elsewhere. 73 illustrations by Peter Arno and others. 183pp. 5⅜ x 8½.   22410-4

YEKL and THE IMPORTED BRIDEGROOM AND OTHER STORIES OF YIDDISH NEW YORK, Abraham Cahan. Film Hester Street based on *Yekl* (1896). Novel, other stories among first about Jewish immigrants on N.Y.'s East Side. 240pp. 5⅜ x 8½.   22427-9

SELECTED POEMS, Walt Whitman. Generous sampling from *Leaves of Grass*. Twenty-four poems include "I Hear America Singing," "Song of the Open Road," "I Sing the Body Electric," "When Lilacs Last in the Dooryard Bloom'd," "O Captain! My Captain!"—all reprinted from an authoritative edition. Lists of titles and first lines. 128pp. 5³⁄₁₆ x 8¼.   26878-0

THE BEST TALES OF HOFFMANN, E. T. A. Hoffmann. 10 of Hoffmann's most important stories: "Nutcracker and the King of Mice," "The Golden Flowerpot," etc. 458pp. 5⅜ x 8½. 21793-0

FROM FETISH TO GOD IN ANCIENT EGYPT, E. A. Wallis Budge. Rich detailed survey of Egyptian conception of "God" and gods, magic, cult of animals, Osiris, more. Also, superb English translations of hymns and legends. 240 illustrations. 545pp. 5⅜ x 8½. 25803-3

FRENCH STORIES/CONTES FRANÇAIS: A Dual-Language Book, Wallace Fowlie. Ten stories by French masters, Voltaire to Camus: "Micromegas" by Voltaire; "The Atheist's Mass" by Balzac; "Minuet" by de Maupassant; "The Guest" by Camus, six more. Excellent English translations on facing pages. Also French-English vocabulary list, exercises, more. 352pp. 5⅜ x 8½. 26443-2

CHICAGO AT THE TURN OF THE CENTURY IN PHOTOGRAPHS: 122 Historic Views from the Collections of the Chicago Historical Society, Larry A. Viskochil. Rare large-format prints offer detailed views of City Hall, State Street, the Loop, Hull House, Union Station, many other landmarks, circa 1904-1913. Introduction. Captions. Maps. 144pp. 9⅜ x 12¼. 24656-6

OLD BROOKLYN IN EARLY PHOTOGRAPHS, 1865-1929, William Lee Younger. Luna Park, Gravesend race track, construction of Grand Army Plaza, moving of Hotel Brighton, etc. 157 previously unpublished photographs. 165pp. 8⅞ x 11¾. 23587-4

THE MYTHS OF THE NORTH AMERICAN INDIANS, Lewis Spence. Rich anthology of the myths and legends of the Algonquins, Iroquois, Pawnees and Sioux, prefaced by an extensive historical and ethnological commentary. 36 illustrations. 480pp. 5⅜ x 8½. 25967-6

AN ENCYCLOPEDIA OF BATTLES: Accounts of Over 1,560 Battles from 1479 B.C. to the Present, David Eggenberger. Essential details of every major battle in recorded history from the first battle of Megiddo in 1479 B.C. to Grenada in 1984. List of Battle Maps. New Appendix covering the years 1967-1984. Index. 99 illustrations. 544pp. 6½ x 9¼. 24913-1

SAILING ALONE AROUND THE WORLD, Captain Joshua Slocum. First man to sail around the world, alone, in small boat. One of great feats of seamanship told in delightful manner. 67 illustrations. 294pp. 5⅜ x 8½. 20326-3

ANARCHISM AND OTHER ESSAYS, Emma Goldman. Powerful, penetrating, prophetic essays on direct action, role of minorities, prison reform, puritan hypocrisy, violence, etc. 271pp. 5⅜ x 8½. 22484-8

MYTHS OF THE HINDUS AND BUDDHISTS, Ananda K. Coomaraswamy and Sister Nivedita. Great stories of the epics; deeds of Krishna, Shiva, taken from puranas, Vedas, folk tales; etc. 32 illustrations. 400pp. 5⅜ x 8½. 21759-0

THE TRAUMA OF BIRTH, Otto Rank. Rank's controversial thesis that anxiety neurosis is caused by profound psychological trauma which occurs at birth. 256pp. 5⅜ x 8½. 27974-X

A THEOLOGICO-POLITICAL TREATISE, Benedict Spinoza. Also contains unfinished Political Treatise. Great classic on religious liberty, theory of government on common consent. R. Elwes translation. Total of 421pp. 5⅜ x 8½. 20249-6

MY BONDAGE AND MY FREEDOM, Frederick Douglass. Born a slave, Douglass became outspoken force in antislavery movement. The best of Douglass' autobiographies. Graphic description of slave life. 464pp. 5⅜ x 8½.   22457-0

FOLLOWING THE EQUATOR: A Journey Around the World, Mark Twain. Fascinating humorous account of 1897 voyage to Hawaii, Australia, India, New Zealand, etc. Ironic, bemused reports on peoples, customs, climate, flora and fauna, politics, much more. 197 illustrations. 720pp. 5⅜ x 8½.   26113-1

THE PEOPLE CALLED SHAKERS, Edward D. Andrews. Definitive study of Shakers: origins, beliefs, practices, dances, social organization, furniture and crafts, etc. 33 illustrations. 351pp. 5⅜ x 8½.   21081-2

THE MYTHS OF GREECE AND ROME, H. A. Guerber. A classic of mythology, generously illustrated, long prized for its simple, graphic, accurate retelling of the principal myths of Greece and Rome, and for its commentary on their origins and significance. With 64 illustrations by Michelangelo, Raphael, Titian, Rubens, Canova, Bernini and others. 480pp. 5⅜ x 8½.   27584-1

PSYCHOLOGY OF MUSIC, Carl E. Seashore. Classic work discusses music as a medium from psychological viewpoint. Clear treatment of physical acoustics, auditory apparatus, sound perception, development of musical skills, nature of musical feeling, host of other topics. 88 figures. 408pp. 5⅜ x 8½.   21851-1

THE PHILOSOPHY OF HISTORY, Georg W. Hegel. Great classic of Western thought develops concept that history is not chance but rational process, the evolution of freedom. 457pp. 5⅜ x 8½.   20112-0

THE BOOK OF TEA, Kakuzo Okakura. Minor classic of the Orient: entertaining, charming explanation, interpretation of traditional Japanese culture in terms of tea ceremony. 94pp. 5⅜ x 8½.   20070-1

LIFE IN ANCIENT EGYPT, Adolf Erman. Fullest, most thorough, detailed older account with much not in more recent books, domestic life, religion, magic, medicine, commerce, much more. Many illustrations reproduce tomb paintings, carvings, hieroglyphs, etc. 597pp. 5⅜ x 8½.   22632-8

SUNDIALS, Their Theory and Construction, Albert Waugh. Far and away the best, most thorough coverage of ideas, mathematics concerned, types, construction, adjusting anywhere. Simple, nontechnical treatment allows even children to build several of these dials. Over 100 illustrations. 230pp. 5⅜ x 8½.   22947-5

THEORETICAL HYDRODYNAMICS, L. M. Milne-Thomson. Classic exposition of the mathematical theory of fluid motion, applicable to both hydrodynamics and aerodynamics. Over 600 exercises. 768pp. 6⅛ x 9¼.   68970-0

SONGS OF EXPERIENCE: Facsimile Reproduction with 26 Plates in Full Color, William Blake. 26 full-color plates from a rare 1826 edition. Includes "The Tyger," "London," "Holy Thursday," and other poems. Printed text of poems. 48pp. 5¼ x 7.
        24636-1

OLD-TIME VIGNETTES IN FULL COLOR, Carol Belanger Grafton (ed.). Over 390 charming, often sentimental illustrations, selected from archives of Victorian graphics—pretty women posing, children playing, food, flowers, kittens and puppies, smiling cherubs, birds and butterflies, much more. All copyright-free. 48pp. 9¼ x 12¼.
        27269-9

PERSPECTIVE FOR ARTISTS, Rex Vicat Cole. Depth, perspective of sky and sea, shadows, much more, not usually covered. 391 diagrams, 81 reproductions of drawings and paintings. 279pp. 5⅜ x 8½. 22487-2

DRAWING THE LIVING FIGURE, Joseph Sheppard. Innovative approach to artistic anatomy focuses on specifics of surface anatomy, rather than muscles and bones. Over 170 drawings of live models in front, back and side views, and in widely varying poses. Accompanying diagrams. 177 illustrations. Introduction. Index. 144pp. 8⅜ x11¼. 26723-7

GOTHIC AND OLD ENGLISH ALPHABETS: 100 Complete Fonts, Dan X. Solo. Add power, elegance to posters, signs, other graphics with 100 stunning copyright-free alphabets: Blackstone, Dolbey, Germania, 97 more–including many lower-case, numerals, punctuation marks. 104pp. 8⅛ x 11. 24695-7

HOW TO DO BEADWORK, Mary White. Fundamental book on craft from simple projects to five-bead chains and woven works. 106 illustrations. 142pp. 5⅜ x 8. 20697-1

THE BOOK OF WOOD CARVING, Charles Marshall Sayers. Finest book for beginners discusses fundamentals and offers 34 designs. "Absolutely first rate . . . well thought out and well executed."–E. J. Tangerman. 118pp. 7¾ x 10⅝. 23654-4

ILLUSTRATED CATALOG OF CIVIL WAR MILITARY GOODS: Union Army Weapons, Insignia, Uniform Accessories, and Other Equipment, Schuyler, Hartley, and Graham. Rare, profusely illustrated 1846 catalog includes Union Army uniform and dress regulations, arms and ammunition, coats, insignia, flags, swords, rifles, etc. 226 illustrations. 160pp. 9 x 12. 24939-5

WOMEN'S FASHIONS OF THE EARLY 1900s: An Unabridged Republication of "New York Fashions, 1909," National Cloak & Suit Co. Rare catalog of mail-order fashions documents women's and children's clothing styles shortly after the turn of the century. Captions offer full descriptions, prices. Invaluable resource for fashion, costume historians. Approximately 725 illustrations. 128pp. 8⅜ x 11¼. 27276-1

THE 1912 AND 1915 GUSTAV STICKLEY FURNITURE CATALOGS, Gustav Stickley. With over 200 detailed illustrations and descriptions, these two catalogs are essential reading and reference materials and identification guides for Stickley furniture. Captions cite materials, dimensions and prices. 112pp. 6½ x 9¼. 26676-1

EARLY AMERICAN LOCOMOTIVES, John H. White, Jr. Finest locomotive engravings from early 19th century: historical (1804–74), main-line (after 1870), special, foreign, etc. 147 plates. 142pp. 11⅜ x 8¼. 22772-3

THE TALL SHIPS OF TODAY IN PHOTOGRAPHS, Frank O. Braynard. Lavishly illustrated tribute to nearly 100 majestic contemporary sailing vessels: Amerigo Vespucci, Clearwater, Constitution, Eagle, Mayflower, Sea Cloud, Victory, many more. Authoritative captions provide statistics, background on each ship. 190 black-and-white photographs and illustrations. Introduction. 128pp. 8⅞ x 11¾. 27163-3

LITTLE BOOK OF EARLY AMERICAN CRAFTS AND TRADES, Peter Stockham (ed.). 1807 children's book explains crafts and trades: baker, hatter, cooper, potter, and many others. 23 copperplate illustrations. 140pp. 4⅝ x 6.   23336-7

VICTORIAN FASHIONS AND COSTUMES FROM HARPER'S BAZAR, 1867–1898, Stella Blum (ed.). Day costumes, evening wear, sports clothes, shoes, hats, other accessories in over 1,000 detailed engravings. 320pp. 9⅜ x 12¼.   22990-4

GUSTAV STICKLEY, THE CRAFTSMAN, Mary Ann Smith. Superb study surveys broad scope of Stickley's achievement, especially in architecture. Design philosophy, rise and fall of the Craftsman empire, descriptions and floor plans for many Craftsman houses, more. 86 black-and-white halftones. 31 line illustrations. Introduction 208pp. 6½ x 9¼.   27210-9

THE LONG ISLAND RAIL ROAD IN EARLY PHOTOGRAPHS, Ron Ziel. Over 220 rare photos, informative text document origin (1844) and development of rail service on Long Island. Vintage views of early trains, locomotives, stations, passengers, crews, much more. Captions. 8⅞ x 11¾.   26301-0

VOYAGE OF THE LIBERDADE, Joshua Slocum. Great 19th-century mariner's thrilling, first-hand account of the wreck of his ship off South America, the 35-foot boat he built from the wreckage, and its remarkable voyage home. 128pp. 5⅜ x 8½.
40022-0

TEN BOOKS ON ARCHITECTURE, Vitruvius. The most important book ever written on architecture. Early Roman aesthetics, technology, classical orders, site selection, all other aspects. Morgan translation. 331pp. 5⅜ x 8½.   20645-9

THE HUMAN FIGURE IN MOTION, Eadweard Muybridge. More than 4,500 stopped-action photos, in action series, showing undraped men, women, children jumping, lying down, throwing, sitting, wrestling, carrying, etc. 390pp. 7⅞ x 10⅝.
20204-6 Clothbd.

TREES OF THE EASTERN AND CENTRAL UNITED STATES AND CANADA, William M. Harlow. Best one-volume guide to 140 trees. Full descriptions, woodlore, range, etc. Over 600 illustrations. Handy size. 288pp. 4½ x 6⅜.   20395-6

SONGS OF WESTERN BIRDS, Dr. Donald J. Borror. Complete song and call repertoire of 60 western species, including flycatchers, juncoes, cactus wrens, many more—includes fully illustrated booklet.   Cassette and manual 99913-0

GROWING AND USING HERBS AND SPICES, Milo Miloradovich. Versatile handbook provides all the information needed for cultivation and use of all the herbs and spices available in North America. 4 illustrations. Index. Glossary. 236pp. 5⅜ x 8½.
25058-X

BIG BOOK OF MAZES AND LABYRINTHS, Walter Shepherd. 50 mazes and labyrinths in all—classical, solid, ripple, and more—in one great volume. Perfect inexpensive puzzler for clever youngsters. Full solutions. 112pp. 8⅛ x 11.   22951-3

CATALOG OF DOVER BOOKS

PIANO TUNING, J. Cree Fischer. Clearest, best book for beginner, amateur. Simple repairs, raising dropped notes, tuning by easy method of flattened fifths. No previous skills needed. 4 illustrations. 201pp. 5⅜ x 8½.   23267-0

HINTS TO SINGERS, Lillian Nordica. Selecting the right teacher, developing confidence, overcoming stage fright, and many other important skills receive thoughtful discussion in this indispensible guide, written by a world-famous diva of four decades' experience. 96pp. 5⅜ x 8½.   40094-8

THE COMPLETE NONSENSE OF EDWARD LEAR, Edward Lear. All nonsense limericks, zany alphabets, Owl and Pussycat, songs, nonsense botany, etc., illustrated by Lear. Total of 320pp. 5⅜ x 8½. (Available in U.S. only.)   20167-8

VICTORIAN PARLOUR POETRY: An Annotated Anthology, Michael R. Turner. 117 gems by Longfellow, Tennyson, Browning, many lesser-known poets. "The Village Blacksmith," "Curfew Must Not Ring Tonight," "Only a Baby Small," dozens more, often difficult to find elsewhere. Index of poets, titles, first lines. xxiii + 325pp. 5⅜ x 8¼.   27044-0

DUBLINERS, James Joyce. Fifteen stories offer vivid, tightly focused observations of the lives of Dublin's poorer classes. At least one, "The Dead," is considered a masterpiece. Reprinted complete and unabridged from standard edition. 160pp. 5³⁄₁₆ x 8¼.   26870-5

GREAT WEIRD TALES: 14 Stories by Lovecraft, Blackwood, Machen and Others, S. T. Joshi (ed.). 14 spellbinding tales, including "The Sin Eater," by Fiona McLeod, "The Eye Above the Mantel," by Frank Belknap Long, as well as renowned works by R. H. Barlow, Lord Dunsany, Arthur Machen, W. C. Morrow and eight other masters of the genre. 256pp. 5⅜ x 8½. (Available in U.S. only.)   40436-6

THE BOOK OF THE SACRED MAGIC OF ABRAMELIN THE MAGE, translated by S. MacGregor Mathers. Medieval manuscript of ceremonial magic. Basic document in Aleister Crowley, Golden Dawn groups. 268pp. 5⅜ x 8½.   23211-5

NEW RUSSIAN-ENGLISH AND ENGLISH-RUSSIAN DICTIONARY, M. A. O'Brien. This is a remarkably handy Russian dictionary, containing a surprising amount of information, including over 70,000 entries. 366pp. 4½ x 6⅛.   20208-9

HISTORIC HOMES OF THE AMERICAN PRESIDENTS, Second, Revised Edition, Irvin Haas. A traveler's guide to American Presidential homes, most open to the public, depicting and describing homes occupied by every American President from George Washington to George Bush. With visiting hours, admission charges, travel routes. 175 photographs. Index. 160pp. 8¼ x 11.   26751-2

NEW YORK IN THE FORTIES, Andreas Feininger. 162 brilliant photographs by the well-known photographer, formerly with *Life* magazine. Commuters, shoppers, Times Square at night, much else from city at its peak. Captions by John von Hartz. 181pp. 9¼ x 10¾.   23585-8

INDIAN SIGN LANGUAGE, William Tomkins. Over 525 signs developed by Sioux and other tribes. Written instructions and diagrams. Also 290 pictographs. 111pp. 6⅛ x 9¼.   22029-X

ANATOMY: A Complete Guide for Artists, Joseph Sheppard. A master of figure drawing shows artists how to render human anatomy convincingly. Over 460 illustrations. 224pp. 8⅜ x 11¼. 27279-6

MEDIEVAL CALLIGRAPHY: Its History and Technique, Marc Drogin. Spirited history, comprehensive instruction manual covers 13 styles (ca. 4th century through 15th). Excellent photographs; directions for duplicating medieval techniques with modern tools. 224pp. 8⅜ x 11¼. 26142-5

DRIED FLOWERS: How to Prepare Them, Sarah Whitlock and Martha Rankin. Complete instructions on how to use silica gel, meal and borax, perlite aggregate, sand and borax, glycerine and water to create attractive permanent flower arrangements. 12 illustrations. 32pp. 5⅜ x 8½. 21802-3

EASY-TO-MAKE BIRD FEEDERS FOR WOODWORKERS, Scott D. Campbell. Detailed, simple-to-use guide for designing, constructing, caring for and using feeders. Text, illustrations for 12 classic and contemporary designs. 96pp. 5⅜ x 8½. 25847-5

SCOTTISH WONDER TALES FROM MYTH AND LEGEND, Donald A. Mackenzie. 16 lively tales tell of giants rumbling down mountainsides, of a magic wand that turns stone pillars into warriors, of gods and goddesses, evil hags, powerful forces and more. 240pp. 5⅜ x 8½. 29677-6

THE HISTORY OF UNDERCLOTHES, C. Willett Cunnington and Phyllis Cunnington. Fascinating, well-documented survey covering six centuries of English undergarments, enhanced with over 100 illustrations: 12th-century laced-up bodice, footed long drawers (1795), 19th-century bustles, 19th-century corsets for men, Victorian "bust improvers," much more. 272pp. 5⅝ x 8¼. 27124-2

ARTS AND CRAFTS FURNITURE: The Complete Brooks Catalog of 1912, Brooks Manufacturing Co. Photos and detailed descriptions of more than 150 now very collectible furniture designs from the Arts and Crafts movement depict davenports, settees, buffets, desks, tables, chairs, bedsteads, dressers and more, all built of solid, quarter-sawed oak. Invaluable for students and enthusiasts of antiques, Americana and the decorative arts. 80pp. 6½ x 9¼. 27471-3

WILBUR AND ORVILLE: A Biography of the Wright Brothers, Fred Howard. Definitive, crisply written study tells the full story of the brothers' lives and work. A vividly written biography, unparalleled in scope and color, that also captures the spirit of an extraordinary era. 560pp. 6⅛ x 9¼. 40297-5

THE ARTS OF THE SAILOR: Knotting, Splicing and Ropework, Hervey Garrett Smith. Indispensable shipboard reference covers tools, basic knots and useful hitches; handsewing and canvas work, more. Over 100 illustrations. Delightful reading for sea lovers. 256pp. 5⅜ x 8½. 26440-8

FRANK LLOYD WRIGHT'S FALLINGWATER: The House and Its History, Second, Revised Edition, Donald Hoffmann. A total revision–both in text and illustrations–of the standard document on Fallingwater, the boldest, most personal architectural statement of Wright's mature years, updated with valuable new material from the recently opened Frank Lloyd Wright Archives. "Fascinating"–*The New York Times*. 116 illustrations. 128pp. 9¼ x 10¾. 27430-6

CATALOG OF DOVER BOOKS

PHOTOGRAPHIC SKETCHBOOK OF THE CIVIL WAR, Alexander Gardner. 100 photos taken on field during the Civil War. Famous shots of Manassas Harper's Ferry, Lincoln, Richmond, slave pens, etc. 244pp. 10⅝ x 8¼. 22731-6

FIVE ACRES AND INDEPENDENCE, Maurice G. Kains. Great back-to-the-land classic explains basics of self-sufficient farming. The one book to get. 95 illustrations. 397pp. 5⅜ x 8½. 20974-1

SONGS OF EASTERN BIRDS, Dr. Donald J. Borror. Songs and calls of 60 species most common to eastern U.S.: warblers, woodpeckers, flycatchers, thrushes, larks, many more in high-quality recording. Cassette and manual 99912-2

A MODERN HERBAL, Margaret Grieve. Much the fullest, most exact, most useful compilation of herbal material. Gigantic alphabetical encyclopedia, from aconite to zedoary, gives botanical information, medical properties, folklore, economic uses, much else. Indispensable to serious reader. 161 illustrations. 888pp. 6½ x 9¼. 2-vol. set. (Available in U.S. only.) Vol. I: 22798-7
Vol. II: 22799-5

HIDDEN TREASURE MAZE BOOK, Dave Phillips. Solve 34 challenging mazes accompanied by heroic tales of adventure. Evil dragons, people-eating plants, blood-thirsty giants, many more dangerous adversaries lurk at every twist and turn. 34 mazes, stories, solutions. 48pp. 8¼ x 11. 24566-7

LETTERS OF W. A. MOZART, Wolfgang A. Mozart. Remarkable letters show bawdy wit, humor, imagination, musical insights, contemporary musical world; includes some letters from Leopold Mozart. 276pp. 5⅜ x 8½. 22859-2

BASIC PRINCIPLES OF CLASSICAL BALLET, Agrippina Vaganova. Great Russian theoretician, teacher explains methods for teaching classical ballet. 118 illustrations. 175pp. 5⅜ x 8½. 22036-2

THE JUMPING FROG, Mark Twain. Revenge edition. The original story of The Celebrated Jumping Frog of Calaveras County, a hapless French translation, and Twain's hilarious "retranslation" from the French. 12 illustrations. 66pp. 5⅜ x 8½. 22686-7

BEST REMEMBERED POEMS, Martin Gardner (ed.). The 126 poems in this superb collection of 19th- and 20th-century British and American verse range from Shelley's "To a Skylark" to the impassioned "Renascence" of Edna St. Vincent Millay and to Edward Lear's whimsical "The Owl and the Pussycat." 224pp. 5⅜ x 8½. 27165-X

COMPLETE SONNETS, William Shakespeare. Over 150 exquisite poems deal with love, friendship, the tyranny of time, beauty's evanescence, death and other themes in language of remarkable power, precision and beauty. Glossary of archaic terms. 80pp. 5³⁄₁₆ x 8¼. 26686-9

THE BATTLES THAT CHANGED HISTORY, Fletcher Pratt. Eminent historian profiles 16 crucial conflicts, ancient to modern, that changed the course of civilization. 352pp. 5⅜ x 8½. 41129-X

THE WIT AND HUMOR OF OSCAR WILDE, Alvin Redman (ed.). More than 1,000 ripostes, paradoxes, wisecracks: Work is the curse of the drinking classes; I can resist everything except temptation; etc. 258pp. 5⅜ x 8½. 20602-5

SHAKESPEARE LEXICON AND QUOTATION DICTIONARY, Alexander Schmidt. Full definitions, locations, shades of meaning in every word in plays and poems. More than 50,000 exact quotations. 1,485pp. 6½ x 9¼. 2-vol. set.
Vol. 1: 22726-X
Vol. 2: 22727-8

SELECTED POEMS, Emily Dickinson. Over 100 best-known, best-loved poems by one of America's foremost poets, reprinted from authoritative early editions. No comparable edition at this price. Index of first lines. 64pp. 5³⁄₁₆ x 8¼. 26466-1

THE INSIDIOUS DR. FU-MANCHU, Sax Rohmer. The first of the popular mystery series introduces a pair of English detectives to their archnemesis, the diabolical Dr. Fu-Manchu. Flavorful atmosphere, fast-paced action, and colorful characters enliven this classic of the genre. 208pp. 5³⁄₁₆ x 8¼. 29898-1

THE MALLEUS MALEFICARUM OF KRAMER AND SPRENGER, translated by Montague Summers. Full text of most important witchhunter's "bible," used by both Catholics and Protestants. 278pp. 6⅝ x 10. 22802-9

SPANISH STORIES/CUENTOS ESPAÑOLES: A Dual-Language Book, Angel Flores (ed.). Unique format offers 13 great stories in Spanish by Cervantes, Borges, others. Faithful English translations on facing pages. 352pp. 5⅜ x 8½. 25399-6

GARDEN CITY, LONG ISLAND, IN EARLY PHOTOGRAPHS, 1869–1919, Mildred H. Smith. Handsome treasury of 118 vintage pictures, accompanied by carefully researched captions, document the Garden City Hotel fire (1899), the Vanderbilt Cup Race (1908), the first airmail flight departing from the Nassau Boulevard Aerodrome (1911), and much more. 96pp. 8⅞ x 11¾. 40669-5

OLD QUEENS, N.Y., IN EARLY PHOTOGRAPHS, Vincent F. Seyfried and William Asadorian. Over 160 rare photographs of Maspeth, Jamaica, Jackson Heights, and other areas. Vintage views of DeWitt Clinton mansion, 1939 World's Fair and more. Captions. 192pp. 8⅞ x 11. 26358-4

CAPTURED BY THE INDIANS: 15 Firsthand Accounts, 1750-1870, Frederick Drimmer. Astounding true historical accounts of grisly torture, bloody conflicts, relentless pursuits, miraculous escapes and more, by people who lived to tell the tale. 384pp. 5⅜ x 8½. 24901-8

THE WORLD'S GREAT SPEECHES (Fourth Enlarged Edition), Lewis Copeland, Lawrence W. Lamm, and Stephen J. McKenna. Nearly 300 speeches provide public speakers with a wealth of updated quotes and inspiration–from Pericles' funeral oration and William Jennings Bryan's "Cross of Gold Speech" to Malcolm X's powerful words on the Black Revolution and Earl of Spenser's tribute to his sister, Diana, Princess of Wales. 944pp. 5⅜ x 8⅜. 40903-1

THE BOOK OF THE SWORD, Sir Richard F. Burton. Great Victorian scholar/adventurer's eloquent, erudite history of the "queen of weapons"–from prehistory to early Roman Empire. Evolution and development of early swords, variations (sabre, broadsword, cutlass, scimitar, etc.), much more. 336pp. 6⅛ x 9¼. 25434-8

CATALOG OF DOVER BOOKS

AUTOBIOGRAPHY: The Story of My Experiments with Truth, Mohandas K. Gandhi. Boyhood, legal studies, purification, the growth of the Satyagraha (nonviolent protest) movement. Critical, inspiring work of the man responsible for the freedom of India. 480pp. 5⅜ x 8½. (Available in U.S. only.) 24593-4

CELTIC MYTHS AND LEGENDS, T. W. Rolleston. Masterful retelling of Irish and Welsh stories and tales. Cuchulain, King Arthur, Deirdre, the Grail, many more. First paperback edition. 58 full-page illustrations. 512pp. 5⅜ x 8½. 26507-2

THE PRINCIPLES OF PSYCHOLOGY, William James. Famous long course complete, unabridged. Stream of thought, time perception, memory, experimental methods; great work decades ahead of its time. 94 figures. 1,391pp. 5⅜ x 8½. 2-vol. set.
Vol. I: 20381-6   Vol. II: 20382-4

THE WORLD AS WILL AND REPRESENTATION, Arthur Schopenhauer. Definitive English translation of Schopenhauer's life work, correcting more than 1,000 errors, omissions in earlier translations. Translated by E. F. J. Payne. Total of 1,269pp. 5⅜ x 8½. 2-vol. set.   Vol. 1: 21761-2   Vol. 2: 21762-0

MAGIC AND MYSTERY IN TIBET, Madame Alexandra David-Neel. Experiences among lamas, magicians, sages, sorcerers, Bonpa wizards. A true psychic discovery. 32 illustrations. 321pp. 5⅜ x 8½. (Available in U.S. only.) 22682-4

THE EGYPTIAN BOOK OF THE DEAD, E. A. Wallis Budge. Complete reproduction of Ani's papyrus, finest ever found. Full hieroglyphic text, interlinear transliteration, word-for-word translation, smooth translation. 533pp. 6½ x 9¼. 21866-X

MATHEMATICS FOR THE NONMATHEMATICIAN, Morris Kline. Detailed, college-level treatment of mathematics in cultural and historical context, with numerous exercises. Recommended Reading Lists. Tables. Numerous figures. 641pp. 5⅜ x 8½. 24823-2

PROBABILISTIC METHODS IN THE THEORY OF STRUCTURES, Isaac Elishakoff. Well-written introduction covers the elements of the theory of probability from two or more random variables, the reliability of such multivariable structures, the theory of random function, Monte Carlo methods of treating problems incapable of exact solution, and more. Examples. 502pp. 5⅜ x 8½. 40691-1

THE RIME OF THE ANCIENT MARINER, Gustave Doré, S. T. Coleridge. Doré's finest work; 34 plates capture moods, subtleties of poem. Flawless full-size reproductions printed on facing pages with authoritative text of poem. "Beautiful. Simply beautiful."–*Publisher's Weekly.* 77pp. 9¼ x 12. 22305-1

NORTH AMERICAN INDIAN DESIGNS FOR ARTISTS AND CRAFTSPEOPLE, Eva Wilson. Over 360 authentic copyright-free designs adapted from Navajo blankets, Hopi pottery, Sioux buffalo hides, more. Geometrics, symbolic figures, plant and animal motifs, etc. 128pp. 8⅜ x 11. (Not for sale in the United Kingdom.) 25341-4

SCULPTURE: Principles and Practice, Louis Slobodkin. Step-by-step approach to clay, plaster, metals, stone; classical and modern. 253 drawings, photos. 255pp. 8⅛ x 11. 22960-2

THE INFLUENCE OF SEA POWER UPON HISTORY, 1660–1783, A. T. Mahan. Influential classic of naval history and tactics still used as text in war colleges. First paperback edition. 4 maps. 24 battle plans. 640pp. 5⅜ x 8½. 25509-3

CATALOG OF DOVER BOOKS

THE STORY OF THE TITANIC AS TOLD BY ITS SURVIVORS, Jack Winocour (ed.). What it was really like. Panic, despair, shocking inefficiency, and a little heroism. More thrilling than any fictional account. 26 illustrations. 320pp. 5⅜ x 8½.
20610-6

FAIRY AND FOLK TALES OF THE IRISH PEASANTRY, William Butler Yeats (ed.). Treasury of 64 tales from the twilight world of Celtic myth and legend: "The Soul Cages," "The Kildare Pooka," "King O'Toole and his Goose," many more. Introduction and Notes by W. B. Yeats. 352pp. 5⅜ x 8½.
26941-8

BUDDHIST MAHAYANA TEXTS, E. B. Cowell and others (eds.). Superb, accurate translations of basic documents in Mahayana Buddhism, highly important in history of religions. The Buddha-karita of Asvaghosha, Larger Sukhavativyuha, more. 448pp. 5⅜ x 8½.
25552-2

ONE TWO THREE . . . INFINITY: Facts and Speculations of Science, George Gamow. Great physicist's fascinating, readable overview of contemporary science: number theory, relativity, fourth dimension, entropy, genes, atomic structure, much more. 128 illustrations. Index. 352pp. 5⅜ x 8½.
25664-2

EXPERIMENTATION AND MEASUREMENT, W. J. Youden. Introductory manual explains laws of measurement in simple terms and offers tips for achieving accuracy and minimizing errors. Mathematics of measurement, use of instruments, experimenting with machines. 1994 edition. Foreword. Preface. Introduction. Epilogue. Selected Readings. Glossary. Index. Tables and figures. 128pp. 5⅜ x 8½.   40451-X

DALÍ ON MODERN ART: The Cuckolds of Antiquated Modern Art, Salvador Dalí. Influential painter skewers modern art and its practitioners. Outrageous evaluations of Picasso, Cézanne, Turner, more. 15 renderings of paintings discussed. 44 calligraphic decorations by Dalí. 96pp. 5⅜ x 8½. (Available in U.S. only.)   29220-7

ANTIQUE PLAYING CARDS: A Pictorial History, Henry René D'Allemagne. Over 900 elaborate, decorative images from rare playing cards (14th–20th centuries): Bacchus, death, dancing dogs, hunting scenes, royal coats of arms, players cheating, much more. 96pp. 9¼ x 12¼.
29265-7

MAKING FURNITURE MASTERPIECES: 30 Projects with Measured Drawings, Franklin H. Gottshall. Step-by-step instructions, illustrations for constructing handsome, useful pieces, among them a Sheraton desk, Chippendale chair, Spanish desk, Queen Anne table and a William and Mary dressing mirror. 224pp. 8⅛ x 11¼.
29338-6

THE FOSSIL BOOK: A Record of Prehistoric Life, Patricia V. Rich et al. Profusely illustrated definitive guide covers everything from single-celled organisms and dinosaurs to birds and mammals and the interplay between climate and man. Over 1,500 illustrations. 760pp. 7½ x 10⅛.
29371-8

Paperbound unless otherwise indicated. Available at your book dealer, online at www.doverpublications.com, or by writing to Dept. GI, Dover Publications, Inc., 31 East 2nd Street, Mineola, NY 11501. For current price information or for free catalogues (please indicate field of interest), write to Dover Publications or log on to www.doverpublications.com and see every Dover book in print. Dover publishes more than 500 books each year on science, elementary and advanced mathematics, biology, music, art, literary history, social sciences, and other areas.